10-14-69

Communications Control

Communications Control

Readings in the Motives and Structures of Censorship

Edited with an Introduction by

JOHN PHELAN

Sheed and Ward : New York

Library of Congress Catalog Card Number 70–89477
Standard Book Number 8362–0273–2

Manufactured in the United States of America

Contents

Preface

This collection of writings is about censorship. It is not about the evil of suppression of ideas and the untrammeled worth of freedom of expression. It is not even an impartial balancing of opposing views on censorship and freedom. It is about the phenomenon of censorship, the sources from which it springs, the forms that it assumes, and the manner in which it operates. Its primary aim is understanding, not advocacy, although as the reader progresses it will be abundantly clear for what the editor and the contributors stand.

In the strict sense, censorship means the prior restraint, by adequate physical or psychological pressure, of any communication that would be published and distributed were that restraint not applied. The clearest case of strict censorship would be the blank white spaces, or blacked-out paragraphs of newspapers in totalitarian countries. Only slightly less strict is censorship understood as subsequent punishment of those responsible for a communication after it has been transmitted. The fear of likely subsequent punishment, as in libel laws or sedition legislation, acts as a potent psychological prior restraint.

This book certainly includes the strict sense of censorship, but it takes a broader view. Censorship in these pages is taken to mean any control that limits the intended content of any communication. The control may be exercised by a legal institution, by a whole culture, by special interest groups, by single individuals. As opposed to propaganda, which creates contents for communication to bring about a result in the target audience regardless of the truth or falsity of the content, censorship shapes and limits already existing contents for many purposes, prescinding from the truth or falsity of the communication content.

In practice, censorship has been preponderantly exercised in three content fields: politics, religion, and sex. As in the familiar obscenity question, these three contents frequently overlap. The three parts of this reader do not correspond to these three content fields. The rubric of division has rather been based on the different relationships of censorship to the services it performs for society and the individual in providing protection from change.

Part I, Censorship and Social Structure, shows how communication, as the cognitive net that enables societies to function coherently, is inevitably institutionalized in such a way as to automatically shape the content of all communications to meet the needs of the society and culture it serves. The articles by Kamen, Lifton, and Carey illustrate this thesis from the historical, social-psychological, and anthropological-sociological viewpoints. MacNeil's article on contemporary television journalism offers a provocative case study of institutional control of communication.

Part II, Censorship and Aesthetics, shows how individuals allow their own needs, philosophies, and aspirations to shape and color the messages they send and the messages they receive. C. S. Lewis' article on the reading of literature reveals how a work of art is frequently made to serve ends for which it was never intended by the author. Abraham Kaplan takes us through the labyrinthine path between an author's intention and the labeling of his efforts as "obscene." The film camera, John Howard Lawson tells us, in the hands of a true artist must create a reality of its own.

Part III, Censorship and Conflict, examines the relationship between communication and conflict. Here we see the obvious exercise of censorship in concrete laws and actual cases. The section is introduced, however, by the profound reflections of Walter

Ong on the nature of verbal communication and human conflict.

Each section is thus a combination of theory, critical analysis, and case study. Three basic media—print, television, and film—are seen in relationship to one or more forms of censorship.

The editor does not pretend that these three divisions do not overlap. There is close affinity, for instance, between Ong's discussion of oral cultures and Carey's elucidation of Harold Innis' theory of social change and dominant media. But the divisions are more than mere conveniences. They allow us to see censorship for the incorrigibly plural thing that it is, from three different viewpoints. For too long censorship has been praised or blamed without being described or defined.

Introduction

One of the oldest definitions of the human person takes as the essential attributes of man his capacity and desire for knowledge and his capacity and desire for love. One of the oldest descriptions of society is in terms of these functions: the organization of men to facilitate and foster growth in knowledge and love within man and between men by providing all the material prerequisites that separate savagery from civilization. From the classic libertarians Milton and Mill increasingly to modern philosopher-psychologists such as Erikson and Kenniston, the role of society in developing human personality and potential has been seen as indispensable and not merely enormously facilitative. Modern psychology has put added stress on the passive voice of knowledge and love: Man desires to be known and to be loved and these desires define him as well as his yearning to understand and to give love.

J. S. Mill passionately felt that an individual could not even think if he were deprived of his capacity to express his thoughts to others. Harold Lasswell, the political psychologist, sees society as a network of organized channels of communication. However one locates the role of communication in society and in individual human lives, it is not peripheral. Without communication, knowledge and love, and thus true humanity, are impossible; and society is unrealizable.

The history of man and the personal experience of all men are bright with the fires of cognitive discovery and conquest, of triumphs and sacrifices of love. But both history and experience are also dark with failure and isolation, to say nothing of perverse blindness to the truth and sadistic destruction. But most of life is without the dramatic contrast of light and dark; it is the gray of imperfection and mediocrity. Man is imperfect and his society is a tissue of inevitable compromises that have not overcome conflict and prejudice. His failure to communicate fully is at the heart of his tragedy.

The reasons for this failure are manifold, some within us, some outside of us, some under our control, some defying our comprehension let alone mastery. This book is about our failure to communicate for only one reason: our desire to control our environment and thus be secure from danger, real or imagined. Social control of communication is a reasonable desire, but the history of censorship shows it has been carried to unreasonable lengths. The more important the content of the communication to the central concerns of men, the more feverish is their tendency to smother what might threaten their beliefs. Thus, censorship has always been associated with the three great cares of man and civilization: politics, sex, and religion. The cliché characterization of the censorious society has been "smug and comfortable and complacent." The opposite has been more nearly the case. Dictators, cold warriors, orthodox bishops, reigning critics, imperious editors, television executives, film producers, college professors, and Students for a Democratic Society all act as censors when and because they are frightened or outraged or both.

The above catalogue of censors, incomplete, uneven, and almost random, is designed to indicate what this book is about. The censorious mind does go to outrageous lengths to avoid knowledge for the sake of a fragile peace, or a needed reform, or merely to exercise power. But this book is not so much about the lengths to which censorship goes as it is about the unexpected places it calls home and the protean forms the censorious mind takes. The authors represented in this book were not chosen because they condemn censorship and uncover its disguises. They were chosen because they offer understanding of a timeless and ubiquitous human practice of choosing what one knows and of societies' mechanisms for maintaining the cognitive choices of the ruling class, whether that class be an authoritarian elite or a liberal majority.

The control of communication is a human necessity and a social inevitability. The question is not to censor or not to censor. The question is how much to censor, who should exercise the power of censorship, and for what specific purposes should censorship be employed. The question has never been satisfactorily answered and this book does not pretend to offer an answer. Its only purpose is to expand our notion of what censorship is, what it does, and how various men and media employ control of what they communicate. Censorship, thus understood broadly as control of the content of communication, is practiced by all men and by all societies. Within us, our memories suppress reminders of our past faults and magnify our triumphs. The golfer who cites his lowest score as his usual game is doing in a trivial way what Soviet history does in its accounts of Stalin's rule on a momentous level. The well-bred gentlewoman chooses to ignore the alcoholic vagrant in her path and the American government has until recently not seen the starving and malnourished millions in the affluent society. The conservative cardinal forbids his priests to speak on birth control and campus radicals shout down professors in the classroom. Pentagon officials classify damaging information and black militants forcibly exclude the press from some of their meetings. John Milton, in the very speech, *Areopagetica,* which is an impassioned brief against censorship, gives equally impassioned assurance to Parliament that the writings of "Popery" will not be tolerated. And John Stuart Mill would not care to extend liberty to obscene publications.

The unexceptionable premise of all censorship is that ideas

have consequences and words lead to action. All legal suppression of free expression has been justified in the name of protection from criminal consequences. This is most clearly seen in the most prominent modern exercises of censorship: the suppression of sexually obscene books and films. As American society has become more sexually permissive with regard to actions: fornication, homosexuality, *etc.*, it has become less restrictive of communication of obscene material. As the sexual ethos of America has grown bewilderingly pluralistic, the meaning of the word "obscene" has become infuriatingly vague for would-be censors and amusingly meaningless for libertarians. Conversely, the fear of violence and war and racism have led to the application of the "obscene" label to Vietnam, ethnic slurs, and even *Tom and Jerry* cartoons. No one complains of vagueness in these cases.

Orthodoxy is thus intimately related to orthopraxy—ideas and expressions are acceptable to society if they encourage the established modes of behavior or if they do not seem to foster conflict with the reigning system. In this age of pluralism, each nation, class, religion, profession, and interest group has its own orthodoxy. Indeed, each individual has his own private version of the orthodoxy he shares with others, although he would like to believe his version is the authentic one for his group. Some few individuals, prophets, geniuses, and madmen have a vision of reality so unique that they share it with no one. They are the social, political, artistic, religious, or scientific heretics, if you will. Theirs is an antiorthodoxy, and they introduce a new mode of thought and behavior by recruiting disciples.

Control of communication, censorship, is exercised by the orthodox and the antiorthodox. It is easily recognized when employed by those in political power, by medieval bishops, totalitarian generalissimos, politburos, congressional committees and editorial boards. It is even more noticeable among the politically antiorthodox who cannot afford to speak with more than one voice, and whose beleaguered cause demands total allegiance. It is practiced to a ludicrous extreme by the scientific heretics, who may believe the earth is flat, or that voltage meters will cure mental illness, or that visitors from Venus founded our civilization. No contradictory evidence can be put forth at their dedicated meetings.

Between these obvious extremes of rigid orthodoxies and their strict censorships lies a vast land of subtler prejudices that seek to stifle and silence criticism and causes for doubt. There is the artistic creed of the critic which hinders him from seeing a work of art for what it is. There is the ideological commitment of the film-maker that compels him to narrow his focus and edit his frames into stereotypes in order to make a point. There is the multiform accusation of "obscenity" made against such diverse forms of expression as burlesque shows and documentaries of war atrocities. The contributions of Lewis, Lawson, and Kaplan explain the psychology and philosophies of these and other forms of the censorious mind at work.

Historically and properly, the terms orthodoxy and heresy are applied to religious beliefs. But orthodoxies and heresies have always been inextricably linked with politics. For the Jewish nation, then as now, its religious beliefs were very much involved with its sense of social cohesion as a people. The leaders of the nation were also custodians of belief and they were opposed to Jesus, according to John's gospel, as much for the political threat he presumably posed as for the undoubted heresies he espoused. Christianity, viewed not as a Platonic idea but as a movement of men through time and place, offers a history of disputatious acrimony which is without parallel. The Councils may have been much more than mere political meetings, but they were undoubtedly and intensely political meetings. This was so because the content of one's religious beliefs, up until this century, determined one's fate in this very tangible world of men and institutions as well as, so it was believed, in the next world. The first selection in this reader, Kamen's study of the problem of toleration, surveys the paradoxical fate of the Christian ideal of charity at the hands of mortal men whose commitment to truth as they saw it demanded community and unity—at whatever price.

The old Comtean notion of intellectual progress from the arcane depths of dogmatic theological obscurantism to the clear and fresh openness of scientifically impartial investigation has not fared very well in the light of twentieth-century ideological conflict. The almost accomplished separation of church and state has eased and muted the sharp confrontation of religious orthodoxy and heresies. We are perhaps beginning to see that it is not concern for the Absolute that invariably demands absolute allegiance and absolute conformity. It is rather concern for order and control of our environment. The same mechanism is at work today on less pretentious ideas. Men do not suppress contrary notions of the Grand Design of the Universe any more, if only because most of them are not interested. National policies and parties now have for some men assumed the mantle of the absolute—as Robert Jay Lifton describes totalism in the second selection in this book.

The censorious creeds and codes of men and their institutions, whether subtle or blatant, are not the only restrictive pressures that all communication is heir to. There are the instrinsic limitations, often disguised or unrealized, of the modes and media of communication utilized in society. These limitations act as built-in censors which pre-select the matter of communication to suit the manner of its transmission. Harold Innis, as James Carey lucidly interprets this difficult and sadly unacclaimed scholar of communications, goes so far as to postulate that the dominant media of a society determine its ethical and political institutions, as well as its religious beliefs and social ideologies. Political and social reformers, this provocative analysis suggests, must fight the media monopoly of the establishment by either gaining control of it or making it obsolete by using new media which will supplant the received system. Carey himself imaginatively extends Innis' thesis to illuminate the current generational gap and concern for "relevancy." Robert MacNeil chronicles the intrinsic pre-selection of electronic journalism in reporting and interpreting contemporary society due to both the business structure of the networks and the bias of the medium itself. The medium may not be the message, but all messages must be made to fit the medium.

Unlike McLuhan, neither Carey nor MacNeil accepts the thesis that the intrinsic bias of the media has us trapped or precludes conscious and moral choice of what we can say to one another (or see of one another). Indeed, both suggest corrective measures to overcome the automatic censoring function of different media. The fact that the special biases of different media can be, and have been, consciously exploited by the censorious mind justifies and demands the inclusion of Carey and MacNeil in a reader about the control of communication.

On a deeper level, and complementing Innis' study of oral and visual cultures, Walter Ong probes the nature of the word itself, the un-medium of communication, and shows how it lends itself to both destructive and truly communicative human employment. Communication, paradoxically, has always been caught between communion and combat. In states of complete communion, symbolic communication is unnecessary; in out-and-out combat, it is futile.

It is the thesis of this writer that the censorious mind will always be present in all men, good and evil, great and small. It is based on fears that we all share: the fear of combat and the fear of communion. Both threaten to annihilate our identity, the sense of ourselves that we have built up patiently over our lives, through our decisions, our hopes, our despairs, and our accomplishments. By keeping our cognitive field swept clear of the truths and lies that may unmake our precious selves, we have a measure of security. We are possibly secure from danger and we are certainly safeguarded against change and growth. Censorship arising from our fear of combat is necessary for our survival—up to a point. Certainly society is justified in instituting controls over utterances that will destroy the social fabric, unless the fabric is rotting. Certainly an individual is justified in screening out information that will introduce conflict in his life, if his life is so harmonious and free without it.

It is the fear of communion that is the cause of the worst kind of censorship, the fear that turned Eden into the human condition. Cain slew Abel because he did not wish to share God with him, wanted to have an exclusive channel to the divine, uncluttered by Abel's sacrifices. There seems to be a bit of Cain in all of us. We try to ignore the views and plans and hopes of other men who may be better than we not because they may be better, but because they are not we. If we joined them, if we listened, if we communicated, it might lead to communion. We would be—terrible fate—changed into something other than ourselves.

The last three selections in this reader deal with recognized and obvious forms of legal censorship. Hudon surveys the history of censorship in early Anglo-Saxon law, Chafee narrates the dramatic Abrams case and illuminates the issues of the case, and of all political censhorship cases, by his perceptive understanding of fundamental human rights as well as of legal procedures. These empirical histories are designed to complement the theoretical investigations of the reader. It is hoped that he will not merely see the battle of free expression against the forces of censorious repression. He will see what he now knows to be the top of an iceberg, whose unexpected size and mammoth shape this book has helped him to appreciate more fully.

Lastly, it is hoped, he will recognize part of himself in the censor as well as the rebel.

John Phelan

Communications Control

CENSORSHIP AND SOCIAL STRUCTURE

1 The Problem of Toleration

Henry Kamen

This essay is taken from the first chapter of Kamen's study of religious tolerance and intolerance in Europe and the American colonies during the sixteenth and seventeenth centuries, *The Rise of Toleration*. The relevance of Kamen's work to this collection is that the contribution reproduced here is a concise statement of the clash between private visions and public order. The interpenetration of religious belief and political practices that Kamen chronicles affords the best historical illustration of censorship as a social institution as well as a human inevitability. Kamen's book addresses itself to two questions about one issue:

> The issue at stake is the liberty of an individual to dissent from an official truth. Has the State, in its function as an auxiliary of the Church, or even in its own right as guardian of the social order, any right to repress heresy? And does the individual—if he appeals to the principle that belief cannot be forced—have any right to freedom of conscience?

This reader addresses itself to the problem and process of social control of communication. Kamen's essay locates the problem as a central concern of man and describes the process in the history of men.

Henry Kamen has also published *The Spanish Inquisition* and has translated the poems of Boris Pasternak. Educated at Oxford (University College and St. Anthony's College), Mr. Kamen has lectured in history at the University of Warwick since 1966.

In its broadest sense, toleration can be understood to mean the concession of liberty to those who dissent in religion. It can be seen as part of the process in history which has led to a gradual development of the principle of human freedom. What should be remembered is that this development has been by no means regular. Even the great English historian Lord Acton, for whom the evolution of freedom lay at the heart of history, was obliged to recognise that toleration has pursued not a linear but a cyclic development; it has not evolved progressively but has suffered periodic and prolonged reverses. The belief that religious liberty is an exclusively modern achievement is of course untrue, and it should cause no great surprise to find that some countries today are further from full liberty than they were five centuries ago. Attitudes are in any case conditioned by social and political circumstances, developing erratically according to their milieu, so that there is no inherent reason why a modern doctrine should be any more progressive than a distant one.

By giving due consideration to the social context of philosophies we can come closer to understanding the contemporary significance of doctrines. It is above all important when studying the protagonists of toleration to realise that they were not merely landmarks in the history of ideas. They were themselves often representative of social forces that cannot be ignored. We may talk of Zwingli and Locke, and yet forget the burgher class in Zurich or the landed aristocracy in England. Rarely indeed do we come across an advocate of toleration as a voice crying in the wilderness; there were some such, no doubt, but they are outnumbered by the voices that represent the vanguard of movements in process of evolution or even dissolution.

Liberalism in religion is not the same thing as tolerance, but historically it was often a prerequisite, and is of considerable importance in helping us to arrive at a general idea of the often vague concept of 'tolerance'. Though the many proponents of toleration were seldom if ever in agreement on general principles, it should be possible to outline the distinguishing features of toleration up to the sixteenth century.

Christianity and Tolerance

Catholic Christianity occupies the whole religious background with which we are concerned. 'The Church', Acton claimed, 'began with the principle of liberty, both as her claim and as her rule'. There can be no doubt about this. The liberty proclaimed by the apostles was both external and internal. Internally, the grace of Christ had redeemed and acquitted man, giving him the absolute freedom of the sons of God. A Christian must correspondingly respect others in a spirit of charity based on freedom: the conscience of one's neighbour must not be hurt. 'When you sin against the brethren and wound their weak conscience, you sin against Christ', Saint Paul warned the Corinthians (1 Cor. 8:12). There was to be no forcing of consciences, since the freedom brought by Christ applied to all men. In the Church there was 'no more Jew or Gentile, no more slave and freeman, no more male and female; you are all one person in Jesus Christ' (Gal. 3:28).

Externally, Christians were to be free from political repression and persecution, since, according to Christ, they were to fulfil all their obligations blamelessly, so as to 'give back to Caesar what is Caesar's and to God what is God's' (Matt. 22:21). In other words, the spheres of secular government and religions were separate, and the State had no right to force acceptance of religion so long as one fulfilled faithfully all obligations to it. Absolute distinction of Church and State, so unequivocally laid down by Christ, became the charter of Christian claims to toleration under the Roman Empire. As long as Christians, like members of other religions, carried out their secular duties, the State had no right to interfere with the consciences of individual Christians, nor indeed did the State possess any authority in religious matters. For two centuries the fathers of the Catholic Church continued to demand toleration on this basis. 'By both human and natural law', Tertullian protested in the early third century, 'each one is free to adore whom he wants. The religion of an individual neither harms nor profits anybody else. It is against the nature of religion to force religion'.

The intolerance of the early Church to its own members was to be of importance later when the Church had triumphed in Europe. Authorities who favoured persecution would cite the instance when Saint Peter had struck down Ananias and Saphira because of their dishonesty. There is little doubt that the discipline of the Christian communities was often harsh and narrow. Yet the doctrinal position of the Church in respect of errant members was clear. The use of capital punishment was totally disallowed. 'The weapons we fight with are not human weapons' (2 Cor. 10:4), wrote St. Paul. Following the advice of Christ, the apostles made use instead of excommunication as a method of discipline; 'Give a heretic one warning, then a second, and after that avoid his company' (Titus 3:10). This was often practised, but the discipline was to be charitable, in the spirit of Christ's admonition to 'love one another' (John 15:12). There would certainly be differences of opinion, but these were not infringements of discipline and should be borne with. As Saint Paul emphasized, 'parties there must needs be among you [*oportet haereses esse*] so that those who are true metal may be distinguished from the rest' (I Cor.

11:19). With a strict adherence to these scriptural tenets, the early Church managed to win a reputation for charity and non-violence of a kind rarely achieved by later heterodox Christian sects. 'See how these Christians love one another', an observation first made in the time of Tertullian, became a commentary on their success and a judgment on their successors.

Texts from the Bible came to be used widely in later controversies on toleration. The golden rule laid down by Christ. 'Do to other men all that you would have them do to you' (Matt. 7.12) became a standard plea for charity among Christians. There were in addition three texts that played a major part in writings on the subject. The most famous of them is the parable of the tares (Matt. 13:24–30, 36–43). 'There was a man who sowed his field with clean seed; but while all the world was asleep an enemy of his came and scattered tares among the wheat'. When this was discovered, the men offered to weed out the tares. 'But he said, No; or perhaps while you are gathering the tares you will root up the wheat with them. Leave them to grow side by side till harvest, and when harvest-time comes I will give the word to the reapers. Gather up the tares first and tie them in bundles to be burned, and store the wheat in my barn'. According to Christ's own explanation of the parable, he meant that the good and bad should be allowed to coexist until the Last Judgment. The common interpretation given to it in later times was that the Church should be tolerant to its own errant children until Christ should come again. Later the interpretation was broadened to mean that Christians should be tolerant to those not of the household of the faith. On either count, it was clear that extreme measures such as the death penalty were not to be applied to heretics or pagans.

The next text, in direct reference to Christ, takes a passage from Isaiah and claims of the Messiah that 'the bruised reed he shall not break, the smoking flax he shall not extinguish' (Matt. 12:20). This was commonly understood to mean that errant sinners ('the smoking flax') would not be cut off by Christ, but would benefit from his mercy. In this, the Church was seen to act in the place of Christ. Several other passages like this, all pointing directly to the extreme mercy of God, were interpreted in the same way, to show that leniency must be practised towards heretics.

A final text concerns the preaching of the apostles in Jerusalem. Their teaching infuriated the Sadducees, who denounced them to the Council and demanded punishment. In Council, however, the rabbi Gamaliel rose and asked for reconsideration. The ground of his argument has become classic. 'If this is man's design or man's undertaking', he said, 'it will be overthrown; if it is God's you will have no power to overthrow it. You would not willingly be found fighting against God' (Acts 5:38–9).

Christianity and Intolerance

In AD 313 the Roman Empire under Constantine finally gave official toleration to Christians. This achievement of emancipation prepared the way for compromise in the role of the Church. Assimilated into the society of the Empire, Christians adapted themselves to the social norms. The revolutionary philosophy of the Church had brought with it a liberty that extended beyond nation and class: at the *agape* and at the Eucharist all men were equal. But this equality was no more than an accidental achievement of Christian freedom, and when political realities had to be faced the Church became a potentially conservative force, resigned to the inevitable evils of what was, after all, a transitory world, and concerned more and more exclusively with the salvation of souls alone. By the end of the fourth century the Church had grown to accept the exercise of punitive constraint against heterodox Christians, and Catholics looked with approval on the measures taken by the secular authorities against Arians and Donatists. As the established religion, Christianity was drawn irresistibly toward an alliance of interest with the secular power. Despite the regular protests of distinguished prelates, the new Church-State alliance began a programme of selective persecution. The Roman emperors proscribed paganism and pulled down its altars. At the close of the fourth century the noble but vain protests of a few distinguished pagans could still be heard speaking in favour of the liberty of cults. *Uno itinere non potest perveniri ad tam grande secretum*—'It is not by one path alone', cried Symmachus in the Roman Senate in the year 384, 'that men can attain the heart of so great a mystery!' But the day had passed to champions of an exclusive truth.

Historians have dated the acceptance of persecution to Saint Augustine's campaign against the Donatists of North Africa in the early fifth century. In justice to the bishop of Hippo, it should be recalled that he was an unswerving opponent of extreme torture and of the death penalty. As one who had himself been a Manichean heretic, Augustine was willing to understand the difficulties encountered by Manichees in relinquishing heresy. Moreover, he opposed all coercion which aimed at enforcing belief, and distilled this position in the fundamental principle: *credere non potest homo nisi volens,* man cannot believe against his will. But it remains true that by his appeal to the secular authorities for help against the outrages committed by the Donatists; by the way in which he wrested the phrase *compelle intrare* from its context in the parable of the supper (Luke 14:23), so as to make it read as a command to enforce the submission of heretics and unbelievers, and by his intolerant exclamation, 'What death is worse for the soul than the liberty to err?'—*Quae peior mors animae quam libertas erroris?*—; he established a precedent which fortified the practice of repression by the mediaeval Church.

The parable of the tares he interpreted to mean that tares should be uprooted if it was clear that no wheat would be uprooted with them. His final position, unbending in its claim to exclusive truth, was uncompromising: 'There is an unjust persecution, which the ungodly operate against the Church of Christ; and a just persecution which the Churches of Christ make use of towards the ungodly . . . The Church persecutes out of love, the ungodly out of cruelty'. The bishop of Hippo was to prove a powerful authority for later protagonists of religious intolerance.

The basis of intolerance in the Middle Ages was the alliance between Church and State. The Church on its side taught patient subjection to the powers of the world, and the State stepped in to eradicate religious heterodoxy wherever it reared its head. Theoretically the ecclesiastical authorities held to the Christian view that the Church should exercise no undue restraint and have no recourse to the shedding of blood. In practice they were willing to resort to the 'secular arm', as the Christian ruler was termed, to carry out that 'just persecution' of which Saint Augustine had spoken. The excuse for this lay in the enormous success of Christian expansion. In the fifth century it was still possible to distinguish between the relative spheres of the Church and the Empire. By the eighth century the old Empire was a memory and the Church had become the unique upholder of civilisation in Europe. The new Empire of Charlemagne consequently came into being under the aegis of the Church, whose presence in all the lands of the West created the concept of an international Christendom embracing the whole population and both secular and ecclesiastical authorities. The theoreticians of this Christendom were not slow to give it a theocratic character, and soon prince and bishop became joint authorities in a sacral society where all authority was divine and therefore entrusted to the Church.

Pope Gelasius I in the fifth century had taught the duality of secular and spiritual power in the world, but it was an uneven duality: 'the world is ruled over by two great powers, that of the pontiffs and that of the Kings, but the authority of the pontiffs is far greater, since they must give account to God of he souls of Kings'. By the time of Innocent III in the late twelfth century theocratic pretensions were at their peak: 'The royal power', claimed this Pope, 'derives from the pontifical authority the splendour of its dignity'. In his bull *Unam Sanctam* in 1302 Boniface VIII claimed that all authority on earth was vested in the Church; two swords ruled the world, but 'both swords, the spiritual and the material, are in the power of the Church'.

Fortified by this sovereignty in temporal matters, the Church did not hesitate to persecute heresies that allegedly threatened the temporal order. Prelates and lords made common cause against seditious preaching and rebellion among the lower classes, so as to preserve the dogmatic and social unity of Christendom. The result was that dissident sects were obliged to reject the coercive power of the Church in temporal matters, as the only way to establish toleration for themselves. On occasion the sectarians placed themselves under the control of some great magnate, in the hope that his protection would suffice to ward off the vengeance of the Church. This defensive tactic might imply the political disobedience of the magnate to his feudal superiors and would call for retribution on both political and religious grounds. Toleration in this context could not fail to be a political problem, of which the thirteenth century crusades against the Albigensians in France are a classic example.

Society and Heresy

Set in political terms, the pattern of mediaeval heresy provides a continuous development down into the Reformation period. Conformity in faith implied unity and therefore security in society. Conversely, to differ in faith meant to threaten the fabric of society. Both Church and State consequently set their face against ideological minorities. On their side, mediaeval heretics saw rightly that in questioning dogmas they must also come to question the world superstructure erected on these dogmas. Not surprisingly, religious innovators often became social rebels and social rebels adopted theology as the vehicle of their protest. The religious Reformation was consequently conditioned by, and in its turn led towards, social movements which were not necessarily in entire sympathy with its aims, particularly since the religious changes of the sixteenth century were often brought about against the wishes of the mass of the people.

Illustrations of this social background to heresy are provided in peasant and doctrinal movements of the later Middle Ages. The influence of the fourteenth-century English heretic John Wycliffe permeated some of the lower social grades of fifteenth-century England, and rebels adopted many of Wycliffe's tenets as part of their economic protest. Doctrine also played a large part in the Czech communities that adopted Hussite teachings after the death of the great Bohemian heretic John Hus at Constance in 1415. One of these, the Hussite Unity of Brethren, founded by Chelčický, followed a communistic programme that rejected the authority of the State in religious matters and called for a complete separation of the spheres of Church and State. These two principles, later to be adopted as a fundamental feature of Anabaptism, would have secured the Hussites freedom of belief. What the authorities objected to in such a doctrine was, of course, that the Hussites by their own principles made religious liberty dependent on radical alterations in the political structure. The struggle for toleration obviously involved a denial of the whole mediaeval framework of government.

By the early sixteenth century this mediaeval world was being perceptibly transformed. The climate of thought in educated circles; the redistribution of political power among the nationalities of Europe; the expansion of commerce and banking; the rise to power of the bourgeoisie in the Netherlands and their decline in Germany, Italy and Spain; were all part of the process. It is to this period that historians have dated the rise of nation states and the New Monarchy, in which individual realms, by their claim to autonomy, caused the fragmentation of the feudal world-system so long upheld by theoreticians of the papacy and the Empire. The cultural Renaissance, diffused from Italy, made a particular contribution to the reorganisation of social norms, while preachers, pamphleteers and political theorists began to revise and reject the preconceptions of their predecessors.

Although the Middle Ages had not tolerated dissent, it would be misleading to portray this as monolithic intolerance. Non-Christians, for example, were theoretically quite free. Saint Thomas Aquinas had maintained that heretics alone deserve the death penalty, on the analogy that if those who counterfeit money are liable to execution, 'it is far more serious to prevent the faith which ensures the life of the soul than to counterfeit money which is only necessary for our temporal needs'. A different standard of values existed for pagans: 'non-believers must not be compelled to believe, because believing is a matter of free will'. On this basis, Catholics could and did coexist peaceably with Jews and Muslims in several parts of the Mediterranean world. It became a common argument in favour of toleration in the sixteenth century that the papacy itself suffered Jews in Rome and allowed them to use their synagogues. Heterodoxy, however, was punished where paganism was not, for the simple reason that heretics had presumably turned their backs on the light and had consequently sinned against the Holy Ghost and against their own conscience. Heretics, Aquinas said, 'must be compelled, even physically, to fulfil what they have promised, and to maintain what they have once accepted'.

The question of toleration, in the form it took at the end of the mediaeval period, may be approached from two principal angles. The issue at stake is the liberty of an individual to dissent from an official truth. Has the State, in its function as an auxiliary of the Church or even in its own right as guardian of the social order, any right to repress heresy? And does the individual—if he appeals to the principle that belief cannot be forced—have any right to freedom of conscience? It was on these two issues that most of the debate turned after the sixteenth century, all other arguments being largely subordinate to these.

The rights of conscience were not explicitly recognised by mediaeval theologians. Error, claimed the scholastics, has no rights; denial of the truth can never coexist with the truth. Certainly it might be objected that those who were sincere in their error necessarily looked on their error as truth. Peter Abelard, for instance, in the twelfth century went so far as to maintain that sin committed in ignorance is not truly sin, because the culprits knew no better. But his views were condemned as heresy, and subsequent theologians came down heavily in favour of the argument that the objective law of God, as laid down by the Church, was the sole criterion of right action, and that a conscience which went against that law, sinned. The duty of someone who saw his own conscience conflict with the law of God, was to reject his conscience, which had obviously been corrupted, and to follow the objective law. This harsh and rigorous position was to some extent modified by Aquinas, who admitted that a conscience in error could plead ignorance of the relevant act or situation, but he narrowed down the possibilities of invincible ignorance to virtually only the weak-minded and insane, so that in effect his position differed hardly at all from that of his predecessors. Before the sixteenth century there were no influential philosophers to support the cause of the erroneous conscience. This intransigent position continued to be taught in official quarters of the Catholic Church down to modern times. In 1832 Gregory XVI described liberty of conscience as a 'delirium' (*deliramentum*), and in 1864 it was condemned in the Syllabus of Errors.

2 Ideological Totalism

Robert Jay Lifton, M.D.

The quest for truth and the need for order are intimately connected. They frequently work as partners in the scientific search for pattern and predictability in the welter of data the inquiring mind must process. They frequently conflict when individual beliefs threaten the social fabric. Kamen has shown how forceful the combination of Church and State can be in establishing order, by imposing both doctrine and behavior in mutually reinforcing forms. When political behaviour is not merely allied with religious belief but itself becomes deeply internalized with the depth of demand that has characterized religion, the social control of communication is awesome and the quest for truth is not only subordinated to, but submerged in, the need for order.

Chinese "brainwashing" has combined the power of the state with the internal demands of religion in an attempt to wholly subordinate the thinking of men, indeed, their whole being, to the need for solidarity and political order. It is the ultimate—thus far—in attempts of social control of communication. Dr. Lifton, psychiatrist and social psychologist, has carefully studied the techniques and philosophy of "brainwashing" over a period of years by painstaking psychiatric interviews with "graduates" of the Chinese thought reform program. His book, *Thought Reform and the Psychology of Totalism*, is a detailed summary of the experiences of the "reformed" and those who failed to become "reformed." From these case studies and other sources, Dr. Lifton has synthesized the basic principles and practices of "brainwashing" from a psychological point of view. The essay you are about to read is the twenty-second chapter of his book. Thoughtful readers will return to this essay

with the realization that many practices of our own society are but milder forms of the extreme measures revealed in it.

Dr. Lifton, Foundations' Fund for Research Professor of Psychiatry at Yale, was formerly associated with Harvard's Department of Psychiatry and Center for Far Eastern Studies. He has spent nearly a decade in the Far East researching the social-psychological impact of cultural change in China and Japan.

Thought reform has a psychological momentum of its own, a self-perpetuating energy not always bound by the interests of the program's directors. When we inquire into the sources of this momentum, we come upon a complex set of psychological themes, which may be grouped under the general heading of *ideological totalism.* By this ungainly phrase I mean to suggest the coming together of immoderate ideology with equally immoderate individual character traits—an extremist meeting ground between people and ideas.

In discussing tendencies toward individual totalism within my subjects, I made it clear that these were a matter of degree, and that some potential for this form of all-or-nothing emotional alignment exists within everyone. Similarly, any ideology—that is, any set of emotionally-charged convictions about man and his relationship to the natural or supernatural world—may be carried by its adherents in a totalistic direction. But this is most likely to occur with those ideologies which are most sweeping in their content and most ambitious—or messianic—in their claims, whether religious, political, or scientific. And where totalism exists, a religion, a political movement, or even a scientific organization becomes little more than an exclusive cult.

A discussion of what is most central in the thought reform

environment can thus lead us to a more general consideration of the psychology of human zealotry. For in identifying, on the basis of this study of thought reform, features common to all expressions of ideological totalism, I wish to suggest a set of criteria against which any environment may be judged—a basis for answering the ever-recurring question: "Isn't this just like 'brainwashing'?"

These criteria consist of eight psychological themes which are predominant within the social field of the thought reform milieu. Each has a totalistic quality, each depends upon an equally absolute philosophical assumption, and each mobilizes certain individual emotional tendencies, most of a polarizing nature. Psychological theme, philosophical rationale, and polarized individual tendencies are interdependent; they require, rather than directly cause, each other. In combination they create an atmosphere which may temporarily energize or exhilarate, but which at the same time poses the gravest of human threats.

Milieu Control

The most basic feature of the thought reform environment, the psychological current upon which all else depends, is the control of human communication. Through this milieu control the totalist environment seeks to establish domain over not only the individual's communication with the outside (all that he sees and hears, reads and writes, experiences, and expresses), but also—in its penetration of his inner life—over what we may speak of as his communication with himself. It creates an atmosphere uncomfortably reminiscent of George Orwell's 1984; but with one important difference. Orwell, as a Westerner, envisioned milieu control accomplished by a mechanical device, the two-way "telescreen." The Chinese, although they utilize whatever mechanical means they have at their disposal, achieve control of greater psychological depth through a human recording and transmitting apparatus. It is probably fair to say that the Chinese Communist prison and revolutionary university produce about as thoroughly controlled a group environment as has ever existed. The milieu control exerted over the broader social environment of Communist China, while considerably less intense, is in its own way unrivalled in its combination of extensiveness and depth; it is, in fact, one of the distinguishing features of Chinese Communist practice.

Such milieu control never succeeds in becoming absolute, and its own human apparatus can—when permeated by outside information—become subject to discordant "noise" beyond that of any mechanical apparatus. To totalist administrators, however, such occurrences are no more than evidence of "incorrect" use of the apparatus. For they look upon milieu control as a just and necessary policy, one which need not be kept secret: thought reform participants may be in doubt as to who is telling what to whom, but the fact that extensive information about everyone is being conveyed to the authorities is always known. At the center of this self-justification is their assumption of omniscience, their conviction that reality is their exclusive possession. Having experienced the impact of what they consider to be an ultimate truth (and having the need to dispel any possible inner doubts of their own), they consider it their duty to create an environment containing no more and no less than this "truth." In order to be the engineers of the human soul, they must first bring it under full observational control.

Many things happen psychologically to one exposed to milieu control; the most basic is the disruption of balance between self and outside world. Pressured toward a merger of internal and external milieux, the individual encounters a profound threat to his personal autonomy. He is deprived of the combination of external information and inner reflection which anyone requires to test the realities of his environment and to maintain a measure of identity separate from it. Instead, he is called upon to make an absolute polarization of the real (the prevailing ideology) and the unreal (everything else). To the extent that he does this, he undergoes a *personal closure*[1] which frees him from man's incessant struggle with the elusive subtleties of truth. He may even share his environment's sense of omniscience and assume a "God's-eye view"[2] of the universe; but he is likely instead to feel himself victimized by the God's-eye view of his environment's controllers. At this point he is subject to the hostility of suffocation of which we have already spoken—the resentful awareness that his strivings toward new information, independent judgment, and self-expression are being thwarted. If his intelligence and sensibilities carry him toward realities outside the closed ideological system, he may resist these as not fully legitimate—until the milieu control is sufficiently diminished for him to share these realities with others. He is in either case profoundly hampered in the perpetual human quest for what is true, good, and relevant in the world around him and within himself.

Mystical Manipulation

The inevitable next step after milieu control is extensive personal manipulation. This manipulation assumes a no-holds-barred character, and uses every possible device at the milieu's command, no matter how bizarre or painful. Initiated from above, it seeks to provoke specific patterns of behavior and emotion in such a way that these will appear to have arisen spontaneously from within the environment. This element of planned spontaneity, directed as it is by an ostensibly omniscient group, must assume, for the manipulated, a near-mystical quality.

Ideological totalists do not pursue this approach solely for the purpose of maintaining a sense of power over others. Rather they are impelled by a special kind of mystique which not only justifies such manipulations, but makes them mandatory. Included in the mystique is a sense of "higher purpose," of having "directly perceived some imminent law of social development," and of being themselves the vanguard of this development.[3] By thus becoming the instruments of their own mystique, they create a mystical aura around the manipulating institutions—the Party, the Government, the Organization. They are the agents "chosen" (by history, by God, or by some other supernatural force) to carry out the "mystical imperative,"[4] the pursuit of which must supersede all considerations of decency or of immediate human welfare. Similarly, any thought or action which questions the higher purpose is considered to be stimulated by a lower purpose, to be backward, selfish, and petty in the face of the great, overriding mission. This same mystical imperative produces the apparent extremes of idealism and cynicism which occur in connection with the manipulations of any totalist environment: even those actions which seem cynical in the extreme can be seen as having ultimate relationship to the "higher purpose."

At the level of the individual person, the psychological responses to this manipulative approach revolve about the basic polarity of trust and mistrust. One is asked to accept these manipulations on a basis of ultimate trust (or faith): "like a child in the arms of its mother," as Father Luca accurately perceived. He who trusts in this degree can experience the manipulations within the idiom of the mystique behind them: that is, he may welcome their mysteriousness, find pleasure in their pain, and feel them to be necessary for the fulfillment of the "higher purpose" which he endorses as his own. But such elemental trust is difficult to maintain; and even the strongest can be dissipated by constant manipulation.

When trust gives way to mistrust (or when trust has never existed) the higher purpose cannot serve as adequate emotional sustenance. The individual then responds to the manipulations through developing what I shall call the *psychology of the pawn.* Feeling himself unable to escape from forces more powerful than himself, he subordinates everything to adapting himself to them. He becomes sensitive to all kinds of cues, expert at anticipating environmental pressures, and skillful in riding them in such a way that his psychological energies merge with the tide rather than turn painfully against himself. This requires that he participate actively in the manipulation of others, as well as in the endless round of betrayals and self-betrayals which are required.

But whatever his response—whether he is cheerful in the face of being manipulated, deeply resentful, or feels a combination of both—he has been deprived of the opportunity to exercise his capacities for self-expression and independent action.

The Demand for Purity

In the thought reform milieu, as in all situations of ideological totalism, the experimental world is sharply divided into the pure and the impure, into the absolutely good and the absolutely evil. The good and the pure are of course those ideas, feelings, and actions which are consistent with the totalist ideology and policy; anything else is apt to be relegated to the bad and the impure. Nothing human is immune from the flood of stern moral judgments. All "taints" and "poisons" which contribute to the existing state of impurity must be searched out and eliminated.

The philosophical assumption underlying this demand is that absolute purity (the "good Communist" or the ideal Communist state) is attainable, and that anything done to anyone in the name of this purity is ultimately moral. In actual practice, however, no one (and no State) is really expected to achieve such perfection. Nor can this paradox be dismissed as merely a means of establishing a high standard to which all can aspire. Thought reform bears witness to its more malignant consequences: for by defining and manipulating the criteria of purity, and then by conducting an all-out war upon impurity, the ideological totalists create a narrow world of guilt and shame. This is perpetuated by an ethos of continuous reform, a demand that one strive permanently and painfully for something which not only does not exist but is in fact alien to the human condition.

At the level of the relationship between individual and environment, the demand for purity creates what we may term a *guilty milieu* and a *shaming milieu.* Since each man's impurities are deemed sinful and potentially harmful to himself and to others, he is, so to speak, expected to expect punishment—which results in a relationship of guilt with his environment. Similarly, when he fails to meet the prevailing standards in casting out such impurities, he is expected to expect humiliation and ostracism—thus establishing a relationship of shame with his milieu. Moreover, the sense of guilt and the sense of shame become highly-valued: they are preferred forms of communication, objects of public competition, and the bases for eventual bonds between the individual and his totalist accusers. One may attempt to simulate them for a while, but the subterfuge is likely to be detected, and it is safer (as Miss Darrow found) to experience them genuinely.

People vary greatly in their susceptibilities to guilt and shame (as my subjects illustrated), depending upon patterns developed early in life. But since guilt and shame are basic to human existence, this variation can be no more than a matter of degree. Each person is made vulnerable through his profound inner sensitivities to his own limitations and to his unfulfilled potential; in other words, each is made vulnerable through his existential guilt. Since ideological totalists become the ultimate judges of good and evil within their world, they are able to use these universal tendencies toward guilt and shame as emotional levers for their controlling and manipulative influence. They become the arbiters of existential guilt, authorities without limit in dealing with others' limitations. And their power is nowhere more evident than in their capacity to "forgive."[5]

The individual thus comes to apply the same totalist polarization of good and evil to his judgments of his own character: he tends to imbue certain aspects of himself with excessive virtue, and condemn even more excessively other personal qualities—all according to their ideological standing. He must also look upon his impurities as originating from outside influences—that is, from the ever-threatening world beyond the closed, totalist ken. Therefore, one of his best ways to relieve himself of some of his burden of guilt is to denounce, continuously and hostilely, these same outside influences. The more guilty he feels, the greater his hatred, and the more threatening they seem. In this manner, the universal psychological tendency toward "projection" is nourished and institutionalized, leading to mass hatreds, purges of heretics, and to political and religious holy wars. Moreover, once an individual person has experienced the totalist polarization of good and evil, he has great difficulty in regaining a more balanced inner sensitivity to the complexities of human morality. For there is no emotional bondage greater than that of the man whose entire guilt potential—neurotic and existential—has become the property of ideological totalists.

The Cult of Confession

Closely related to the demand for absolute purity is an obsession with personal confession. Confession is carried beyond its ordinary religious, legal, and therapeutic expressions to the point of becoming a cult in itself. There is the demand that one confess to crimes one has not committed, to sinfulness that is artificially induced, in the name of a cure that is arbitrarily imposed. Such demands are made possible not only by the ubiquitous human tendencies toward guilt and shame but also by the need to give expression to these tendencies. In totalist hands, confession becomes a means of exploiting, rather than offering solace for, these vulnerabilities.

The totalist confession takes on a number of special meanings. It is first a vehicle for the kind of personal purification which we have just discussed, a means of maintaining a perpetual inner emptying or psychological purge of impurity; this *purging milieu* enhances the totalists' hold upon existential guilt. Second, it is an act of symbolic self-surrender, the expression of the merging of individual and environment. Third, it is a means of maintaining an ethos of total exposure—a policy of making public (or at least known to the Organization) everything possible about the life experiences, thoughts, and passions of each individual, and especially those elements which might be regarded as derogatory.

The assumption underlying total exposure (besides those which relate to the demand for purity) is the environment's claim to total ownership of each individual self within it. Private ownership of the mind and its products—of imagination or of memory—becomes highly immoral. The accompanying rationale (rationalization) is familiar to us (from George Chen's experience); the milieu has attained such a perfect state of enlightenment that any individual retention of ideas or emotions has become anachronistic.

The cult of confession can offer the individual person meaningful psychological satisfactions in the continuing opportunity for emotional catharsis and for relief of suppressed guilt feelings, especially insofar as these are associated with self-punitive tendencies to get pleasure from personal degradation. More than this, the sharing of confession enthusiasms can create an orgiastic sense of "oneness," of the most intense intimacy with fellow confessors and of the dissolution of self into the great flow of the Movement. And there is also, at least initially, the possibility of genuine self-revelation and of self-betterment through the recognition that "the thing that has been exposed is what I am."[6]

But as totalist pressures turn confession into recurrent command performances, the element of histrionic public display takes precedence over genuine inner experience. Each man becomes concerned with the effectiveness of his personal performance, and this performance sometimes comes to serve the function of evading the very emotions and ideas about which one feels most guilty—confirming the statement by one of Camus' characters that "authors of confessions write especially to avoid confessing, to tell nothing of what they know."[7] The difficulty, of course, lies in the inevitable confusion which takes place between the actor's method and his separate personal reality, between the performer and the "real me."

In this sense, the cult of confession has effects quite the reverse of its ideal of total exposure: rather than eliminating personal secrets, it increases and intensifies them. In any situation the personal secret has two important elements: first, guilt and shameful ideas which one wishes to suppress in order to prevent their becoming known by others or their becoming too prominent in one's own awareness; and second, representations of parts of oneself too precious to be expressed except when alone or when involved in special loving relationships formed around this shared secret world. Personal secrets are always maintained in opposition to inner pressures toward self-exposure. The totalist milieu makes contact with these inner pressures through its own obsession with the exposé and the unmasking process. As a result old secrets are revived and new ones proliferate; the latter frequently consist of resentments toward or doubts about the Movement, or else are related to aspects of identity still existing outside of the prescribed ideological sphere. Each person becomes caught up in a continuous conflict over which secrets to preserve and which to surrender, over ways to reveal lesser secrets in order to protect more important ones; his own boundaries between the secret and the known, between the public and the private, become blurred. And around one secret, or a complex of secrets, there may revolve (as we saw with Hu) an ultimate inner struggle between resistance and self-surrender.

Finally, the cult of confession makes it virtually impossible to attain a reasonable balance between worth and humility. The enthusiastic and aggressive confessor becomes like Camus' character whose perpetual confession is his means of judging others: "[I] . . . practice the profession of penitent to be able to end up as a judge . . . the more I accuse myself, the more I have a right to judge you." The identity of the "judge-penitent"[8] thus becomes a vehicle for taking on some of the environment's arrogance and sense of omnipotence. Yet even this shared omnipotence cannot protect him from the opposite (but not unrelated) feelings of humiliation and weakness, feelings especially prevalent among those who remain more the enforced penitent than the all-powerful judge.

The "Sacred Science"

The totalist milieu maintains an aura of sacredness around its basic dogma, holding it out as an ultimate moral vision for the ordering of human existence. This sacredness is evident in the prohibition (whether or not explicit) against the questioning of basic assumptions, and in the reverence which is demanded for the originators of the Word, the present bearers of the Word, and the Word itself. While thus transcending ordinary concerns of logic, however, the milieu at the same time makes an exaggerated claim of airtight logic, of absolute "scientific" precision. Thus the ultimate moral vision becomes an ultimate science; and the man who dares to criticize it, or to harbor even unspoken alternative ideas, becomes not only immoral and irreverent, but also "unscientific." In this way, the philosopher kings of modern ideological totalism reinforce their authority by claiming to share in the rich and respected heritage of natural science.

The assumption here is not so much that man can be God, but rather that man's *ideas* can be God: that an absolute science of ideas (and implicitly, an absolute science of man) exists, or is at least very close to being attained; that the science can be combined with an equally absolute body of moral principles; and that the resulting doctrine is true for all men at all times. Although no ideology goes quite this far in overt statement, such assumptions are implicit in totalist practice.[9]

At the level of the individual, the totalist sacred science can offer much comfort and security. Its appeal lies in its seeming unification of the mystical and the logical modes of experience (in psychoanalytic terms, of the primary and secondary thought processes). For within the framework of the sacred science, there is room for both careful step-by-step syllogism, and sweeping, nonrational "insights." Since the distinction between the logical and the mystical is, to begin with, artificial and man-made, an opportunity for transcending it can create an extremely intense feeling of truth. But the posture of unquestioning faith—both rationally and nonrationally derived—is not easy to sustain, especially if one discovers that the world of experience is not as absolute as the sacred science claims it to be.

Yet so strong a hold can the sacred science achieve over his mental processes that if one begins to feel himself attracted to ideas which either contradict or ignore it, he may become guilty and afraid. His quest for knowledge is consequently hampered, since in the name of science he is prevented from engaging in the receptive search for truth which characterizes the genuinely scientific approach. And his position is made more difficult by the absence, in a totalist environment, of any distinction between the sacred and the profane: there is no thought in action which cannot be related to the sacred science. To be sure, one can usually find areas of experience outside its immediate authority; but during periods of maximum totalist activity (like thought reform) any such areas are cut off, and there is virtually no escape from the milieu's ever-pressing edicts and demands. Whatever combination of continued adherence, inner resistance, or compromise co-existence the individual person adopts toward this blend of counterfeit science and back-door religion, it represents another continuous pressure toward personal closure, toward avoiding, rather than grappling with, the kinds of knowledge and experience necessary for genuine self-expression and for creative development.

Loading the Language

The language of the totalist environment is characterized by the thought-terminating cliché. The most far-reaching and complex of human problems are compressed into brief, highly reductive, definitive-sounding phrases, easily memorized and easily expressed. These become the start and finish of any ideological analysis. In thought reform, for instance, the phrase "bourgeois mentality" is used to encompass and critically dismiss ordinarily troublesome concerns like the quest for individual expression, the exploration of alternative ideas, and the search for perspective and balance in political judgments. And in addition to their function as interpretive shortcuts, these clichés become what Richard Weaver has called "ultimate terms": either "god terms," representative of ultimate good; or "devil terms," representative of ultimate evil. In thought reform, "progress," "progressive," "liberation," "proletarian standpoints" and "the dialectic of history" fall into the former category; "capitalist," "imperialist," "exploiting classes," and "bourgeois" (mentality, liberalism, morality, superstition, greed) of course fall into the latter.[10] Totalist language, then, is repetitiously centered on all-encompassing jargon, prematurely abstract, highly categorical, relentlessly judging, and to anyone but its most devoted advocate, deadly dull: in Lionel Trilling's phrase, "the language of nonthought."

To be sure, this kind of language exists to some degree within any cultural or organizational group, and all systems of belief depend upon it. It is in part an expression of unity and exclusiveness: as Edward Sapir put it, " 'He talks like us' is equivalent to saying 'He is one of us':"[11] The loading is much more extreme in ideological totalism, however, since the jargon expresses the claimed certitudes of the sacred science. Also involved is an underlying assumption that language—like all other human products—can be owned and operated by the Movement. No compunctions are felt about manipulating or loading it in any fashion; the only consideration is its usefulness to the cause.

For an individual person, the effect of the language of ideological totalism can be summed up in one word: constriction. He is, so to speak, linguistically deprived; and since language is so central to all human experience, his capacities for thinking and feeling are immensely narrowed. This is what Hu meant when he said, "using the same pattern of words for so long . . . you feel chained." Actually, not everyone exposed *feels* chained, but in effect everyone *is* profoundly confined by these verbal fetters. As in other aspects of totalism, this loading may provide an initial sense of insight and security, eventually followed by uneasiness. This uneasiness may result in a retreat into a rigid orthodoxy in which an individual shouts the ideological jargon all the louder in order to demonstrate his conformity, hide his own dilemma and his despair, and protect himself from the fear and guilt he would feel should he attempt to use words and phrases other than the correct ones. Or else he may adopt a complex pattern of inner division, and dutifully produce the expected clichés in public performances while in his private moments he searches for more meaningful avenues of expression. Either way, his imagination becomes increasingly dissociated from his actual life experiences and may even tend to atrophy from disuse.

Doctrine Over Person

This sterile language reflects another characteristic feature of ideological totalism; the subordination of human experience to the claims of doctrine. The primacy of doctrine over person is evident in the continual shift between experience itself and the highly abstract interpretation of such experience—between genuine feelings and spurious cataloguing of feelings. It has much to do with the peculiar aura of half-reality which a totalist environment seems, at least to the outsider, to possess.

This tendency in the totalist approach to broad historical events was described in relationship to Chinese Communism by John K. Fairbank and Mary C. Wright:

> . . . stock characters like capitalist imperialists from abroad, feudal and semi-feudal reaction at home, and the resistance and liberation movements of "the people" enact a morality play. This melodrama sees aggression, injustice, exploitation, and humiliation engulf the Chinese people until salvation comes at last with Communism. Mass revolutions require an historical myth as part of their black and white morality, and this is the ideological myth of one of the great revolutions of world history.[12]

The inspiriting force of such myths cannot be denied, nor can one ignore their capacity for mischief. For when the myth becomes fused with the totalist sacred science, the resulting "logic" can be so compelling and coercive that it simply replaces the realities of individual experience. Consequently, past historical events are retrospectively altered, wholly rewritten, or ignored, to make them consistent with the doctrinal logic. This alteration becomes especially malignant when its distortions are imposed upon individual memory as occurred in the false confessions extracted during thought reform (most graphically Father Luca's).

The same doctrinal primacy prevails in the totalist approach to changing people: the demand that character and identity be reshaped, not in accordance with one's special nature or potentialities, but rather to fit the rigid contours of the doctrinal mold. The human is thus subjugated to the ahuman. And in this manner, the totalists, as Camus phrases it, "put an abstract idea above human life, even if they call it history, to which they themselves have submitted in advance and to which they will decide quite arbitrarily to submit everyone else as well."[13]

The underlying assumption is that the doctrine—including its mythological elements—is ultimately more valid, true, and real than is any aspect of actual human character or human experience. Thus, even when circumstances require that a totalist movement follow a course of action in conflict with or outside of the doctrine, there exists what Benjamin Schwartz has described as a "will to orthodoxy"[14] which requires an elaborate façade of new rationalizations designed to demonstrate the unerring consistency of the doctrine and the unfailing foresight which it provides. The public operation of this will to orthodoxy is seen in the Party's explanation of the Hundred Flowers Campaign. But its greater importance lies in more hidden manifestations, particularly the totalists' pattern of imposing their doctrine-dominated remolding upon people in order to seek confirmation of (and again, dispel their own doubts about) this same doctrine. Rather than modify the myth in accordance with experience, the will to orthodoxy requires instead that men be modified in order to reaffirm the myth. Thus, much of prison thought reform was devoted to making the Westerner conform to the pure image of "evil imperialist," so that he could take his proper role in the Communist morality play of Chinese history.

The individual person who finds himself under such doctrine-dominated pressure to change is thrust into an intense struggle with his own sense of integrity, a struggle which takes place in relation to polarized feelings of sincerity and insincerity. In a totalist environment, absolute "sincerity" is demanded; and the major criterion for sincerity is likely to be one's degree of doctrinal compliance—both in regard to belief and to direction of personal change. Yet there is always the possibility of retaining an alternative version of sincerity (and of reality), the capacity to imagine a different kind of existence and another form of sincere commitment (as did Grace Wu when she thought, "the world could not be like this"). These alternative visions depend upon such things as the strength of previous identity, the penetration of the milieu by outside ideas, and the retained capacity for eventual individual renewal. The totalist environment, however, counters such "deviant" tendencies with the accusation that they stem entirely from personal "problems" ("thought problems" or "ideological problems") derived from untoward earlier ("bourgeois") influences. The outcome will depend largely upon how much genuine relevance the doctrine has for the individual emotional predicament. And even for those to whom it seems totally appealing, the exuberant sense of well-being it temporarily affords may be more a "delusion of wholeness"[15] than an expression of true and lasting inner harmony.

The Dispensing of Existence

The totalist environment draws a sharp line between those whose right to existence can be recognized, and those who possess no such right. In thought reform, as in Chinese Communist practice generally, the world is divided into the "people" (defined as "the working class, the peasant class, the petite bourgeoisie, and the national bourgeoisie"), and the "reactionaries" or "lackeys of imperialism" (defined as "the landlord class, the bureaucratic capitalist class, and the KMT reactionaries and their henchmen"). Mao Tse-tung makes the existential distinction between the two groups quite explicit:

> Under the leadership of the working class and the Communist Party, these classes [the people] unite together to form their own state and elect their own government [so as to] carry out a dictatorship over the lackeys of imperialism. . . . These two aspects, namely, democracy among the people and dictatorship over the reactionaries, combine to form the people's democratic dictatorship . . . to the hostile classes that state apparatus is the instrument of oppression. It is violent, and not "benevolent." . . . Our benevolence applies only to the people, and not to the reactionary acts of the reactionaries and reactionary classes outside the people.[16]

Being "outside the people," the reactionaries are presumably nonpeople. Under conditions of ideological totalism, in China and elsewhere, nonpeople have often been put to death, their executioners then becoming guilty (in Camus' phrase) of "crimes of logic." But the thought reform process is one means by which nonpeople are permitted, through a change in attitude and personal character, to make themselves over into people. The most literal example of such dispensing of existence and nonexistence is to be found in the sentence given to certain political criminals: execution in two years' time, unless during that two-year period they have demonstrated genuine progress in their reform. . .

Are not men presumptuous to appoint themselves the dispensers of human existence? Surely this is a flagrant expression of what the Greeks called *hubris*, of arrogant man making himself God. Yet one underlying assumption makes this arrogance mandatory: the conviction that there is just one path to true existence, just one valid mode of being, and that all others are perforce invalid and false. Totalists thus feel themselves compelled to destroy all possibilities of false existence as a means of furthering the great plan of true existence to which they are committed. Indeed, Mao's words suggest that all of thought reform can be viewed as a way to eradicate such allegedly false modes of existence—not only among the nonpeople, within whom they supposedly originate, but also among legitimate people allegedly contaminated by them.

> The [function of the] people's state is to protect the people. Only where there is the people's state, is it possible for the people to use democratic methods or a nationwide and all-round scale to educate and reform themselves, to free themselves from the influence of reactionaries at home and abroad . . . to unlearn the bad habits and ideas acquired from the old society and not to let themselves travel on the erroneous path pointed out by the reactionaries, but to continue to advance and develop towards a Socialist and Communist Society accomplishing the historic mission of completely eliminating classes and advancing toward a universal fraternity.[17]

For the individual, the polar emotional conflict is the ultimate existential one of "being versus nothingness." He is likely to be drawn to a conversion experience, which he sees as the only means of attaining a path of existence for the future (as did George Chen). The totalist environment—even when it does not resort to physical abuse—thus stimulates in everyone a fear of extinction or annihilation much like the basic fear experienced by Western prisoners. A person can overcome this fear and find (in Martin Buber's term) "confirmation," not in his individual relationships, but only from the fount of all existence, the totalist Organization. Existence comes to depend upon creed (I believe, therefore I am), upon submission (I obey, therefore I am) and beyond these, upon a sense of total merger with the ideological movement. Ultimately of course one compromises and combines the totalist "conformation" with independent elements of personal identity; but one is ever made aware that, should he stray too far along this "erroneous path," his right to existence may be withdrawn.

The more clearly an environment expresses these eight psychological themes, the greater its resemblance to ideological totalism; and the more it utilizes such totalist devices to change people, the greater its resemblance to thought reform (or "brainwashing"). But facile comparisons can be misleading. No milieu ever achieves complete totalism, and many relatively moderate environments show some signs of it. Moreover, totalism tends to be recurrent rather than continuous: in China, for instance, its fullest expression occurs during thought reform; it is less apparent during lulls in thought reform, although it is by no means absent. And like the "enthusiasm" with which it is often associated, totalism is more apt to be present during the early phases of mass movements than later—Communist China in the 1950's was generally more totalist than Soviet Russia. But if totalism has at any time been prominent in a movement, there is always the possibility of its reappearance, even after long periods of relative moderation.

Then too, some environments come perilously close to totalism but at the same time keep alternative paths open; this combination can offer unusual opportunities for achieving intellectual and emotional depth. And even the most full-blown totalist milieu can provide (more or less despite itself) a valuable and enlarging life experience—*if* the man exposed has both the opportunity to leave the extreme environment and the inner capacity to absorb and make inner use of the totalist pressures (as did Father Vechten and Father Luca).

Also, ideological totalism itself may offer a man an intense peak experience; a sense of transcending all that is ordinary and prosaic, of freeing himself from the encumbrances of human ambivalence, of entering a sphere of truth, reality, trust, and sincerity beyond any he had ever known or even imagined. But these peak experiences, the result as they are of external pressure, distortion, and threat, carry a great potential for rebound, and for equally intense opposition to the very things which initially seem so liberating. Such imposed peak experiences[18]—as contrasted with those more freely and privately arrived at by great religious leaders and mystics—are essentially experiences of personal closure. Rather than stimulating greater receptivity and "openness to the world," they encourage a backward step into some form of "embeddedness"—a retreat into doctrinal and organizational exclusiveness, and into all-or-nothing emotional patterns more characteristic (at least at this stage of human history) of the child than of the individuated adult.[19]

And if no peak experience occurs, ideological totalism does even greater violence to the human potential: it evokes destructive emotions, produces intellectual and psychological constrictions, and deprives men of all that is most subtle and imaginative—under the false promise of eliminating those very imperfections and ambivalences which help to define the human condition. This combination of personal closure, self-destructiveness, and hostility toward outsiders leads to the dangerous group excesses so characteristic of ideological totalism in any form. It also mobilizes extremist tendencies in those outsiders under attack, thus creating a vicious circle of totalism.

What is the source of ideological totalism? How do these extremist emotional patterns originate? These questions raise the most crucial and the most difficult of human problems. Behind ideological totalism lies the ever-present human quest for the omnipotent guide—for the supernatural force, political party, philosophical ideas, great leader, or precise science—that will bring ultimate solidarity to all men and eliminate the terror of death and nothingness. This quest is evident in the mythologies, religions, and histories of all nations, as well as in every individual life. The degree of individual totalism involved depends greatly upon factors in one's personal history: early lack of trust, extreme environmental chaos, total domination by a parent or parent-representative, intolerable burdens of guilt, and severe crises of identity. Thus an early sense of confusion and dislocation, or an early experience of unusually intense family milieu control, can produce later a complete intolerance for confusion and dislocation, and a longing for the reinstatement of milieu control. But these things are in some measure part of every childhood experience; and therefore the potential for totalism is a continuum from which no one entirely escapes, and in relationship to which no two people are exactly the same.

It may be that the capacity for totalism is most fundamentally a product of human childhood itself, of the prolonged period of helplessness and dependency through which each of us must pass. Limited as he is, the infant has no choice but to imbue his first nurturing authorities—his parents—with an exaggerated omnipotence, until the time he is himself capable of some degree of independent action and judgment. And even as he develops into the child and the adolescent, he continues to require many of the all-or-none polarities of totalism as terms with which to define his intellectual, emotional, and moral world. Under favorable circumstances (that is, when family and culture encourage individuation) these requirements can be replaced by more flexible and moderate tendencies; but they never entirely disappear.

During adult life, individual totalism takes on new contours as it becomes associated with new ideological interests. It may become part of the configuration of personal emotions, messianic ideas, and organized mass movement which I have described as ideological totalism. When it does, we cannot speak of it as simply a form of regression. It is partly this, but it is also something more: a new form of adult embeddedness, originating in patterns of security-seeking carried over from childhood, but with qualities of ideas and aspirations that are specifically adult. During periods of cultural crisis and of rapid historical change, the totalist quest for the omnipotent guide leads men to seek to become that guide.

Totalism, then, is a widespread phenomenon, but it is not the only approach to re-education. We can best use our knowledge of it by applying its criteria to familiar processes in our own cultural tradition and in our own country.

Notes

[1] Personal "closure" implies abandoning man's inherent strivings toward the outer world as well as much of his receptivity to his own inner impulses, and retreating into what Ernest Schachtel has called "the closed pattern of relatedness to the world institutionalized in . . . [a] particular culture or cultural subgroup," *Metamorphosis* (New York: Basic Books, 1959), p. 75.

[2] Helen Lynd, *On Shame and the Search for Identity* (New York: Harcourt, Brace & Co., 1958), p. 57.

[3] Alex Inkeles, "The Totalitarian Mystique. Some Impressions of the Dynamics of Totalitarian Society," *Totalitarianism,* edited by Carl Friedrich (Cambridge, Mass.: Harvard University Press, 1953), pp. 88 and 91.

[4] *Ibid.*, p. 91.

[5] In Camus' novel, *The Fall* (New York: Alfred A. Knopf, 1957), p. 127, Clamence states: "My great idea is that one must forgive the Pope. To begin with, he needs it more than anyone else. Secondly, that's the only way to set oneself above him. . . ."

[6] Helen Lynd, *op. cit.*, p. 57.

[7] Camus, *The Fall,* p. 120.

[8] *Ibid.*, pp. 8 and 138.

[9] A somewhat similar point of view is expressed by Hannah Arendt in her comprehensive study, *The Origins of Totalitarianism* (New York: Meridian Books, 1958), pp. 468–474.

[10] In this respect, thought reform is clearly a child of its era, for Weaver claims that "progress is the 'god term' of the present age," and also lists "progressive," "science," "fact," and "modern" as other widely-used "god terms" ("Ultimate Terms in Contemporary Rhetoric," *Perspectives* (1955), pp. 11, 1–2, 141). All these words have a similar standing in thought reform. Thought reform's "devil terms" are more specifically Communist, but also included are such general favorites as "aggressor" and "fascist."

[11] Edward Sapir, "Language," *Culture, Language and Personality* (Berkeley, Calif.: University of California Press, 1956), p. 17.

[12] John K. Fairbank and Mary C. Wright, "Documentary Collections on Modern Chinese," *The Journal of Asian Studies* (1957) 17:55–56, intro.

[13] Camus, *The Rebel* (New York: Alfred A. Knopf, 1954), p. 141.

[14] Benjamin Schwartz, *Chinese Communism and the Rise of Mao* (Cambridge: Harvard University Press, 1951), pp. 4–5.

[15] Erik Erikson, "Wholeness and Totality," in Friedrich, ed., *op. cit.*, p. 165.

[16] Mao Tse-tung, "One the People's Democratic Dictatorship," Brandt, Schwartz, and Fairbank, *A Documentary History of Chinese Communism* (Cambridge: Harvard University Press, 1951), pp. 456–457.

[17] *Ibid.*, p. 457.

[18] I have borrowed the term "peak experiences" from A. H. Maslow (Presidential Address, Division of Personality and Social Psychology, American Psychological Association, Chicago, Ill., September 1, 1956, mimeographed), although my use of it is perhaps somewhat broader than his. In his terminology, he might see the imposed "peak experience" as lacking in genuine "cognition of being."

[19] "Openness to the world," or "world-openness," and "embeddedness" are conceptualized by Schachtel (*Metamorphosis*, pp. 22–77), as perpetually antagonistic human emotional tendencies.

3 Harold Adams Innis and Marshall McLuhan

James W. Carey

This lucid analysis of two difficult thinkers is not presented in its entirety. For the purpose of Professor Carey, contrasting the insights of Innis and McLuhan, is not the purpose of our reader. The selection here, which does in fact represent the bulk of Carey's essay, concentrates on the thought of Innis, who relates the use of media of communication to the control of social change.

Both Kamen and Lifton deal with the conscious efforts of some men to control other men by controlling the communication between men. Carey and Innis are interested in the structure and biases of the media of communication which invite some forms of control and stimulate certain kinds of social ideals, regardless of the intention of the controllers. For neither does this bias render moral choice illusory or irrelevant, but it does make the exercise of free choice in using and receiving communication a complex procedure.

Reprinted by permission of the publishers from *The Antioch Review*, Vol. XXVII, No. 1 (Spring 1967). By permission of the Antioch Press, Ohio.

DR. CAREY is both a professor of journalism and communications research at the College of Communications and the Institute of Communications Research at the University of Illinois in Urbana.

Harold Adams Innis was a Canadian economist and historian who devoted most of his scholarly life to producing marvelously detailed studies of Canadian industries—the fur trading industry, the cod fisheries, the Canadian Pacific Railway, for example. During the last decade of his life (Innis died in 1952), he undertook an extensive analysis of all forms of human communication and produced two major works—*The Bias of Communication* and *Empire and Communications*—and two important collections of essays, *Changing Concepts of Time* and *Political Economy and the Modern State.* His interest in communications was not, however, independent of his concerns for economic history. Rather, the former grew out of the latter. In his studies of the economic history of Canada, Innis was confronted by two important questions: (1) What are the underlying causes of change in social organization, defined broadly to include both culture and social institutions? (2) What are the conditions which promote stability in any society? Stability here is defined as both the capacity to adapt to changing realities in politics and the economy and also as the capacity to preserve the integrity of culture, the continuity of attitude, sentiment, and morality upon which civilization is based. Further, Innis wanted to answer those questions in a manner that would capture not only the major currents of history in the West but also the eddies and tributaries, streams and backwaters of social change.[1]

Innis felt that the answer to his first question—the question of the source of social change—was to be found in technological innovation. He was, like McLuhan, a technological determinist, though unlike McLuhan a rather soft determinist. Innis and McLuhan agree that while there are various kinds of technology—military, industrial, administrative—these technologies were not equal in their impact on society or in their ontological status. For Innis, the technology of communication was central to all other technology. He does not make at all clear why this should be so. However, let me make this suggestion. There are presumably two reasons for the centrality of communications technology—one logical, one historical. Innis assumes that man stands in a unique, symbiotic relationship to his technology. In McLuhan's phrase, technology is literally an extension of man, as the ax is an extension of the hand, the wheel of the foot. Most instruments are attempts to extend man's physical capacity, a capacity shared with other animals. Communications technology, on the other hand, is an extension of thought, of consciousness, of man's unique perceptual capacities. Thus communication media, broadly used to include all modes of symbolic representation, are literally extensions of mind.

Innis also suggests that historically fundamental breakthroughs in technology are first applied to the process of communication. The age of mechanics was ushered in by the printing press, the age of electronics by the telegraph. The explanation for this historical fact Innis derived from a conception of society based upon a model of competition appropriated from economics and extended to all social institutions. And in this competitive model, competition for new means of communication was a principal axis of the competitive struggle. Innis argued that the available media of communication influence very strongly the forms of social organization that are possible. The media thus influence the kinds of human associations that can develop in any period. Because these patterns of association are not independent of the knowledge men have of themselves and others—indeed, consciousness is built on these associations—control of communications implies control of both consciousness and social organization. Thus, whenever a medium of communication and the groups which control the media have a hegemony in society, Innis assumes that a principal axis of competition will be the search for competing media of communication. New media are designed to undercut existing centers of power and to facilitate the creation of new patterns of association and the articulation of new forms of knowledge. I will return to this point later. Let me only note now that Innis assumed that disenfranchised groups in society would lead the search for new forms of technology in seeking to compete for some form of social power.

The bulk of Innis' work was devoted to analyzing the kinds of control inherent in communications media. He considered, as near as one can tell, all forms of communication from speech through printing, including what he took to be the four dominant pre-printing media—clay, papyrus, parchment, and paper. With each of these media he also considered the types of script employed and the kinds of writing instruments used. Innis argued that various stages of Western civilization could be characterized by the dominance of a particular medium of communication. The medium had a determinate influence on the form of social organization typical of the stage of society and on the character of the culture of that stage. Further, the succession of stages in Western civilization could be seen in terms of a competition between media of communication for dominance. The results of this competition among media progressively transformed the character of social institutions and the nature of culture.

I think it important to note Innis' emphasis on both culture and social organization. He was concerned not only with the ways in which culture and institutions were interrelated but also the sense in which they were *both* epiphenomena of communications technology. Usually the social history of the West takes either the route of August Comte, emphasizing the progressive transformation of culture from the theological to the metaphysical to the positivistic, or the route taken by Lewis Mumford, emphasizing the transformations in social organization from the tribe to the town to the city. Innis, however, attempts to marry these two traditions into a unified view of social change. Moreover, he attaches changes in both social organization and culture to changes in the technology of communication. The generality of Innis' argument is seldom recognized, I think, because of a failure to appreciate the meaning of the phrase "the bias of communication" and the dual sense in which he defines his two principal variables, space and time.

Innis argues that any given medium of communication is biased in terms of the control of time or space. Media which are durable and difficult to transport—parchment, clay, and stone—are time-binding or time-biased. Media which are light and less durable are space-binding or spatially biased. For example, paper and papyrus are space-binding, for they are light, easily transportable, can be moved across space with reasonable speed and great accuracy, and they thus favor administration over vast distance.

Any given medium will bias social organization, for it will favor the growth of certain kinds of interests and institutions at the expense of others and will also impose on these institutions a form of organization. Media which are space-binding facilitate and encourage the growth of empire, encourage a concern with expansion and with the present, and thus favor the hegemony of secular political authority. Space-binding media encourage the growth of the state, the military, and decentralized and expansionist institutions. Time-binding media foster concern with history and tradition, have little capacity for expansion of secular authority, and thus favor the growth of religion, of hierarchical organization, and of contractionist institutions. The hegemony of either religion or the state imposes a characteristic pattern on all secondary institutions, such as education, and also leads to a search for competing, alternative modes of communication to undercut this hegemony. Thus, the dynamic of social change resided in the search for alternative forms of communication alternately supporting the kingdom of God or man.

At the level of social structure, a time bias meant an emphasis upon religion, hierarchy, and contraction, whereas a space bias meant an emphasis upon the state, decentralization, and expansion. But the terms "time" and "space" also had a cultural meaning.

In cultural terms, time meant the sacred, the moral, the historical; space the present and the future, the technical and the secular. As media of communication favored the growth of certain kinds of institutions, it also assured the domination of the culture characteristic of those institutions. On the cultural level, his principal contrast was between the oral and written traditions. Let me try to develop the contrast.

Although speech is not the only means of communication in traditional societies, it certainly is the principal means. Traditional societies are organized in terms of, or are at least severely constrained by, certain features of speech. For example, spoken language can traverse only relatively short distances without being altered and distorted, giving rise to dialects. Speech not only moves over short distances but travels slowly compared with other means of communication. Speech also has a low capacity for storage; there is no way of preserving information except by storing it in the memories of individuals or by symbolizing it in some material form. Life in traditional societies must be collective, communal, and celebrative as the medium of communication requires it to be.

Innis argues that speech encourages the development of a society with a strong temporal bias, a society which focuses on the past and which emphasizes tradition, which attempts to conserve and preserve the existing stock of knowledge and values. Such societies are likely to have limited conceptions of space, conceptions restricted to the village or geographical area currently occupied by the tribe. Space beyond that is invested with magical qualities, frequently being the home of the gods; for example, cargo cults. While the mind of primitive man can traverse extraordinary reaches of time, it is radically limited in traversing space. The hegemony of speech is likely to also lead to magical beliefs in language. Words become icons, they do not represent things, they are themselves things. The care, nurture, and preservation of language is likely to occupy much collective energy of the society.

Oral cultures, then, are time-binding cultures. They have consequently a limited capacity for technical change. The imbalance toward time rooted in the available means of communication emphasizes the cohesion of people in the present by their "remembrances of things past." With media such as speech, Innis associated tradition, the sacred, and the institutionalization of magic and religion.

Speech as the dominant mode of communication gave rise to an oral tradition, a tradition that Innis not only described but admired. By an oral tradition Innis meant a "selection from the history of a people of a series of related events, culturally defined as significant, and their transmission from generation to generation." The recitation of artistic works within the oral tradition was a social ceremony which linked audiences to the past and celebrated their social cohesion in the present. While individual performers would modify an oral tradition to make it more serviceable in present circumstances, they began with the tradition and thus became indissolubly linked to it.

Furthermore, the oral tradition was flexible and persistent. Linked as it was to the collective and communal life of a people, built into their linguistic habits and modes of symbolic expression, the oral tradition was difficult to destroy. Through endless repetition an oral tradition "created recognized standards and lasting moral and social institutions; it built up the soul of social organization and maintained their continuity. . . ."

Oral traditions and time-binding media led to the growth of a culture oriented toward a sacred tradition, which built consensus on the sharing of mutually affirmed and celebrated attitudes and values, and placed morals and metaphysics at the center of civilization.

Written traditions, in general, led to quite different cultures. They were usually space-binding and favored the growth of political authority and secular institutions and a culture appropriate to them. Let me warn you that Innis did not admire oral cultures and derogate written ones. Some of his language could easily lead one to that conclusion, but, as I hope to show, that was decidedly not the case.

Written traditions and their appropriate culture ground relations among men not on tradition but on attachment to secular authority. Rather than emphasizing the temporal relations among kinship, written tradition emphasizes spatial relationships. Rather than emphasizing the past, it emphasizes the present and the future, particularly the future of empire. Rather than emphasizing knowledge grounded in moral order, it emphasizes the technical order and favors the growth of science and technical knowledge. Whereas the character of storage and reception of the oral tradition favor continuity over time, the written tradition favors discontinuity in time though continuity over space.

What Innis recognized was the hostility that seemed inevitably to develop between the written and the oral tradition. The innovation of writing would first lead to a recording of the oral tradition. It would thus freeze it and make it of interest to subsequent generations largely for antiquarian reasons. The written tradition, after its initial contact with the oral, would go its own way. It would favor change and innovation and progressive attenuation from the past as a residue of knowledge, values, and sentiment. The hostility between these traditions and between time-binding and space-binding media generally led to the creation of a monopoly of knowledge. He used the term monopoly in a straightforward economic sense. Very simply, Innis contended that the culture of the favored institution would infiltrate every aspect of social life and ultimately drive out, define as illegitimate, or radically transform competing traditions. Only knowledge that conformed to the concerns and cultural predispositions of the dominant medium would persist. In a written tradition, knowledge must be technical, secular, and future-oriented for it to be defined as legitimate or recognized as valid.

By now it should be obvious that Innis defined as the central problem of social science and social change the same problem which was the focus of Max Weber's work: the problem of authority. Innis wanted to know what, in general, determines the location of ultimate authority in a society and what will be recognized as authoritative knowledge. His answer was this: That media of communication, depending on their bias, confer monopolies of authority and knowledge on the state, the technical order, and civil law or on religion, the sacred order, and moral law.[2]

Innis believed that an overemphasis or monopoly of either time or space, religion or the state, the moral or the technical, was the principal dynamic of the rise and fall of empire. Time and space were thus related as conjugant variables in which the progressive presence of one led to the progressive absence of the other. The bias toward time or space produced instability in society. A stable society was possible only with the development of mechanisms that preserved both temporal and spatial orientations, that preserved competition between religion and the state, and that preserved independence and tension between the moral and the technical. In *The Bias of Communication* Innis commented that

> in western civilization a stable society is dependent on an appreciation of a proper balance between the concepts of space and time. We are concerned with control over vast areas of space but also over vast stretches of time. We must appraise civilization in relation to its territory and in relation to its duration. The character of the medium of communication tends to create a bias in civilization favorable to an overemphasis on the time concept or on the space concept and only at rare intervals are the biases offset by the influence of another medium and stability achieved.

Classical Greece was such a rare interval. The relative isolation of Greece from the older civilizations of Egypt and the Near East enabled her to develop an oral tradition. The written tradition was slowly introduced into Greece from these neighboring cultures, but it did not destroy the oral tradition. The tradition was committed to writing, but the oral tradition continued to flourish. For example, the dialogue remained the principal instrument of Greek culture, and an oral literature constituted the common moral consciousness. The written tradition with its spatial emphasis encouraged the growth of political authority and allowed Greece to deal with problems of administration. Eventually, writing triumphed over the oral tradition in the latter part of the fifth century B.C., and the spatial bias gave rise to a divisive individualism.

Generalizing from the experience of classical Greece, Innis argued that a healthy society requires competition not only in the marketplace but also in ideas, traditions, and institutions. Typically, media favor the development of cultural and institutional monopolies. Unless media favoring time and space exist as independent traditions offsetting and checking the biases of one another, the society will be dominated by a narrow monopoly. In such biased states, politics becomes sacralized or religion secularized; science destroys morality or morality emasculates science; tradition gives way to the notion of progress or chronic change obliterates tradition.

The history of the modern West, Innis argues, is the history of a bias of communication and a monopoly of knowledge founded on print. In one of his most quoted statements, Innis characterized modern Western history as beginning with temporal organization and ending with spatial organization. The introduction of printing attacked the temporal monopoly of the medieval church. Printing fostered the growth of nationalism and empire; it favored the extension of society in space. It encouraged the growth of bureaucracy and militarism, science and secular authority. Printing infiltrated all institutions, being the major force in creating what is currently celebrated as "the secular society." Not only did print destroy the oral tradition but it also drove underground the principal concerns of the oral tradition—morals, values, and metaphysics. While print did not destroy religion, it did, as Max Weber has argued, transform religion to meet the needs of the state and economy. Ultimately, the obsession with space, with the nation, with the moment, exposed the relativity of all values and led Western civilization, in Innis' eyes, to the brink of nihilism. The death of the oral tradition, the demise of concern with time, not only shifted the source of authority from the church to the state and of ultimate knowledge from religion to science; it also insisted on a transformation of religious concerns and language from the theological and sacred to the political and secular.

Innis viewed the rampaging nationalism of the twentieth century with anger and anguish, attitudes not untypical of contemporary intellectuals. But his emotion-charged writing should not obscure his central argument. The primary effect of changes in communication media is on the form of social organization that can be supported. Social organization produces a characteristic culture which constitutes the predispositions of individuals. The centrality of communication media to both culture and social structure implies that the principal axis of change, of the rise and fall of empire, will be alternations in the technologies of communication upon which society is principally reliant.

There are many similarities between the thought of Innis and that of Marshall McLuhan. Although I do not intend to obscure those similarities, I would like to emphasize, at least in this paper, some significant points of difference. The question I am asking is this: What is absolutely central to Innis' argument and how does it compare with the central notion in McLuhan's work? Although McLuhan has occasionally characterized his work as an extension of Innis', I want to suggest that McLuhan has taken a relatively minor but recurring theme of Innis' work (perhaps only a suggestion) and made it central to his entire argument. Conversely,

McLuhan has neglected or ignored the principal argument developed by Innis.

Both Innis and McLuhan agree that historically "the things on which words were written down count more than the words themselves"; that is, the medium is the message. Starting from this proposition, they engage in quite different kinds of intellectual bookkeeping, however, and are seized by quite different kinds of implications.

Both McLuhan and Innis assume the centrality of communication technology; where they differ is in the principal kinds of effects they see deriving from this technology. Whereas Innis sees communication technology principally affecting social organization and culture, McLuhan sees its principal effect on sensory organization and thought. McLuhan has much to say about perception and thought but little to say about institutions; Innis says much about institutions and little about perception and thought.

While McLuhan is intellectually linked to Innis, I think he can be more clearly and usefully tied to a line of speculation in sociolinguistics usually referred to as the Sapir-Whorf hypothesis.

The Sapir-Whorf hypothesis proposes that the language a speaker uses has a determining influence on the character of his thought. While it is a truism that men think with and through language, Edward Sapir and Benjamin Lee Whorf proposed that the very structure of reality—if I may use that grandiose and overworked phrase—is presented to individuals through language. When a person acquires a language he not only acquires a way of talking but also a way of seeing, a way of organizing experience, a way of discriminating the real world. Language, so the argument goes, has built into its grammar and lexicon the very structure of perception. Individuals discriminate objects and events in terms of the vocabulary provided by language. Further, individuals derive their sense of time, their patterns of classifications, their categories for persons, their perception of action, in terms of the tenses, the genders, the pronouns, the pluralizations that are possible in their language. This argument, then, largely reduces the structure of perception and thought to the structure of language.

McLuhan adopts the form of argument provided by the Sapir-Whorf hypothesis with two important modifications. First, he adopts a quite unorthodox characterization of the grammar of a language. Second, he extends the "grammatical analysis" to modes of communication such as print and television which are normally not treated as types of languages.

McLuhan does not view the grammar of a medium in terms of the formal properties of language, the parts of speech or morphemes, normally utilized in such an analysis. Instead, he argues that the grammar of a medium derives from the particular mixture of the senses that an individual characteristically uses in the utilization of the medium. For example, language—or better, speech—is the first of the mass media. It is a device for externalizing thought and for fixing and sharing perceptions. As a means of communication, speech elicits a particular orchestration of the sense. While speech is an oral phenomenon and gives rise to "ear-oriented cultures" (cultures in which people more easily believe what they hear than what they see), oral communication synthesizes or brings into play other sensual faculties. For example, in conversation men are aware not only of the sound of words but also of the visual properties of the speaker and the setting of the tactile qualities of various elements of the setting, and even certain olfactory properties of the person and the situation. These various faculties constitute parallel and simultaneous modes of communication, and thus McLuhan concludes that oral cultures synthesize these various modalities, elicit them all or bring them all into play in a situation utilizing all the sensory apparatus of the person. Oral cultures, then, involve the simultaneous interplay of sight, sound, touch, and smell and thus produce, in McLuhan's view, a depth of involvement in life as the principal communications medium—oral speech—simultaneously activates all the sensory faculties through which men acquire knowledge and share feeling.

However, speech is not the only mass medium, nor must it necessarily be the dominant mass medium. In technologically advanced societies, print, broadcasting, and film can replace speech as the dominant mode through which knowledge and feeling are communicated. In such societies speech does not disappear, but it assumes the characteristics of the dominant medium. For example, in literate communities oral traditions disappear and the content of spoken communication is the written tradition. Speech no longer follows its own laws. Rather it is governed by the laws of the written tradition. This means not only that the "content" of speech is what has previously been written but that the cadence and imagery of everyday speech is the cadence and imagery of writing. In literate communities, men have difficulty believing that the rich, muscular, graphic, almost multidimensional speech of Oscar Lewis' illiterate Mexican peasants was produced by such "culturally deprived" persons. But for McLuhan speech as an oral tradition, simultaneously utilizing many modes of communication, is almost exclusively the province of the illiterate.

McLuhan starts from the biological availability of parallel modes for the production and reception of messages. These modes —sight, touch, sound, and smell—do not exist independently but are interdependent with one another. Thus, to alter the capacity of one of the modes changes the total relations among the senses and thus alters the way in which individuals organize experience and fix perception. All this is clear enough. To remove one sense from a person leads frequently to the strengthening of the discriminatory powers of the other senses and thus to a rearrangement of not only the senses but of the kind of experience a person has. Blindness leads to an increasing reliance on and increasing power of smell and touch as well as hearing as modes of awareness. Loss of hearing particularly increases one's reliance on sight. But, McLuhan argues, the ratios between the senses and the power of the senses is affected by more than physical impairment or, to use his term, amputation. Media of communication also lead to the amputation of the senses. Media of communication also encourage the over-reliance on one sense faculty to the impairment or disuse of others. And thus, media of communication impart to persons a particular way of organizing experience and a particular way of knowing and understanding the world in which they travel.

Modes of communication, including speech, are, then, devices for fixing perception and organizing experience. Print, by its technological nature, has built into it a grammar for organizing experience, and its grammar is found in the particular ratio of sensory qualities it elicits in its users. All communications media are, therefore, extensions of man, or, better, are extensions of some mix of the sensory capacities of man. Speech is such an extension and thus the first mass medium. As an extension of man, it casts individuals in a unique, symbiotic relation to the dominant mode of communication in a culture. This symbiosis is not restricted to speech but extends to whatever medium of communication dominates a culture. This extension is by way of projecting certain sensory capacities of the individual. As I have mentioned, speech involves an extension and development of all the senses. Other media, however, are more partial in their appeal to the senses. The exploitation of a particular communications technology fixes particular sensory relations in members of society. By fixing such a relation, it determines a society's world view; that is, it stipulates a characteristic way of organizing experience. It thus determines the forms of knowledge, the structure of perception, and the sensory equipment attuned to absorb reality.

Media of communication, consequently, are vast social metaphors that not only transmit information but determine what is knowledge; that not only orient us to the world but tell us what kind of world exists; that not only excite and delight our sense but, by altering the ratio of sensory equipment that we use, actually change our character.

This is, I think, the core of McLuhan's argument. It can be most conveniently viewed as an attempt, albeit a creative and imaginative attempt, to extend the Sapir-Whorf hypothesis to include all forms of social communication.

Let me attempt to illustrate this abstruse argument with McLuhan's analysis of print. Print, the dominant means of communication in the West, depends on phonetic writing. Phonetic writing translated the oral into the visual; that is, it took sounds and translated them into visual symbols. Printing enormously extended and speeded up this process of translation, turning societies historically dependent upon the ear as the principal source of knowledge into societies dependent upon the eye. Print cultures in which seeing is believing, in which oral traditions are translated into written form, in which men have difficulty believing or remembering oral speech—names, stories, legends—unless they first see it written. In short, in print cultures knowledge is acquired and experience is confirmed by sight: as they say, by seeing it in writing. Men confirm their impressions of Saturday's football game by reading about it in Sunday morning's paper.

Besides making us dependent on the eye, printing imposes a particular logic on the organization of visual experience. Print organizes reality into discrete, uniform, harmonious, causal relations. The visual arrangement of the printed page becomes a perceptual model by which all reality is organized. The mental set of print—the desire to break things down into elementary units (words), the tendency to see reality in discrete units, to find causal relations and linear serial order (left to right arrangement of the page), to find orderly structure in nature (the orderly geometry of the printed page)—is transferred to all other social activities. Thus, science and government, art and architecture, work and education become organized in terms of the implicit assumption built into the dominant medium of communication.

Moreover, print encourages individualism and specialization. To live in an oral culture, one acquires knowledge only in contact with other people in terms of communal activities. Printing, however, allows individuals to withdraw, to contemplate and meditate outside of communal activities. Print thus encourages privatization, the lonely scholar, and the development of private, individual points of view.

McLuhan thus concludes that printing detribalizes man. It removes him from the necessity of participating in a tightly knit oral culture. In a notion apparently taken from T. S. Eliot, McLuhan contends that print disassociates the senses, separating sight from sound; encourages a private and withdrawn existence; and supports the growth of specialization.

Above all, print leads to nationalism, for it allows for the visual apprehension of the mother tongue and through maps a visual apprehension of the nation. Printing allows the vernacular to be standardized and the mother tongue to be universalized through education.

While the book ushered in the age of print, developments such as newspapers and magazines have only intensified the implications of print: extreme visual nationalism, specialist technology and occupations, individualism and private points of view.

By such argument McLuhan insists that the meaning and effect of any communications innovation is to be found in the way it structures thought and perception. The excitement which currently surrounds McLuhan derives from his extension of this argument to the newer media of communication, particularly television, and the effect these newer media have on the venerated tradition of print and on the mental life of contemporary man.

For McLuhan, the civilization based on print is dead. A science based on its assumptions, which searches for causal relations, encourages orderly, non-contradictory argument, fosters the specialization and compartmentalization of knowledge, is obsolete. Education which relies on the book and the lecture—itself merely reading from written script—and the traditional modes of sciences is likewise obsolete.

Print culture was doomed, so McLuhan argues, by the innovation of telegraphy, the first of the electronic media. Radio further undercut the hegemony of print, but the triumph of electronic communication over print awaited the permeation of the entire society by television. We are now observing, McLuhan concludes, the first generation weaned on television for whom the book and printing are secondary, remote, and ephemeral kinds of media. It is not only that television, as Storm Jameson has recently argued, leads to a devaluation of the written word. Television is not only another means for transmitting information; it is also a radically new way of organizing experience. Unlike print, television is not merely an eye medium but utilizes a much broader range of sensory equipment. That television marries sight and sound is obvious; but McLuhan also argues that television is a tactile medium as well. Television, as a result of the scanning system on which it operates, is capable of conveying or eliciting a sense of touch. Thus, in the apprehension of television not only the eye but the ear and the hand are brought into play. Television re-orchestrates the senses; it engages, if you will, the whole man, the entire range of sensory qualities of the person.

Moreover, television is, in one of McLuhan's inimitable phrases, a cool medium. By this McLuhan means only that television, like the cartoon and line drawing, is low in information. You don't merely watch a television screen. You engage it; you are forced to add information to complete the message. The capacity of the screen to transmit information is determined by the number of lines in the scanning system. In American television the scanning system is particularly low, 525 lines, and thus the medium is low in information relative to say, movies. Thus the viewer must get involved; he must fill in auditory, visual, and tactile cues for the message on the screen to be completed. Because television appeals to all the senses, because it is a cool or active, participational medium in front of which a viewer cannot remain passive, a culture in which television is the dominant medium will produce a person characteristically different than will a culture based on print.

McLuhan observes we are now witnessing in maturity the first generation who were suckled on television, who acquired the conventions of television long before it acquired traditional print literacy. The generational gap we now observe by contrasting the withdrawn, private, specializing student of the fifties with the active, involved, generalist student of the sixties McLuhan rests at the door of television. For the characteristic difference in these generations are paralleled by the differences between print and television as devices of communication. The desire of students for involvement and participation, for talking rather than reading, for seminars rather than lectures, for action rather than reflection, in short for participation and involvement rather than withdrawal and observation he ascribes to the re-orchestration of the senses provoked by television.

The conflict between generations of which we are now so acutely aware is ultimately a conflict between a generation bred on the book and a generation bred on the tube and related forms of electronic communication. The generational gap involves much more than politics and education, of course. In every area of life McLuhan observes youth asserting forms of behavior, demanding kinds of experience, which engage the total self. Dance and dress, music and hair styles, must not only have a "look"; they must also have a "sound" and above all a "touch." They must appeal to all the senses simultaneously. It is not only that youth wants experience; it wants experience that unifies rather than dissociates the senses. Moreover, in the new styles of literature which destroy all the conventions of print, in the new argots which destroy all the conventions of traditional grammar, in the new styles of political action which demean the traditionally radical forms of ideology and organization, in the demands for change in education, in music, in art, in dance, in dress, McLuhan sees the re-tribalization of man restoring him to the integrated condition of the oral culture in which the sensual capacities of men are again made whole.

This re-tribalization presumably involves the extension in space of the entire nervous system. Sight, hearing, and tactility derive from a nervous system originally contained within the skin. Each of the media has in turn extended these mechanisms, these aspects of the nervous system, beyond the skin. They have externalized them. The book and camera extend the eye, radio and the listening device extend the ear, television extends not only the eye and the ear but also the hand. Electric circuitry in general represents an extension of the entire nervous system. Think, for example, of the imagery of the computer with its network of wires and nodes linked to a television system. This is the sense in which communications media are extensions of man—extending with the aid of the computer the entire sensory and neurological system of the person in space, heightening the capacity of the organism to receive and digest information, literally turning the person now extended by his technology into an information processing system.

It is through such an analysis that McLuhan arrives at or expresses his central point: every medium of communication possesses a logic or grammar which constitutes a set of devices for organizing experience. The logic or grammar of each medium which dominates an age impresses itself on the users of the medium, thus dictating what is defined as truth and knowledge. Communication media, then, determine not only what one thinks about but literally how one thinks.

In the exposition of this notion McLuhan, of course, treats more than print and television. There are merely the endpoints in an exposition that includes commentary on films, radio, cartoons, light bulbs, political candidates, and virtually every other technique and folly of man. But in each case he attempts to determine the grammar inherent in the technology of the medium. While McLuhan normally defines the grammar of a medium in terms of the sense ratios it elicits, he frequently resorts to the more simplified method of designating media as "hot" or "cold." A hot medium is one that presents a lot of information in one sense; it bombards the receiver with information or, in another favorite phrase, is in high definition. A cool medium, or one in low definition, is a medium that presents relatively little information; the receiver must complete the image, must add values to what is presented to him and is thus more involving or participational. The halftone photo in four colors is visually hot; the cartoon is visually cool. Print is a hot medium, television a cool medium. The quality of having temperature applies also to persons and culture, dance and dress, autos and sports. Temperature, then, is another way of designating grammar. However, it is the least satisfactory of all McLuhan's concepts and arguments. This is unfortunate, because for most critics it is the terms "hot" and "cool" which are taken to be McLuhan's principal contribution to the study of media, and a lot of unanswerable critical fire can be heaped on McLuhan at this point. The terms "hot" and "cool" are applied in very haphazard ways. Media that are hot one minute seem to be cool another. It is impossible to tell if temperature is an absolute property of a medium or whether a medium is hot or cool relative only to some other medium. And the classification of media into these categories seems to be always quite arbitrary.

McLuhan's argument does not, however, stand or fall on the usage of the terms "hot" and "cool." One can simply agree that while media do possess an inherent grammar, the exact structure and logic of this grammar has not, as yet, been particularly well worked out. Some latitude should be allowed McLuhan at this point anyway. He obviously is doing a good deal of experimenting with the classification of media. There is little resemblance between the classification one finds in the "first edition" of *Understanding Media* (a report to the United States Office of Education, 1960) and that in the McGraw-Hill edition currently in circulation. His argument must, I think, be assessed in terms of its most general point: men stand in a symbiotic relation to all media, and consequently the dominant mode of communication dictates the character of perception and through perception the structure of mind.

At this point I would like to make some critical notes on the arguments that have been presented. My only reluctance in doing so is that Innis and McLuhan present rather convenient targets for criticism if only because their arguments are so unconventional. Also, criticism, let us be reminded, is easy. It is still harder to write novels than to write reviews. Further, not only the structure of McLuhan's argument but also his current popularity stand as an incautious invitation to criticism and thus most critical fire that I might muster would inevitably be aimed at McLuhan. Marshall McLuhan is, after all, not only a social analyst; he is also a prophet, a phenomenon, a happening, a social movement. His work has given rise to an ideology—*mcluhanisme*—and a mass movement producing seminars, clubs, art exhibits, and conferences in his name.

Besides, I'm convinced that a technical critique of McLuhan is a rather useless undertaking. If Robert Merton cannot dent his armor by pointing out inconsistencies in his argument and lacunae in his observations, I'm quite sure that my own lesser intellectual luminosity shall have little effect on McLuhan or his devotees. I am thinking here of such inconsistencies as the fact that while he is a serious critic of traditional logic and rationality, his argument is mechanistic, built upon linear causality, and illustrative of all the deficiencies of this type of analysis. His terminology is ill-defined and inconsistently used and maddeningly obtuse. More seriously, he has a view of mind, directly adopted from the *tabula rasa* of John Locke, that is not only simple-minded but contradicted by much of the work currently being done in linguistics, psychology, and psychotherapy. But I sense that such criticism is analogous to criticizing Christianity by pointing out contradictions in the Bible.

McLuhan is beyond criticism not only because he defines such activity as illegitimate but also because his work does not lend itself to critical commentary. It is a mixture of whimsy, pun, and innuendo. These things are all right in themselves, but unfortunately one cannot tell what he is serious about and what is mere whimsy. His sentences are not observations or assertions but, in his own language, "probes." Unfortunately, a probe is a neutral instrument about which one can say nothing but congratulate its inquisitiveness. One may resist his probes or yield to their delights, but to quarrel with them is rather beside the point.

Despite these disclaimers, a manageable enterprise remains. I would like to judge McLuhan's argument not in absolute or universal terms but only in relation to the work of Innis. If we can for the moment grant the central assumption on the role of communications technology in social change, who has presented us with the more powerful and useful arguments? This is a question both manageable and germane to the paper. Less germane but at least of importance to me is the concluding question I would like to raise: what is it that makes McLuhan an acceptable prophet of our times? I think the answer to this question will also shed some important light on the argument of Innis.

I have suggested that Innis argued that the most visible and important effects of media technology were on social organization and through social organization on culture. Radio and television, I assume Innis would argue, are light media that quickly and easily transmit large amounts of information. Moreover, electronic signals, while highly perishable, are difficult to control. Unlike print, electronic media do not recognize national boundaries, as the Canadians have discovered. Thus, the effect of the electronic media is to extend the spatial bias of print, to make new forms of human association possible, and to foreshorten one's sense of time. As spatially biased media, radio and television, even when used by religious institutions, contribute to the growing hegemony of secular authority and to the extension of political influence in space. Further, they have contributed to the weakening of tradition and to the secularization of religion. Or so Innis might have it.

McLuhan treats quite a different effect of the media—the effect of the media not on social organization but on sensory organization. As I have previously mentioned, Innis and McLuhan do treat both kinds of effects. The effect of the media on sensory organization is a minor but persistent theme in Innis' writings.[3] McLuhan also treats the effects of media on social organization, as the previous discussion of nationalism, specialization, science, and education illustrated. However, the major direction and thus the implication of the two arguments is quite different. Moreover, McLuhan, deliberately or otherwise, confuses these two quite different effects of media technology. Much of his evidence is not directed at nor does it support his analysis of the sensory bias of media. Rather it supports Innis' claim for the institutional or organizational bias of media. For example, xerography, a process which very much interests McLuhan, is an important innovation in communication. While the innovation is based upon discoveries in electronic technology, its usual product nonetheless is the orderly, linear type of the printed page. The effect of xerography is not on sensory organization. However, by increasing the rate of speed at which information can be transmitted and reproduced, by allowing for the rapid recombination of printed materials, xerography does encourage the creation of novel vehicles of communication and novel groups of readers. That is, xerography encourages or at least permits certain structural reorganizations of social groups. Developments in offset printing have a similar effect.

My argument is simply that the most visible effects of communications technology are on social organization and not on sensory organization. Much of McLuhan's evidence can be more plausibly, directly, and productively used in support of the form of argument offered by Innis. I will subsequently return to this point. Here I much want to suggest that Innis provides a more plausible accounting of the principal phenomena in question and is of greater usefulness to students of the history of mass communication. My preferences for Innis are partly aesthetic; they stem partly from a simple aversion to much of what McLuhan represents. In addition I feel that Innis' argument will be ultimately productive of more significant scholarship. Finally, I feel that McLuhan's position awaits the same fate as the Sapir-Whorf hypothesis to which it is so closely tied. The Sapir-Whorf hypothesis, while it is a perfectly plausible notion, has never turned out to be productive of much insight or research or to have particularly advanced the study of language and perception.

The same fate awaits McLuhan, I fear, and stems from an argumentative similarity between the positions. For McLuhan states his case on very general grounds and defends it on very narrow grounds. Because he views the effect of the media as principally acting on the senses, his entire argument ultimately rests on the narrow grounds of the psychology of perception. This is, I think, a very weak foundation to support such a vast superstructure. This is not only because many of his comments on the psychology of perception are highly questionable, but also because given what we know about the complexity of behavior, it is hard to understand how such a vast range of social phenomena are to be so simply explained. When McLuhan is writing about the oral tradition and about print, areas where he is backed by the extensive scholarship of Innis, his work has a cogency and integration and is sensitive to the complexity of the problems at hand (for example, in large portions of *The Gutenberg Galaxy*). When he probes beyond these shores into the world of television and the computer, the water gets very muddy indeed, for here he attempts to explain every twitch in contemporary society on the basis of the sensory reorganization brought about by the media. I do not have the time, nor the knowledge, to examine McLuhan's theory of perception. However, a couple of problems should be pointed out.[4] The phenomenon of sensory closure upon which McLuhan's theory is built is a very primitive perceptual mechanism. It is found in all experiments on perception, though not always in predictable ways. Moreover, the gestalt movement in psychology was based upon the operation of this mechanism, though it was largely limited to the study of visual closure. An obvious strength of McLuhan's argument is his isolation of this primitive and important perceptual phenomenon and his generalization of the phenomenon beyond visual closure to include the relations among all the senses. However, the assumption that the pattern of sensory closure is dictated by the structure of the media seems to be an unnecessary and unwarranted oversimplification.

For example, McLuhan severely overestimates the inflexibility of media of communication. While any given medium confronts an artist with certain inherent constraints, media still allow wide latitude for innovation and artistic manipulation. McLuhan does not consider, for example, that any medium can be used, in any historical period, either discursively or presentationally. Speech and writing, while they have a bias toward discursive presentation, can also be used presentationally. It is difficult to imagine why McLuhan does not utilize the distinction between presentational and discursive forms, a distinction of some importance in modern aesthetic theory.[5] Elements in a presentational form have no individuated meaning but take on meaning only in relation to the whole. Elements in a discursive form have individuated meaning and the elements can be combined by formal rules. Ordinary language is highly discursive, but it can be used presentationally. And "this is the distinguishing mark of poetry. The significance of a poetic symbol can be appreciated only in the context of the entire poem."

The same can be said of other forms. A given medium of communication may favor discursive presentation of the presentation of perceptual gestalts, but they can be and are manipulated in either genre. These media are, of course, constraining forces: they limit and control to some degree the expressive capacities of men. But the history of these forms is the history of attempts to overcome the deficiencies seemingly inherent in media of communication, to make the media bend to thought and imagination rather than allowing thought and imagination to be imprisoned by them. Thus, metaphor and simile, incongruity and hyperbole, personification and irony, are all devices, imaginative and productive devices, for overcoming the formal constraints of speech and writing. Similarly, while print, radio and television, and movies have inherent technological constraints, artists within these media have constantly struggled to overcome the limitations of the form through invention of new modes of symbolic representation. Think only of the history of film editing.

While McLuhan frequently excludes artists from the laws of perceptual determinism, he does not exclude audiences. However, I want to suggest that devices such as metaphor, simile, and personification are used not only by artists but are part of the linguistic repertoire of every five-year-old child. They are devices through which all of us attempt to overcome the inherent constraints of speech. There is, I suspect, much more freedom in perception and invention in everyday communication than Mc-

Luhan is willing to admit. To propose the audience as an empty vessel, a black box, that has no significant autonomous existence but is, instead, filled or wired up by sources exclusively external to the self is not only to deny an enormous amount of everyday evidence but also to casually dismiss a significant amount of reasonably sound scientific evidence. The empty organism view of the self is, I think, not only pernicious but also unsupportable from the evidence at hand on perception.

But the most important criticism to make of McLuhan is that much of the argument he wants to make and most of the contemporary phenomena he wants to explain—particularly the conflict between generations—can be more effectively handled within the framework provided by Innis. Furthermore, the utilization of the perspective of Innis opens up, I think, a number of important and researchable questions and puts the argument once more in a historical context.

In this final section let me tentatively attempt to bring Innis' argument up to date; that is, to extend it from the early 1950's, where he left it, into the 1960's. You will remember that Innis argued that Western history began with temporal bias and was ending with spatial bias. I want to suggest that contemporary developments in the electronic media have intensified this spatial bias. Electronic media, particularly with the innovation of satellite broadcasting, increasingly transcend all national boundaries, thereby weakening nationalism or at least tending to undercut the parochial limitations of national identifications. Further, such media are a potent force in generating a more universal, worldwide culture which is urban, secular, and, in Innis' terms, unstable.

Let me put it this way. Among primitive societies and in earlier stages of Western history, relatively small discontinuities in space led to vast differences in culture and social organization. Tribal societies separated by a hundred miles could have entirely different forms of economic, political, and religious life and grossly dissimilar systems of expressive symbolism, myth, and ritual. However, within these societies there was a great continuity of culture and social structure over generations. Forms of life changed slowly, of course, and the attitudes, hopes, fears, and aspirations of a boy of fourteen and a man of sixty were remarkably similar. This does not mean there were not conflicts between age groups in such societies. Such conflicts are probably inevitable if only because of biological changes accompanying aging. However, the conflict occurred within a system of shared attitudes and values and within a system of mutual dependencies across age groups. Such societies were based on an oral tradition with a strong temporal bias. The continuity of culture was maintained by a shared, collective system of ritual and by the continuity of passage rites marking off the entrance of individuals into various stages of the life cycle. In such a world, then, there were vast differences between societies but relatively little variation between generations within a given society. In Innis' terms, temporal media produce vast continuity in time and great discontinuity in space.

The spatial bias of modern media, initiated by print but radically extended by film and the electronic media, has reversed the relations between time and space. Space in the modern world progressively disappears as a differentiating factor. As space becomes more continuous, regional variations in culture and social structure become ground down. Further, as I have already suggested and as other modern writers have persuasively argued, the rise of a world-wide urban civilization built upon the speed and extensiveness of travel and electronic media have progressively diminished—though they have come nowhere near eliminating—spatial, transnational variation in culture and social structure. It is this fact that has led Claude Levi-Strauss to re-echo the traditional keen of the anthropologist that primitive societies must be intensively studied now because they are rapidly disappearing.

If in fact the spatial bias of contemporary media does lead to a progressive reduction of regional variation within nations and transnational variation between nations, one must not assume that differences between groups are being obliterated as some mass society theorists characterize the process of homogenization. As Levi-Strauss has argued, there may be a principle of diversity built into the species or, from our standpoint, built into the organization of man's communication. I am suggesting that the axis of diversity shifts from a spatial or structural dimension to a temporal or generational dimension. If in primitive societies time is continuous and space discontinuous, in modern societies as space becomes continuous time becomes discontinuous. In what seems like an ironic twist of language, spatially biased media obliterate space while temporally biased media obliterate time. The spatial bias of modern media, which has eliminated many spatial variations in culture and social structure, has simultaneously intensified the differences between generations within the same society. The differences in modern society between a boy of fourteen and a man of sixty—differences in language and values, symbols and meanings—are enormous. It is modern societies that face the problem of generations. It is not only that conflict across age groups continues but there are gross discontinuities between generations in culture and symbols, perhaps best symbolized by the phrase, "Don't trust anyone over thirty."[6] This inversion in the relation of time and space in contemporary society seems to me a logical extension of Innis' argument. The inversion depends on the observation that spatially biased media obliterate space and lead men to live in a non-spatial world. Simultaneously, such media fragment time and make it progressively discontinuous. Temporal media, on the other hand, obliterate time, lead men to live in a non-temporal world, but fragment space.

I think it is important to remember that Innis argued that media possessed a bias or a predisposition toward time or space. He was not arguing for some simple mono-causality. Thus, if generations have become an increasingly important axis of diversity, in modern society, the causes include factors other than the media but to which the media are linked in a syndrome. I cannot, of course, attempt to trace out all such factors here, but a couple should be mentioned if only for their suggestive value. The importance of generations and the phenomena of generational discontinuity is linked most directly to the rate of technical change. In traditional societies, societies that change very slowly, the old are likely to be venerated as the repositories of the oral tradition and, consequently, as the storage banks of tribal wisdom. In societies such as ours, where knowledge and technique change very rapidly, the old are not likely to be so venerated. It is the young, the bearers of the new techniques and knowledge, that are likely to have both the power and the prestige. As the transmission of this knowledge is in the educational system, it is in this institution that generational discontinuities are likely to become most apparent. Also, because rapidly changing technical knowledge is difficult to acquire beyond school, the old are likely to be continually threatened by competition from the young, to be subject to fairly early obsolescence, and conflicts between generations bearing different knowledge and different values are likely to become a fact of life in all institutions.

This conflict is muted and disguised somewhat by the reorganization of the age composition of society. Some 40 per cent of the population is now under twenty, and within the year 50 per cent of the population will be under twenty-five. With the rapid expansion of the economy and institutions such as education, the young overwhelm older generations merely by numbers, and thus the intensity of the conflict is frequently masked by the ease of the political solutions. One thus must not discount the sheer fact of larger numbers in younger generations in heightening our awareness of generational discontinuity. The proportion of youth in the total population is also intensified by the progressive lengthening of adolescence; that is, one is young much longer today than in previous centuries.

Finally, the weakening of tradition caused not only by the media but also by the pace of technical change and progressive dominance of the educational system in the socialization process intensifies, I think, generational discontinuity. I am led to this argument by the belief that structural elements in the society are less able to provide useful and stable identity patterns to youth. Religious, ethnic, regional, and class identifications are weakening, and they are identifications which are *not* temporal in character. As religious and ethnic traditions weaken, generational identity becomes more important as a means of placing oneself and organizing one's own self-conception. This is true not only in the society at large but also in all subordinate institutions. The importance of generational identity is enhanced by the decline of ritual and passage rites which formerly served as devices for confirming and symbolizing structural identity. In addition, these structural identities simply come into conflict with one another, they counterpoint, and the young are frequently led to reject all past identities and seize upon membership in a generation as the key to understanding what is happening to them. This is a phenomenon Erik Erikson has usefully analyzed under the label the "totalism" of youth.

I am suggesting that generations are becoming more important sources of solidarity than other social groups in spite of Harold Rosenberg's observation that being a member of an age group is the lowest form of solidarity. The spread of a world-wide urban civilization built upon rapid and ephemeral means of communication ultimately means that individuals of the same age in Warsaw, Moscow, Tokyo, and New York sense a membership in a common age group and feel they have more in common with one another than with individuals older and younger within their own societies. This is a phenomenon which Innis did not anticipate. When

Innis spoke of competition to establish a monopoly of knowledge, he normally was thinking of competition coming from institutions or structural groups: competition from the clergy, politicians, or the middle classes. Similarly, when other scholars have spoken of the role of groups in social change, they have normally thought of structural groups such as the burghers, the aristocracy, or the Jews. The implication of my suggestion is that the bearers of social change are increasingly age groups or generations rather than structural groups. Instead of groups representing individuals of all ages bound together by a common structural characteristic such as religion, race, or occupation, the most important groups of the future will be those of a common age who are structurally variegated. A generational group finds its solidarity in a common age even though some of its members are Catholic, some Jewish, some Protestant, some northerners, some southerners, some middle class, some working class. If this is correct, then political conflict, to choose just one example, which we have normally thought of in structural terms as conflict between regions, classes, and religions becomes focused instead around generations. If I correctly interpret the behavior of Robert Kennedy, he was aware of the phenomenon.

Now, unfortunately, things are neither as neat, as simple, or as true as I have painted them in these pages. There are still strong differences within generations. One must speak of generations of musicians and novelists, physicists and sociologists, northerners and southerners, Catholics and Jews. Obviously, one has to pay attention to the intersection of structural variables such as class and generational variables or the entire analysis quickly slides into a tautology. But I do think that in modern society generations become more important in all spheres of life. There is a competition to name generations, to symbolize them, to characterize the meaning of a generation. There is a competition within and between generations to choose the culture by which the generation shall be known. Further, there is competition to impose the culture of a generation on the entire society. And this, of course, is what Innis meant by a monopoly of knowledge. It was only a few years ago that David Riesman was suggesting that the media, particularly television, are devices by which the culture of youth is imposed on the entire society. In the competition to determine whose culture shall be the official culture and whose values the official norms, the axis of conflict is between generations.

These perhaps over-long notes on the sociology of generations illustrate, I hope, Innis' central point: the principal effect of media technology is on social organization. The capacity of Innis to deal with such phenomena in a reasonably direct and clear way leads me to prefer his characterization of media effects to that of McLuhan.

Notes

[1] The literary style adopted by Innis to convey the complexity of social change is a principal barrier to any adequate understanding of his work. He amasses on each page such an enormous body of fact, fact rarely summarized or generalized, that one becomes quickly lost in the thicket of data. Further, Innis disdains the conventions of written book scholarship; indeed, he attempts to break out of what he takes to be these limiting conventions by presenting an apparently disconnected kaleidoscope of fact and observation. He avoids arguing in a precise, serial order and instead, like the proprietor of a psychedelic delicatessen, flashes onto the page historic events widely separated in space and time. With such a method, he attempts to capture both the complexities of social existence and its multidimensional change. Nowhere does he present an orderly, systematic argument (except perhaps in the first and last chapters of *Empire and Communications*) depending rather on the reader to impose order, to capture not merely the fact of history but a vision of the dynamics of historic change.

[2] Innis was interested in all forms of monopolies of knowledge. In his teaching he was interested in the tendency of social science research to become focused around one man—a Keynes, Marx, or Freud—or one narrow attitude of speculation. He himself preferred an open and vigorous com-

petition or viewpoints and felt that the reliance of Western education on the book severely reduced the possibility of vigorous debate and discourse in education. See Donald Creighton, *Harold Adams Innis, Portrait of a Scholar* (Toronto: University of Toronto Press, 1957).

[3] Here are some examples culled at random from Innis' writings; "Scholars were concerned with letters rather than sounds and linguistic instruction emphasized eye philology rather than ear philology" (*Empire and Communications*, p. 159). "The discovery of printing in the middle of the 15th century implied the beginning of a return to a type of civilization dominated by the eye rather than the ear" (*The Bias of Communication*, p. 138). "Introduction of the alphabet meant a concern with sound rather than with sight or with the ear rather than the eye" (*The Bias of Communication*, pp. 40–41). "In oral intercourse the eye, ear and brain acted together in busy co-operation and rivalry each eliciting, stimulating and supplementing the other" (*The Bias of Communication*, p. 106). "The ear and the concern with time began to have its influence on the arts concerned with eye and space" (*The Bias of Communication*, p. 110).

[4] Here I am indebted to Sidney Robinovitch of the University of Illinois.

[5] Susanne K. Langer, *Philosophy in a New Key* (Cambridge: Harvard University Press, 1957).

[6] Of course, generational discontinuity is a universal of history. Normally, these discontinuities are explained by the periodic and random shocks to a system caused by relatively unsystematic variables such as wars, depressions, famines, etc. I am suggesting that generational discontinuity no longer depends on these random shocks to the system but that generational discontinuities are now endogenous factors, built into the normal operation of the system and very much "caused" by the bias of contemporary communication.

4 Consensus Journalism

Robert MacNeil

The all-pervasive nature of television as the most mass of mass media in the United States, the intimate connection of its ownership patterns and method of production with the dominant business behavior of American culture and economics, and the built-in biases of television as a visual medium of instantaneous transmission, all these qualities and more make Robert MacNeil's opinions on the problems and procedures of American television journalism an ideal contemporary illustration of the theoretical viewpoints found in the immediately preceding contributions. The following selection is a chapter from Mr. MacNeil's book, *The People Machine: The Influence of Television on American Politics.*

ROBERT MACNEIL is a working journalist with abundant experience in television journalism. Mr. MacNeil covered the Congolese and Algerian conflicts of the early sixties for NBC News as well as the building of the Berlin Wall and the Cuban Missile Crisis. Domestically he also covered the Kennedy assassination in Dallas and Barry Goldwater's presidential campaign. Since 1967 with BBC, he has covered the domestic crises in France and the American presidential election of 1968. Mr. MacNeil now lives in London.

Television journalists are by-products of an industry which prefers to have as little to do with reality as possible, and which sees no value as being more important than business expediency in complying with government. Is it, in fact, possible to maintain the better traditions and values of American journalism inside an industry to which consensus and conformity are the foundations of prosperity? Can journalists drink at the same well as businessmen, entertainers and advertising men, and not be infected with their values?

The ambivalence of their role traumatizes many people in network television journalism, and they compensate by becoming cynically complacent. Such adaptation probably does more to damage originality and curiosity than any direct pressure from outside the profession. By *television* standards anywhere in the world, their product is brilliantly professional: slick, exciting and convincing in its aura of authority. Yet how professional is it by journalistic standards?

Mechanics before Substance

There is little doubt that regular television news programs like *Huntley-Brinkley* and *Walter Cronkite* must have raised the threshold of public awareness of current events over the past ten years. One can assume that they have conditioned in millions of people who were not avid newspaper readers some appetite for serious news and given them a fleeting familiarity with the world.

For people who have given it some thought, however, electronic journalism cares more about form than content. Leslie Slote, who is Governor Rockefeller's press secretary, and who has been dealing with TV newsmen for years, believes that "people responsible for TV news are fairly unimaginative and seem to be preoccupied with the mechanistic as opposed to the substantive."[1] Slote repeats the frequently uttered criticism that "one of the ingredients lacking in TV news coverage is the *why* factor: it is superficial." His particular concern was with what he thought was the failure of TV journalists in New York State to explain Rockefeller's Medicaid program: "They got so involved in the controversy that they never reported what the program was all about and what it was supposed to do."

In May, 1967, when the late Martin Luther King, Jr., was protesting that the Vietnam war was immoral because it interfered with civil rights progress at home, the *Huntley-Brinkley Report* carried a curious item. It began with Brinkley saying that King had alienated himself from other civil rights leaders and from the Administration by his campaign against the war. He then introduced what was called an "interview" with Hubert Humphrey in which the Vice-President, more in sorrow than in anger, chastised Dr. King. No questioner was ever shown or identified. One only saw Humphrey standing against a wood-paneled background, talking. The circumstances of the interview, or at whose initiative it was given, were never mentioned. It is a fundamental rule of journalism that you must give the circumstances of an interview or statement, for otherwise there is no way of evaluating whether it was inspired or spontaneous. This story left a viewer with the strong impression that the Administration had something to say about Dr. King and that NBC had accommodated it in making a gratuitous attack.

Taken in isolation, such technical matters are perhaps not important. Television news programs are not habitually so careless about journalistic standards. What appears more damaging to television news credibility is the atmosphere of outside pressure in which TV journalists must work, a pressure not always overt but of the sort that suffuses one's thinking so delicately that a person writing a story or broadcasting it may not even be aware of how careful he is being. Buried somewhere in his professional psyche is a feeling of caution put there by years of "politic" judgments by his superiors.

The Reassurance Syndrome

From time to time, television journalism appears anxious to sell the chief commodity of entertainment TV—reassurance. Apart from the descent to a tone of somewhat deeper unction on occasions of sadness, as during coverage of the Martin Luther King or Robert Kennedy assassinations, the heavily stylized mode of delivery—half sung, half chanted—of many news broadcasters makes most of the stories sound alike and imparts a quality of artificiality to the content. That, coupled with the tendency for newscasters to punctuate their performances with smiles, conveys a false geniality which drains the news of meaning.

Research into audience preferences in New York and Los Angeles has revealed that newscasters who could reduce the anxiety level of audiences and present the news in a context of reassurance had tremendous appeal. The most successful personalities on the air were those who could take the edge off what was unpleasant.

It could be demonstrated that, deliberately or unconsciously, broadcasting organizations do choose personalities to give such an impression of reassurance in order to attract audience. TV executives might be hard put to define precisely what qualities they are looking for, but basically they want men who will sound authoritative while making the audience feel comfortable.

It would be fascinating to know more about what goes on in the minds of regular viewers. It may be that the broad reaches of the American public have become so inured to falsity in wide areas of the advertising and mass entertainment media that they are incapable of discrimination. From the early days of network radio when movie stars with melodic, sexy voices assured fawning announcers that they always used a certain soap, while both read from a script the audience could not see, to the television newsmen of today may seem a giant and improbable step, but what if the newsman, so impeccably dressed, so calculatedly believable, is a man who simply does not know what he is talking about and is reading from a script on a TelePrompTer the audience cannot see? Are these merely "conventions" of mass communications which Americans in their sophistication accept as unimportant? If viewers are so healthily cynical, where do they start and where do they stop believing? Or are they so buffeted by spurious information, by halftruths and comforting slogans, that they believe everything? Does a viewer believe and respect the newscaster and then a few seconds later greet the commercial announcer with skepticism? These questions represent crucial mysteries which have yet to be clarified.

As we have seen, networks and stations tend to fit journalism into the other big world of television. Thus the news comes not as objective observation of the environment but as *part* of the environment. It is what philosophers would call part of the "flow," part of the "given." When the commentator is also a commercial pitchman, the effect is further reinforced. Can the audience take seriously the pronouncements on world affairs of a man who ingratiatingly tries to sell them barbecue forks or dog food a few minutes later? There have been instances when newsmen refused to read commercials in order to protect their credibility as journalists, and the practice is increasingly less common. That they were asked, however, is typical of the misunderstanding of the journalistic function in the broadcasting industry. Because of this danger of a credibility gap, a case could be made for removing commercials altogether from news programming. The selling could be done in time segments before and after, but not during the news. After years of living with the system, the networks and local broadcasters know how incongruous commercials appear. It is standard practice, for example, to fade out to a few seconds of black if a particularly tragic or moving story appears just before a commercial. There are also arrangements to avoid embarrassing sponsors with the irony of, for instance, a commercial rhapsodizing air travel in a newscast with a report of an airline crash. In such situations, the commercials are not run, although there are occasions when the decision is made only after discussion about whether the news value of the story warrants the loss of revenue.

If, as Marshall McLuhan says, people perceive information on television in an intuitive, "mosaic" form, how do they see the news as they drink in the reassuring voice of the commentators and the surrounding commercials? Surely, many must regard it as part of the numbing, relaxing, mesmerizing "stuff" that comes at them out of the glowing box, a fraction of life size, inseparable from the total "television experience."

Ideas Are Bad Business

There is yet another aspect of television journalism which lends it common identity with the other programs: it has too little opinion about the subjects it covers. Broadcasting has made a virtue of neutrality. Many critics believe that it is not merely neutrality but noninvolvement. V. O. Key and others have theorized that what is controversial is bad business for the mass media. A week's exposure to commercial television would suggest that the networks believe that even ideas are bad business unless they have already been sensationalized in other media. Michael Arlen believes that certain gods have been kept out of television, "the gods of Wit and Unprofessionalism, the nasty gods, the gods that get into noisy arguments, the dissenting gods."[2] The short of it is that television does not want to offend anyone. When Pauline Frederick, NBC's United Nations Correspondent, once interviewed General Maxwell Taylor rather more aggressively than usual on the *Today* show, Hugh Downs later felt it necessary to apologize to the audience for the vigor of her questions: a few people had written in to complain. At the beginning of *Meet the Press* each week, the announcer reminds the audience that the questions the panelists ask do not necessarily reflect their own points of view. Only in extreme cases—as in the period of disillusionment about Vietnam in the spring of 1968—do network commentators burst through the blandness.

The television news departments offer what sound like respectable arguments to defend their avoidance of controversial stands. They operate under the restraints of FCC regulations, which require them to present both sides on matters of controversy. When they do examine controversial matters they are fair, but sometimes fair to the point of irresponsibility. William S. Paley, defending Edward R. Murrow's broadcast on Senator Joseph McCarthy in 1954, said that fairness cannot be reduced to a mathematical formula. He went on: "And it must be recognized that there is a difference between men, ideas and institutions: some are good and some are bad, and it is up to us to know the difference—to know what will hold up democracy and what will undermine it—and then not to do the latter."[3] That was powerful stuff in 1954. It would be today. Unfortunately, today only the critics complain about the absurdity of mathematical fairness, not the broadcasters.

It is exceedingly difficult to believe that it is genuinely a fear of government regulation which keeps broadcasting so sterile of opinion. Government regulation by the FCC does not appear to be nearly as effective in bringing broadcasters to heel as is the occasional direct interference of an elected official or the general awareness of being part of a business community with a large stake in the economy.

Taken together, all these influences suggest that the television industry, including its news operation, does not enjoy rocking the boat, politically or commercially. It enjoys the status quo. It identifies with the establishment, nationally or locally.

Television Can Be Pushed Around

People in government have not been slow to recognize television's desire to stay out of trouble. They have often assumed that the industry could be made to do what this or that government department wanted, without regard for journalistic independence. The instances which have found their way into public knowledge are, of course, those occasions when broadcasters resisted the pressures.

One was in 1959 when the State Department tried to tell the networks when they could, and when they could not, show the Nixon-Khrushchev Kitchen Debate. The film of the encounter actually belonged to NBC because it was at the pavilion of the network's parent company, RCA, that the two statesmen had their famous argument. The State Department had undertaken on its own to make an agreement with the Russians that the film would not be shown on American television until it had been shown on Soviet television. The networks discussed it among themselves. Robert Sarnoff of NBC was doubtful about using it but was persuaded by CBS to run it.

In 1962, the networks were again disturbed to find that the government was committing them in advance, and without consultation, to carry a program on which President Kennedy and Khrushchev would appear jointly. Officials were reported to have rationalized this interference by pointing to the fact that television is licensed by the government while newspapers are not.

Later, the State Department tried very hard to stop NBC from putting on its exclusive and dramatic film of the digging of a tunnel under the Berlin Wall, through which a large group of refugees escaped. Robert E. Kintner, who was then NBC President, said it was the network's "worst encounter with the government" and that they had been subjected to unremitting pressure for a month.[4] NBC's Berlin office had heard of a tunnel being dug and contracted with the diggers to let them film the escape. The building of the tunnel was filmed in its entirety and in great secrecy and so was the climax when the refugees finally slipped through. Before it was completed, however, a Deputy Assistant Secretary of State came to NBC to say that the tunnel had been discovered by the East Germans and that further work on it would be dangerous. He was wrong. Kintner charges that the higher levels of the State Department were "unbelievably timid and remarkably ignorant of what was really happening in Berlin." In spite of the pressure, NBC did air the film, to tremendous critical acclaim, and the United States Information Agency later distributed it overseas. The incident was not marked by consistent boldness within NBC. There was much soul-searching and at one point the network was even proposing that all the faces of the Germans involved should be blacked out (an incredibly tedious and costly procedure on film). In the end, journalistic freedom asserted itself and NBC brought off one of the television coups of the Cold War.

More important than these occasions on which the industry had the fortitude to resist official pressure is the knowledge that such pressure can be brought to bear so often. It is bound to have an influence on the conduct of television executives, and, as we shall see in a subsequent chapter, television does not always resist. Obviously, the susceptibility to yield is present.

Jack Gould pointed out in 1962: "When you operate under a government license, you are never indifferent to the possibility of reprisal." Ferdinand Lundberg suggests in *The Coming World Transformation* that "the private holders of public broadcasting franchises must give government and government personnel so much respectfully neutral and even sympathetic attention that in effect they become semi-government agencies. . . ."[5] How true that is depends very much on how the television industry, most importantly the national networks, views the possibility of government reprisal against its franchises. The fact of the matter is that revoking a license has been so rare a procedure on any grounds that it is scarcely credible today as a threat. When the networks are pusilanimous, the motive is more likely to be a general fear of government than a specific fear about licenses. And that general fear may have a solid commercial foundation.

One example, which has been the subject of comment in the press and in the FCC, is the relationship between large corporations which have multimillion-dollar defense contracts and the broadcasting stations they also own. In July, 1967, *Variety* noted that six such corporations with broadcasting interests—General Electric, Kaiser, Westinghouse, General Tire and Rubber, Radio Corporation of America and International Telephone and Telegraph—had received substantial increases in defense contracts between 1965 and 1966. The trade paper asked: "Can a major news medium like television do a thorough, honest job when it is owned and controlled by a parent corporation that has a financial involvement with the government?" And it added: ". . . it's not unreasonable to conclude that none of the broadcasting subsidiaries of war contracting corporations acquitted its news obligations in a way upsetting to the contractor, the Defense Department."[6]

This fear was very much in the minds of three FCC Commissioners who dissented from the majority decision of the Commission, which approved the merger of ITT and the ABC Television Network. Commissioners Bartley, Cox and Johnson wrote that any threat to the integrity of ABC News must be a matter of serious concern to the FCC and the American people. The fact that ITT had sensitive business relations abroad and at the highest levels of the U.S. Government meant that reporting on any number of industries and economic developments would touch on ITT interests. The dissenting Commissioners then identified what is probably the chief kind of pressure that network news departments feel, the anticipation of trouble through a subtle, almost unconscious process. "The threat is not so much that documentaries or news stories adversely affecting the interests of ITT will be filmed and then killed, or slanted—although that is also a problem," they wrote. "It is that the questionable story idea, or news coverage, will never even be proposed—whether for reasons of fear, insecurity, cynicism, realism or unconscious avoidance."[7] As it turned out, the Justice Department took the merger question to court and, before there was a ruling, ITT withdrew from the agreement.

The whole dispute had been very instructive. It revealed the morality of a large corporation like ITT in the kind of pressure it thought permissible to exercise on the press. Reporters of the *New York Times* and the *Milwaukee Sentinel* declared that ITT had tried directly to influence the stories they were writing on the merger hearings. It also revealed the opinion of several FCC Commissioners that RCA had considerable influence on the public behavior of its broadcasting subsidiary, NBC. The episode reinforces the impression that the broadcasting industry finds itself in a highly sensitive position as regards both its business connections and its relations to government. When this fact is added to the normal commercial orientation of the industry and its connection with the mass advertising business, the extent of the extraordinary pressures on television journalism will be apparent. When it has to program for the widest audience to stay profitable, keep one eye open for displeasure in Washington and occasionally consider the larger interests of parent corporations with a vast stake in government and defense, it is not surprising that TV news is cautious.

Shooting Bloody in Vietnam

By the end of 1967, NBC and CBS were each reported to be spending $2 million a year on covering the Vietnam war, and ABC $1 million. Each network maintained a staff of two dozen or more people in Saigon and the film shot in the jungle battles had appeared prominently on the news programs virtually every night for two years. Much was written about "the first television war" and the probable political effects of having a war which so divided the nation brought so vividly into American homes. No one is certain what that effect has been. Morris Janowitz, a University of Chicago sociologist, has said that television coverage had "hardened and polarized public sentiment." He added: "Those people who are skeptical of the war now have a vehemence in their skepticism. Those who are for the war see Americans being killed and they don't want those sacrifices to be in vain."[8] Other observers have echoed that view.

Another point of view suggests itself, however, if the nature of television's coverage is considered. Overwhelmingly, what has been seen on the home screen has been battle action. Camera teams and reporters in Vietnam found that no matter what they filmed, the networks wanted action footage. At CBS, Vietnam hands used the expression "shooting bloody" to describe the filming they had to do to get on the air. It was not that they were ordered to shoot only war scenes, but when they shot a political story or the progress of the pacification program as well as war scenes, it would be the action film which the program producers selected. Night after night for two years, American families have seen episodes more vivid and gripping than those concocted for entertainment shows later in the evening.

They have seen a considerable amount of horror: badly wounded Americans, sacks of dead Americans being loaded for shipment home, sprawled heaps of small, dead Vietnamese bodies. There are those who believe that this portrayal of horror has sickened Americans and turned many against the war, which has seemed increasingly pointless. Yet the horror has been heavily edited, and that may also have had a political impact. By exposing the mass audience to more vivid and horrible battle events than have ever been brought into American homes before, but by cutting out what is most unbearable, it may be that television has built up a tolerance for the frightful, a feeling that war really is bearable. The grisly truth has been shown in the screening rooms of the network news departments. There would be close-up footage, with sound, of a young soldier, whose leg had been shot away a moment before, screaming obscenities at the medics, pleading with them in desperation to stop his agony. As someone who believed from before 1964 that this war was a futile and stupid waste of American energies, I often wondered as I watched this uncut footage at NBC whether we should not be putting on even more of the horror, so as to arouse people more. We did not because, as one man put it, and not facetiously, "We go on the air at suppertime."

He said that that afternoon we screened a story showing American soldiers cutting the ears off dead Vietcong as souvenirs. A U.S. sergeant took out a straight razor and the zoom lens followed him in. The ear came off like a piece of soft cheese, and the sergeant put it away in his pack as the party went crunching off through the forest. The NBC reporter explained in a careful commentary that this barbaric practice was not uncommon. The story was referred to an executive in the News Department, who said not to use it. We were divided on whether we wanted to, in any case. Again, to have shown such an incident would have said a good deal about the brutalizing effect of the war. Six months later, a CBS crew filmed a similar scene, which was seen on the *Walter Cronkite* program.

The political impact of the war coverage could have been far greater if more such scenes had been shown, possibly causing the American people to protest to their government more strongly that it was too much. The effect of TV coverage, in convincing people they are seeing the worst, may have been to inculcate a spirit of pained but loyal tolerance of the war.

Michael Arlen, of *The New Yorker,* believes that the cumulative effect of all these short film reports has been "bound to provide these millions of people with an excessively simple, emotional and military-oriented point of view." Arlen also feels that the physical size of the screen had diminished the horrors of war

—"a picture of men three inches tall shooting at other men three inches tall and trivialized, or at least tamed, by the enveloping cozy alarms of the household."[9]

It is also possible that the conditioning of the audience to the staged violence of television serials has diminished the emotional impact of the Vietnam footage. Real violence often seems curiously tame and insignificant compared with violence constructed by film producers. It was remarked at the time that Jack Ruby's shooting of Lee Harvey Oswald, as carried by TV, looked amateurish; the action occurred too quickly, there was no buildup. Cameramen risking their lives to record a sudden battle in Vietnam cannot provide intimate close-ups of both sides: they cannot often record all the elements that make for a satisfying film sequence.

Perhaps all these factors have helped to minimize the impact of the nightly war coverage. It was not until the sudden reverses of the Tet offensive in February, 1968, that a majority of Americans seemed decisively moved by the events of the war. Then television appeared to be moving with public opinion rather than leading or molding it.

Until the Tet offensive raised the rate of American deaths to over five hundred a week, television had not treated the story as a crisis or a national emergency. Throughout 1967, when only two hundred Americans were being killed a week, Vietnam tended to appear on television as just another story. Many critics complained that TV had not put the war into perspective. There were efforts at longer treatments of the political and economic issues, but for the most part not when a majority of the television audience was around. NBC ran a *Vietnam Weekly Review* for over a year at midafternoon on Sundays, but finally took it off in 1967 when no sponsors could be interested. The program was hastily resurrected after the Tet offensive. *ABC Scope* was a weekly series of half-hour programs, also run at odd weekend hours, and discontinued for financial reasons in January, 1968. It had first been scheduled on Saturday evening in prime time, was then moved to 7 P.M., and finally pushed off by a teen-age rock-and-roll program to Sunday afternoon. By the end of 1967, the United States was engaged in a major war and the nation's most important news medium was not even reviewing the war week by week.

This business-as-usual attitude probably assisted President Johnson in playing the war down. It is interesting to consider what the effect might have been on the Administration if one network had decided that the war needed greatly expanded coverage and deserved at least one hour of prime time on a weekday evening. Assuming that the other networks would have followed suit, the impact might have been very great.

In 1967, a member of the White House staff told me he thought that network policy was working on two levels. There was a policy filtering down from the top and another policy bubbling up from the bottom. He went on: "The latter may not survive long. It sometimes does not get to the surface. When it does it can be very antiestablishment before the word gets down from the top. For example, Morley Safer's piece on the Marines in Vietnam was antiestablishment and no doubt after that it was decided all over to scrutinize Vietnam pieces more carefully."

Safer's piece (on CBS-TV), showing Marines setting fire to the huts in a Vietnamese village with cigarette lighters, infuriated the Pentagon. Defense Department officials tried to pressure CBS into removing Safer, who is a Canadian, from Vietnam. Perhaps it is significant that the one piece of television war reporting which notoriously went against the grain in the Pentagon appeared on a network which had no affiliations with large defense contractors.

The Vietnam war obviously presented the television networks with a dilemma. It is the best and most exciting story going and therefore merits vivid coverage. At the same time it has seriously divided the country. The industry has reacted in a manner that is now habitual: it has covered the action, done a minimum of explaining and taken no moral stand until very late in the day. One wonders how television would have treated the Second World War. Presumably because the nation was almost unanimous in support of the President's policy, television would have acted as a cheerleader for the country. That is closer to the natural inclinations of the industry than frosty detachment. Thin bits of cheerleading can even be heard through the coverage of the Vietnam war.

Have the networks behaved correctly? Whether the White House wanted it said or not, Vietnam had obviously become a national emergency for the United States by 1967. It was having a profound impact on the economy, on the strength of the dollar overseas and on the race problem at home. Hundreds of Americans were being killed each month. It was not a time in which most intelligent people felt neutral. The best-known TV commentators were by no means neutral in their own minds. Yet there was a curious reaction. Those who were inclined to be hawks let their hawkishness come through on the air. Listening to Chet Huntley, for instance, over many months, one would have little doubt that he was in agreement with Administration policy. David Brinkley was, apparently, opposed to the war, but little evidence of that came across in his broadcasts. In June, 1967, Brinkley told *TV Guide:* "We should stop the bombing—there is not much evidence that it has ever been as effective as the Air Force thinks it is, in this or any war—and I think we should take the first settlement that is even remotely decent and get out without insisting on any kind of victory. It was a mistake to get committed there in the first place, but this country is big enough and secure enough to admit it, survive it and go on to something else."[10]

If a man with David Brinkley's following had said precisely that, at that period, on nationwide television, it would have created quite a stir. The question arises whether a man who is a communicator of such stature should not communicate what he believes when the issue is so important. Why could Brinkley say it in print and not on television? *TV Guide* has an enormous circulation. Why is neutrality necessary in one medium and not in another? It is not a question of compromising the credibility of a news commentator. Comment can easily be separated from what is reported as fact, and even when it is not clearly labeled, a good deal of contraband comment slips through anyway.

If a commentator wishes, he can make his attitude known in a multitude of subtle ways by varying his expression or intonation. More important, however, are the facts the commentator chooses to use and the form of words used to report them. In a situation like the Vietnam story, which appears night after night, it is possible consistently to accentuate the positive elements in the news and to give less emphasis to the negative. Simply by beginning each story with the American initiative that day and the number of Vietcong reported killed, you can create a sense of American achievement and progress. By beginning your story with an account of the *enemy's* initiative, you convey the opposite impression. This is putting it crudely, and I am not imputing to all well-known TV commentators a deliberate attempt to slant the news. Personal attitudes and emotions, however, are a factor in how a story is told.

My complaint is that it took television so long to tell the American people frankly how disastrously the war was going. By the time the industry did, and then almost to a man, in February, 1968, the evidence was so overwhelmingly conclusive that a good proportion of the public had made up its mind anyway.

The Vietnam war is a good case over which to argue the morality of television's refusal to take an editorial position. It is true, as we shall see later, that some stations do present editorials, chiefly on local issues. The networks do not, but it is time they did. What tended to happen, at least over Vietnam, was that stealthy editorializing in support of the Administration slipped through, but criticism did not. There was implied cheerleeding in the nightly preoccupation with battles and body counts and often cursory treatment of Congressional debate.

Television does not have to come on with flags waving to appear in agreement with the Administration. It takes that side by default. If the networks argue that they have no business editorializing, when they serve some two hundred diverse affiliates, that is an argument for changing the system.

Television and the Negro—Revolution or Counterrevolution

On a hot day in late spring, 1963, a police chief named Bull Connor decided he had had enough of civil rights protestors. There was something alarming in the air of Birmingham, Alabama. Day after day, crowds of young Negroes had come marching and singing down the streets demanding an end to racial discrimination in shops, restaurants and employment. Each day, Connor had carted many of them off to jail, but each following day more kept coming. On May 2, schoolchildren were taken to jail. On May 3, still more marchers appeared. Connor turned police dogs and fire hoses on them, on women and children as well as on the men. That evening, film of the dogs lunging at the Negroes and of the high-pressure hoses tearing at the marchers' bodies was seen on television news all over the country. The Negro Revolution became vividly known to white America.

Because we are still living through that revolution, it is too early yet to assess conclusively what role in its course television has played. For several years after the Birmingham explosion, it was conventional to talk about the beneficial impact of television coverage of nonviolent demonstrations. Television was a primary agent in conveying to fair-minded white Americans for the first time the depths of Negro humiliation and frustration. From the days of the Freedom Riders, through the March on Washington of 1963, to the march from Selma, Alabama, in 1965, television moved with the fresh tide of goodwill that swept the country. Through those years, television presented a sympathetic picture of the Negro struggle. It was sympathy dictated by events. In each of the major episodes of those years, the Negro demonstrators were on the defensive. They were taking the initiative in provoking confrontations but they were under physical attack, by the fire hoses of Birmingham, the stone-throwing mobs in Cambridge, Maryland, the charging police in Selma.

Then, after Selma, the mood in America changed. More militant Negroes tried to supplant the moderates in front of the cameras. The tide of goodwill had been stemmed and white intransigence had set in. By the summer of 1966, President Johnson could not get his open-housing bill through a Congress with a more liberal complexion than is likely to exist again for a long time. Now, by the nature of events, television was presenting Negroes, not on the defensive, but attacking, looting, burning and shooting as they rioted in the big cities. It was not a sympathetic picture and undoubtedly it helped to reinforce the fears and hostility of many white people.

More and more Congressmen and others began to claim that television was a bad influence, that it was stimulating and provoking the violence. Theodore White charged that television, "reaching for a distorted dramatic effect," had ignored decent Negro communities for garbage-strewn slums and the moderate Negro leadership for those who were inflammatory and provocative. He was talking about the summer of 1964, when the "white backlash" became an emotional political issue. By the summer of 1967, when big-city riots had assumed the proportion of small wars, many officials were uneasy. Some claimed outright that the riots in Detroit were fanned and inflamed by local TV coverage. There were similar charges in Cleveland, leading to an enquiry which exonerated television news. The Ohio legislature passed a bill permitting newsmen, including television newsmen, free access to scenes of riots and disturbances. The impact of television and the other news media on the riots of 1967 was studied closely by the Commission on Civil Disorders appointed by President Johnson. The Commission reported in March, 1968, that despite some incidents of sensationalism, television and the other media had made a real effort to be balanced and factual in their riot coverage.[11] The media had made the disorders look more widespread, more destructive and more of a black-white confrontation than was the case, the Report said, but could not be generally accused of helping to intensify the rioting. The Commission's chief criticism was that the media tended to reflect too much the attitudes of the white power structure, that they neglected the causes of ghetto unrest beforehand and then, when disorders broke out, concentrated on efforts of the authorities to suppress the violence.

The Commission produced a warning which has particular relevance to television: "Reporters and editors must be sure that descriptions and pictures of violence, and emotional or inflammatory sequences or articles, even though 'true' in isolation, are really representative and do not convey an impression at odds with the overall reality of events."[12] Although the Commission directed this admonition to all news media, one aspect of television news method justifies some apprehension.

When a reporter and camera team go out to cover any story involving action, they are looking for the best of the action. I have covered demonstrations and riots and street fighting for television in many cities here and overseas. The point for television is always the same: to extract the most extreme scenes. One can argue for hours about the ethics of such behavior, but this policy is not far removed from the wire service practice of pulling the most sensational detail up into the lead. Any incident involving crowds of people—a ticker tape parade for John Glenn or battles between French troops and nationalist demonstrators in Algiers—has lulls and pauses. Much of the time little happens; then there is a little violence, which flares up into bigger violence. Unless, by a mixture of bravery, instinct and sheer luck, a TV crew is to film the peaks of the violence, they will not feel they have covered the story; they will have missed what newspapermen call the "lead." From several hours' shooting, they will send back perhaps 1,000 or more feet of film. The longest television news story will use only five minutes of film (180 feet of 16 millimeter) and part of that five minutes will probably be taken up with someone talking. So the editors will obviously select the scenes of peak violence and the television audience will see the very worst of what happened. In a ghetto riot, they will not see that 75 percent of the Negroes were staying in their homes with the doors locked. In a journalistic sense, this is not distorting the story. From the point of view of public order and the good of society, however, it could be very damaging if such selected coverage hardened or stimulated Congressmen to make wild calls for heavier police forces as the solution to urban problems. Television conveys such an intensity of emotion in a few scenes, and is so much more powerful a kindler of emotional reactions in the audience, that its responsibility to society, in this case, is greater than that of print journalism.

The President's Commission dismisses any idea of government restrictions on television and press coverage of racial disorders. It does advocate voluntary adherence to guidelines and codes mutually agreed on by local authorities and the press. The chief feature of such codes is a brief moratorium, of thirty minutes or so, during which the media do not rush out with bulletins. Such an arrangement is useful because it not only gives the law time to mobilize, but permits television and radio stations to check their facts before going on the air.

Television, particularly, must carry through the next generation a great part of the burden of educating white America about the Negro problem. The responsibility is greater even than that which television bears to enlighten Americans about the Vietnam war. The needs are the same, however, in both crises: a major effort toward creative, analytical, exploratory journalism, rather than reliance on a ritualized coverage of violence. If the Vietnam war is again worth a half-hour weekly review, so is the racial crisis. On occasion, the television networks, and some local stations, have made commendable efforts to explore the meaning of Negro unrest in special programs and documentaries. The two programs Stuart Schulberg produced in Watts for the NBC *Experiment in Television* series were a good example of the kind of imaginative effort that is needed to bring sympathetic white understanding to bear on the ghetto.

Notes

[1] Interview with author, June 1, 1967.

[2] *The New Yorker*, December 10, 1966.

[3] Speech to National Association of Broadcasters annual convention in Chicago, quoted by *New York Times*, May 30, 1954.

[4] Robert E. Kintner, "Television and the World of Politics," *Harper's Magazine*, May, 1965, pp. 129f.

[5] (Garden City: Doubleday, 1963), p. 178.

[6] July 6, 1967.

[7] Federal Communications Commission, "Opinion and Order on Petition for Reconsideration, ABC-ITT Merger Proceedings," Release 67–743 2055, June 22, 1967, pp. 65f.

[8] Quoted in *Time*, December 1, 1967.

[9] *The New Yorker*, October 15, 1966.

[10] Quoted by Joan Barthel, "When Will They Say Their Final Goodnights?" *TV Guide*, July 1, 1967, p. 19.

[11] *Report of the National Advisory Commission on Civil Disorders*, The New York Times Company (New York: Bantam Books, 1968).

[12] *Ibid.*, p. 366.

CENSORSHIP AND AESTHETICS

5 On Misreading by the Literary

C. S. Lewis

With the following contribution the focus of the reader narrows to the individual recipient of knowledge and how he applies various devices to make the message suit his "competitive particularity." Lewis' essay is one chapter of a sparklingly provocative little book, *An Experiment in Criticism*. The thesis of the book is that there are two ways of reading literature (and, by extrapolation, of appreciating art or of listening to music). One way is to "use" books as mere mechanics to trigger escapist fantasies about ourselves, what Lewis calls "egoistic castle building." One is also "using" books if one reads dutifully merely to become cultured, or interesting, or knowledgeable. The other way of reading literature is to "receive" it. Here the reader opens himself totally to the viewpoint of the literary artist in truly creative passivity, a procedure Lewis compares with dancing a dance choreographed by a master.

The novel purpose of the late Professor Lewis in this book was to suggest a new criterion for literary critics. Instead of judging how a book was written, they might try to judge how it may be read. If it permits and invites "receiving," it is good literature. If it can only be "used," it is not literature, whatever else it might be.

The purpose of the editor in including one chapter from Lewis' book is not to add to the discussion of literary values. It is included because of Lewis' acute diagnosis of "using" in the cognitive affairs of men. What Lewis says of the communicative process of reading can be extended to all communicative procedures. Censorship springs

from the utilitarian view of communication. We must all "use" communications, but there is a lamentable tendency to extend the "use" to all our cognitive activities. The censor, by definition, cannot "receive."

In the epilogue of *An Experiment in Criticism*, Lewis explains his notion of artistic "reception."

> Good reading, therefore, though it is not essentially an affectional or moral or intellectual activity, has something in common with all three. In love we escape from our self into one other. In the moral sphere, every act of justice or charity involves putting ourselves in the other person's place and thus transcending our own competitive particularity. In coming to understand anything we are rejecting the facts as they are for us in favour of the facts as they are. The primary impulse of each is to maintain and aggrandize himself. The secondary impulse is to go out of the self, to correct its provincialism and heal its loneliness. In love, in virtue, in the pursuit of knowledge, and in the reception of the arts, we are doing this. Obviously this process can be described either as an enlargement or as a temporary annihilation of the self. But that is an old paradox; 'he that loseth his life shall save it.'

The following description of one kind of failure to "receive" illuminates the protean forms of the censorious mind.

Reprinted by permission of the publishers from C. S. Lewis, *An Experiment in Criticism* (London: Cambridge University Press, 1961).

Clive Staples Lewis was an esteemed novelist, critic, and Christian apologist. His works include poems, prayers, and allegories as well as fairy tales. He was a close associate of J. R. R. Tolkien, the author of *The Lord of the Rings* trilogy.

We have to consider a fault in reading which cuts right across our distinction between the literary and the unliterary. Some of the former are guilty of it and some of the latter are not.

Essentially, it involves a confusion between life and art, even a failure to allow for the existence of art at all. Its crudest form is pilloried in the old story of the backwoodsman in the gallery who shot the 'villain' on the stage. We see it also in the lowest type of reader who wants sensational narrative but will not accept it unless it is offered him as 'news.' On a higher level it appears as the belief that all good books are good primarily because they give us knowledge, teach us 'truths' about 'life.' Dramatists and novelists are praised as if they were doing, essentially, what used to be expected of theologians and philosophers, and the qualities which belong to their works as inventions and as designs are neglected. They are reverenced as teachers and insufficiently appreciated as artists. In a word, De Quincey's 'literature of power' is treated as a species within his 'literature of knowledge.'

We may begin by ruling out of consideration one way of treating fictions as sources of knowledge which, though not strictly literary, is pardonable at a certain age and usually transient. Between the ages of twelve and twenty nearly all of us acquired from novels, along with plenty of misinformation, a great deal of information about the world we live in: about the food, clothes, customs and climates of various countries, the working of various professions, about methods of travel, manners, law, and political machinery. We were getting not a philosophy of life but what is called 'general knowledge.' In a particular case a fiction may serve this purpose for even an adult reader. An inhabitant of the cruel countries might come to grasp our principle that a man is innocent till he is proved guilty from reading our detective stories (in that sense such stories are a great proof of real civilisation). But in general this use of fiction is abandoned as we grow older. The curiosities it used to satisfy have been satisfied or simply died away, or, if they survive, would now seek information from more reliable sources. That is one reason why we have less inclination to take up a new novel than we had in our youth.

Having got this special case out of the way, we may now return to the real subject.

It is obvious that some of the unliterary mistake art for an account of real life. As we have seen, those whose reading is conducted, egoistic castle-building will inevitably do so. They wish to be deceived; they want to feel that though these beautiful things have not really happened to them, yet they might. ('He might take a fancy to me like that Duke did to that factory girl in the story.') But it is equally obvious that a great many of the unliterary are not in this state at all—are indeed almost safer from it than anyone else. Try the experiment on your grocer or gardener. You cannot often try it about a book, for he has read few, but a film will do just as well for our purpose. If you complain to him about the gross improbability of its happy ending, he will very probably reply 'Ah. I reckon they just put that in to wind it up like.' If you complain about the dull and perfunctory love-interest which has been thrust into a story of masculine adventure, he will say 'Oh well, you know, they usually got to put in a bit of that. The women like it.' He knows perfectly well that the film is art, not knowledge. In a sense his very unliterariness saves him from confusing the two. He never expected the film to be anything but transitory and not very important, entertainment; he never dreamed that any art could provide more than this. He goes to the pictures not to learn but to relax. The idea that any of his opinions about the real world could be modified by what he saw there would seem to him preposterous. Do you take him for a fool? Turn the conversation from art to life—gossip with him, bargain with him—and you will find he is as shrewd and realistic as you can wish.

Contrariwise, we find the error, in a subtle and especially insidious form, among the literary. When my pupils have talked to me about Tragedy (they have talked much less often, uncompelled, about tragedies), I have sometimes discovered a belief that it is valuable, is worth witnessing or reading, chiefly because it communicates something called the tragic 'view' or 'sense' or 'philosophy' of 'life.' This content is variously described, but in the most widely diffused version it seems to consist of two propositions: (1) That great miseries result from a flaw in the principal sufferer. (2) That these miseries, pushed to the extreme, reveal to us a certain splendour in man, or even in the universe. Though the anguish is great, it is at least not sordid, meaningless, or merely depressing.

No one denies that miseries with such a cause and such a close can occur in real life. But if tragedy is taken as a comment on life in the sense that we are meant to conclude from it 'This is the typical or usual, or ultimate, form of human misery,' then tragedy becomes wishful moonshine. Flaws in character do cause suffering; but bombs and bayonets, cancer and polio, dictators and roadhogs, fluctuations in the value of money or in employment, and mere meaningless coincidence, cause a great deal more. Tribulation falls on the integrated and well adjusted and prudent as readily as on anyone else. Nor do real miseries often end with a curtain and a roll of drums 'in calm of mind, all passion spent.' The dying seldom make magnificent last speeches. And we who watch them die do not, I think, behave very like the minor characters in a tragic death-scene. For unfortunately the play is not over. We have no *exeunt omnes*. The real story does not end: it proceeds to ringing up undertakers, paying bills, getting death certificates, finding and proving a will, answering letters of condolence. There is no grandeur and no finality. Real sorrow ends neither with a bang nor a whimper. Sometimes, after a spiritual journey like Dante's, down to the centre and then, terrace by terrace, up the mountain of accepted pain, it may rise into peace —but peace hardly less severe than itself. Sometimes it remains for life, a puddle in the mind which grows always wider, shallower, and more unwholesome. Sometimes it just peters out, as other moods do. One of these alternatives has grandeur, but not tragic grandeur. The other two—ugly, slow, bathetic, unimpressive—would be of no use at all to a dramatist. The tragedian dare not present the totality of suffering as it usually is in its uncouth mixture of agony with littleness, all the indignities and (save for pity) the uninterestingness, of grief. It would ruin his play. It would be merely dull and depressing. He selects from the reality just what his art needs; and what it needs is the exceptional. Conversely, to approach anyone in real sorrow with these ideas about tragic grandeur, to insinuate that he is now assuming that 'sceptred pall,' would be more than imbecile: it would be odious.

Next to a world in which there were no sorrows we should like one where sorrows were always significant and sublime. But if we allow the 'tragic view of life' to make us believe that we live in such a world, we shall be deceived. Our very eyes teach us better. Where in all nature is there anything uglier and more undignified than an adult male face blubbered and distorted with weeping? And what's behind it is not much prettier. There is no sceptre and no pall.

It seems to me undeniable, that tragedy, taken as a philosophy of life, is the most obstinate and best camouflaged of all wish-fulfillments, just because its pretensions are so apparently realistic. The claim is that it has faced the worst. The conclusion that, despite the worst, some sublimity and significance remains, is therefore as convincing as the testimony of a witness who appears to speak against his will. But the claim that it has faced the worst—at any rate the commonest sort of 'worst'—is in my opinion simply false.

It is not the fault of the tragedians that this claim deceives certain readers, for the tragedians never made it. It is critics who make it. The tragedians chose for their themes stories (often grounded in the mythical and impossible) suitable to the art they practised. Almost by definition, such stories would be atypical, striking, and in various other ways adapted to the purpose. Stories with a sublime and satisfying *finale* were chosen not because such a *finale* is characteristic of human misery, but because it is necessary to good drama.

It is probably from this view of tragedy that many young people derive the belief that tragedy is essentially 'truer to life' than comedy. This seems to me wholly unfounded. Each of these forms chooses out of real life just those sorts of events it needs. The raw materials are all around us, mixed anyhow. It is selection, isolation, and patterning, not a philosophy, that makes the two sorts of play. The two products do not contradict one another any more than two nosegays plucked out of the same garden. Contradiction comes in only when we (not the dramatists) turn them into propositions such as 'This is what human life is like.'

It may seem odd that the same people who think comedy less true than tragedy often regard broad farce as realistic. I have often met the opinion that in turning from the *Troilus* to his *faibliaux* Chaucer was drawing nearer to reality. I think this arises from a failure to distinguish between realism of presentation and realism of content. Chaucer's farce is rich in realism of presentation; not in that of content. Criseyde and Alisoun are equally probable women, but what happens in the *Troilus* is very much more probable than what happens in the *Miller's Tale*. The world of farce is hardly less ideal that that of pastoral. It is a paradise of jokes where the wildest coincidences are accepted and where all works together to produce laughter. Real life seldom succeeds in being, and never remains for more than a few minutes, nearly as funny as a well-invented farce. That is why the people feel that they cannot acknowledge the comicality of a real situation more emphatically than by saying 'It's as good as a play.'

All three forms of art make the abstractions proper to them. Tragedies omit the clumsy and apparently meaningless bludgeoning of much real misfortune and the prosaic littlenesses which usually rob real sorrows of their dignity. Comedies ignore the possibility that the marriage of lovers does not always lead to permanent, nor ever to perfect, happiness. Farce excludes pity for its butts in situations where, if they were real, they would deserve it. None of the three kinds is making a statement about life in general. They are all constructions: things made *out* of the stuff of real life; additions to life rather than comments on it.

At this point I must take pains not to be misunderstood. The great artist—or at all events the great literary artist—cannot be a man shallow either in his thoughts or his feelings. However improbable and abnormal a story he has chosen, it will, as we say, 'come to life' in his hands. The life to which it comes will be impregnated with all the wisdom, knowledge and experience the author has; and even more by something which I can only vaguely describe as the flavour or 'feel' that actual life has for him. It is this omnipresent flavour or feel that makes bad inventions so mawkish and suffocating, and good ones so tonic. The good ones allow us temporarily to share a sort of passionate sanity. And we may also—which is less important—expect to find in them many psychological truths and profound, at least profoundly felt, reflections. But all this comes to us, and was very possibly called out of the poet, as the 'spirit' (using that word in a quasi-chemical sense) of a work of art, a play. To formulate it as a philosophy, even if it were a rational philosophy, and regard the actual play as primarily a vehicle for that philosophy, is an outrage to the thing the poet has made for us.

I use the words *thing* and *made* advisedly. We have already mentioned, but not answered, the question whether a poem 'should not mean but be.' What guards the good reader from treating a tragedy—he will not talk much about an abstraction like 'Tragedy'—as a mere vehicle for truth is his continual awareness that it not only means, but is. It is not merely *logos* (something said) but *poiema* (something made). The same is true of a novel or narrative poem. They are complex and carefully made objects. Attention to the very objects they are is our first step. To value them chiefly for reflections which they may suggest to us or morals we may draw from them, is a flagrant instance of 'using' instead of 'receiving.'

What I mean by 'objects' need not remain mysterious. One of the prime achievements in every good fiction has nothing to do with truth or philosophy or a *Weltanschauung* at all. It is the triumphant adjustment of two different kinds of order. On the one hand, the events (the mere plot) have their chronological and causal order, that which they would have in real life. On the other, all the scenes or other divisions of the work must be related to each other according to principles of design, like the masses in a picture or the passages in a symphony. Our feelings and imaginations must be led through 'taste after taste, upheld with kindliest change.' Contrasts (but also premonitions and echoes) between the darker and the lighter, the swifter and the slower, the simpler and the more sophisticated, must have something like a balance, but never a too perfect symmetry, so that the shape of the whole work will be felt as inevitable and satisfying. Yet this second order must never confuse the first. The transition from the 'platform' to the court scene at the beginning of *Hamlet*, the placing of Aeneas' narrative in *Aeneid* II and III, or the darkness in the first two books of *Paradise Lost* leading to the ascent in the third, are simple illustrations. But there is yet another requisite. As little as possible must exist solely for the sake of other things. Every episode, explanation, description, dialogue—ideally every sentence—must be pleasurable and interesting for its own sake. (A fault in Conrad's *Nostromo* is that we have to read so much pseudo-history before we get to the central matter, for which alone this history exists.)

Some will discount this as 'mere technique.' We must certainly agree that these orderings, apart from that which they order, are worse than 'mere'; they are nonentities, as shape is a nonentity apart from the body whose shape it is. But an 'appreciation' of sculpture which ignored the statue's shape in favour of the sculptor's 'view of life' would be self-deception. It is by the shape that it is a statue. Only because it is a statue do we come to be mentioning the sculptor's view of life at all.

It is very natural that when we have gone through the ordered movements which a great play or narrative excites in us—when we have danced that dance or enacted that ritual or submitted to that pattern—it should suggest to us many interesting reflections. We have 'put on mental muscle' as a result of this activity. We may thank Shakespeare or Dante for that muscle, but we had better not father on them the philosophical or ethical use we make of it. For one thing, this use is unlikely to rise very much—it may rise a little—above our own ordinary level. Many of the comments on life which people get out of Shakespeare could have been reached by very moderate talents without his assistance. For another, it may well impede future receptions of the work itself. We may go back to it chiefly to find further confirmation for our belief that it teaches this or that, rather than for a fresh immersion in what it is. We shall be like a man poking his fire, not to boil the kettle or warm the room, but in the hope of seeing in it the same pictures he saw yesterday. And since a text is 'but a cheverel glove' to a determined critic—since everything can be a symbol, or an irony, or an ambiguity—we shall easily find what we want. The supreme objection to this is that which lies against the popular use of all the arts. We are so busy doing things with the work that we give it too little chance to work on us. Thus increasingly we meet only ourselves.

But one of the chief operations of art is to remove our gaze from that mirrored face, to deliver us from that solitude. When we read the 'literature of knowledge' we hope, as a result, to think more correctly and clearly. In reading imaginative work, I suggest, we should be much less concerned with altering our own opinions—though this of course is sometimes their effect—than with entering fully into the opinions, and therefore also the attitudes, feelings and total experience, of other men. Who in his ordinary senses would try to decide between the claims of materialism and theism by reading Lucretius and Dante? But who in his literary senses would not delightedly learn from them a great deal about what it is like to be a materialist or a theist?

In good reading there ought to be no 'problem of belief.' I read Lucretius and Dante at a time when (by and large) I agreed with Lucretius. I have read them since I came (by and large) to agree with Dante. I cannot find that this has much altered my experience, or at all altered my evaluation, of either. A true lover of literature should be in one way like an honest examiner, who is prepared to give the highest marks to the telling, felicitous and well-documented exposition of views he dissents from or even abominates.

The sort of misreading I here protest against is unfortunately encouraged by the increasing importance of 'English Literature' as an academic discipline. This directs to the study of literature a great many talented, ingenious, and diligent people whose real interests are not specifically literary at all. Forced to talk incessantly about books, what can they do but try to make books into the sort of things they can talk about? Hence literature becomes for them a religion, a philosophy, a school of ethics, a psychotherapy, a sociology—anything rather than a collection of works of art. Lighter works—*divertissements*—are either disparaged or misrepresented as being really far more serious than they look. But to a real lover of literature an exquisitely made *divertissement* is a very much more respectable thing than some of the 'philosophies of life' which are foisted upon the great poets. For one thing, it is a good deal harder to make.

This is not to say that all critics who extract such a philosophy from their favourite novelists or poets produce work without value: Each attributes to his chosen author what he believes to be wisdom; and the sort of thing that seems to him wise will of course be determined by his own calibre. If he is a fool he will find and admire foolishness, if he is a mediocrity, platitude, in all his favourites. But if he is a profound thinker himself, what he acclaims and expounds as his author's philosophy may be well worth reading, even if it is in reality his own. We may compare him to the long succession of divines who have based edifying and eloquent sermons on some straining of their texts. The sermon, though bad exegesis, was often good homiletics in its own right.

6 Denial of Reality

John Howard Lawson

Film making seems quite a distance from book reading, but screen writer Lawson shares a common concern with C. S. Lewis. Both are concerned with the unique vision of the artist. Lewis warns of the filters and screens our personality puts up between the artist and our perception of his work. Lawson describes the theory behind creative film-making that demands the erection of filtering devices by the film-maker in order to have "objective" reality serve the "subjective" concepts of the artist.

Lawson's contribution is one chapter excerpted from his book, *Film: The Creative Process.* This book is a very complete study of the entire film medium. Lawson traces the history of cinema, analyzes the language of the film, the styles of important directors, the political ideas of different schools of cinema, and theorizes about the purpose and form of film as an art. This essay opens Lawson's discussion of film theory.

John Howard Lawson has written a number of important films of political significance, including *Blockade,* a controversial story of the Spanish Civil War released in the late thirties. Besides books on the technique of play and screen writing, he has also written *Film in the Battle of Ideas.*

Some of the attributes of film language have been examined, beginning with specific instruments—camera, microphone, screen, strips of film, and sound track. These are real objects; anyone trying to use them in an unrealistic manner would encounter formidable obstacles. A camera in a room without light would be of no interest to anyone. It cannot function unless there is something which the light touches and illuminates, something having corporeal existence.

Beginning with his tools and with the world of sight and sound, the artist proceeds to arrange and organize the available materials; every step that he takes—the placing of camera and microphone, the duration of each shot, the cutting of film and sound track—create something that is peculiarly his own, bearing the stamp of his personality or purpose. This *something* cannot be absolutely new, because it is made of materials that are already there. What is new is the interpretation or sensibility or vision supplied by the creator of the film. The film artist, like all artists, is impelled by the nature of his task to seek to enrich the meaning and enhance the value of his work. He is affected by the experience of all the arts, because all are part of his heritage, his consciousness of himself and his world. But he has been attracted to cinema, not by its similarity to other arts, but by its unique potentialities.

In exploring and realizing these potentialities, the artist is engaged in a great struggle with reality: there is nothing else that his instruments can see or hear. He faces the vast variety of sights and sounds that can be ordered and organized according to his will. The expansion of cinematic language to its ultimate limits depends on the artist's understanding of the film's relationship to reality. He must relate each image and sound to some concept or feeling concerning the real material with which he is dealing. Otherwise, there would be nothing but disordered movement and noise. What the film-maker thinks or feels may seem personal and subjective. Nonetheless, it involves a more or less systematic attitude toward what is projected on the screen, an image of something that exists.

It is paradoxical to speak of film as a "denial of reality." Yet an impressive movement of cinematic theory and practice has been built around the paradox. The artist who grapples most fiercely with reality may pretend it does not exist. His view is false, yet it springs from the need of his own spirit and therefore contains, paradoxically, an element of human truth. His zeal and feeling bring him in contact with reality even while he is denying it.

Hans Richter, one of the rebels of the early twenties, has devoted his life to what he calls "the free use of the means of cinematographic expression." He wrote in 1955: "It is still too early to speak of a tradition or of a style. . . . The Movement is still too young."[1] Richter does not defend a specific style: he is less concerned with the differences between pure abstraction and surrealism than with the ground they hold in common. He describes the revolt against "realism" in these terms:

> Problems of modern art lead directly into film. Organization and orchestration of form, color, the dynamics of motion, simultaneity, were problems with which Cézanne, the cubists and the futurists had to deal.
>
> The connection to theatre, and literature, was completely severed.[2]

Many painters have turned to film as an extension of their work on canvas. In exploring the dynamics of motion, they have also been influenced by choreographic movement. Ed Emschwiller describes his film *Dance Chromatique* as an attempt to combine "painting and dance in various ways. . . .":

> As a painter, I find that film, with its time dimensions, gives me a wider range of expression than plain painting. . . . I feel that the human figure, moving in dance forms, has a special significance, a basic appeal, which makes dance a particularly powerful visual art.[3]

Human figures as part of a pictorial configuration retain their "special significance," their humanity, the physical beauty of their bodily movement. Unless the artist deals with lines or unrecognizable shapes, he is portraying human beings or objects.

However, people or things can be shown in such a way that they no longer conform to our normal visual experience. The believers in a unique cinematic vision hold that new and more profound aspects of reality are revealed through the creative organization of photographic images. According to Richter, "the object is taken out of its conventional context and is put into new relationships, creating in that way a new content altogether."[4]

Fernand Léger spoke of "A new realism . . . concentrated on bringing out the value of the object":

> Before the invention of the moving picture no one knew the possibilities latent in a foot—a hand, a hat. . . . Take an aluminum saucepan. Let shafts of light play on it from all angles—penetrating and transforming it. . . . The public may never know that this fairy-like effect of light in many forms, that so delights it, is nothing but an aluminum saucepan.[5]

The transformation of reality, as Léger describes it, is an extension of the sleight of hand or magic that delighted Méliès. The artist has not created something "unreal," but he has used the camera to expose new aspects of the external world, communicating his attitude toward it. The literature of "pure cinema" tends to blur the distinction between objective and subjective. The confusion is indicated in the views of Parker Tyler, a leading American theoretician. He insists that it is the true function of film to explore aspects of objective reality to which we are customarily blind. He uses the terms "illusionist realism," or "realist illusion" to describe "a prosaic, unimaginative and reportorial view of the world and the life with which it teems." He holds that "the chief function of the film camera is not to cement and exploit mere appearances, mere 'reality,' but to imply all kinds of changeability, all mutations, whether of time or space."

What is unclear in Tyler's formulation is the role of consciousness. He does not ignore the subjective factor: "To equate photography, still or moving, with the objects which are portrayed by the artificial eye of the lens is as silly as believing that everyone sees (e.g., comprehends what he sees) just alike. Vision is a psychological as well as a mechanical process."[6]

This basic truth cannot be accepted so casually. The crucial issue is the conception of reality.

In a moving tribute to Maya Deren shortly after her death, Rudolph Arnheim says that in her films "the familiar world captures us by its pervasive strangeness."[7] Maya Deren, herself, regarded her work as an expression of psychological experience:

> My films might be called metaphysical, referring to their thematic content. It has required millenniums of tortured evolution for nature to produce the intricate miracle which is man's mind. . . . This metaphysical action of the mind has as much reality and importance as the material and physical activities of his body. My films are concerned with meanings—ideas and concepts—not with matter.[8]

In the same declaration of principles, Maya Deren describes her films as poetic ("a celebration, a singing of values and meanings"), and choreographic (conferring "a ritual dimension upon functional motion"). She defines the structure as "a logic of ideas and qualities, rather than of causes and events."

How does "a logic of ideas and qualities" differ from a logic "of causes and events?" One is subjective and the other is objective. The familiar world in which we live and move is certainly full of events, and it seems to involve a continuous interplay of causes and effects. Our ordinary activities are largely of a social character: jobs and recreation and family situations bring us into constant contact with other people. These are the aspects of reality which are either excluded from "pure cinema" or converted into something strange and unfamiliar. The revolt against the narrative film is not solely motivated by distaste for the vulgarities of commercial production; nor is it solely an opposition to literary or theatrical influences. It is based on the view that cinematic experience is unrelated to *social* reality. Jean Epstein declared in 1923 that "The film should positively avoid any connection with the historical, romantic, moral or immoral, geographic or documentary subjects."[9]

In the film of ideas and sensations, according to Richter, "the external object was used, as in the documentary film, as raw material, but instead of employing it for a rational theme of a social, economic or scientific nature, it has broken away from its habitual environment and was used as material to express irrational visions."[10]

The various schools of avant-garde film are united in their insistence on the primacy of the subjective vision. Nonobjective images form patterns that cannot be identified with objects or people; surrealism shows fragments of reality in arrangements that are unrelated to ordinary experience; purveyors of dreams present fantasies drawn from the depths of the unconscious. Although abstraction is generally used as a technical term in painting and film, it may properly be applied to all these forms: all of them reject what is material and concrete in favor of an abstract configuration. The concept is abstracted from ordinary observation; it is a product of the mind. It is not necessarily irrational: abstract thought can be extremely logical. But aesthetic abstraction asserts the primacy of inner experience; therefore, it rejects on principle the possibility of submitting creative experience to any objective criteria. Science conceives abstract structures, but these must meet the test of reality. The cinema of "ideas and qualities" holds that such a test is unnecessary and destructive.

Nonetheless, we must make the test. If an abstract concept is unrelated to actuality, if it is not an abstract of some facet of someone's real experience, then it cannot be verified and we might as well abandon our attempt to build a theory of film. A work of art cannot be judged, or even understood, if it has no meaning outside the mind of its creator. The opponents of "illusionist realism" meet this objection with a paradox: everything is to some extent illusory, they say, but subjective experience can be more real than what we see with our eyes. This is a statement of their philosophy, but by the same token it is a flat denial that there is any means of determining the validity of subjective experience.

Maya Deren resolves the problem by a poetic affirmation: "I believe that I am a part of, not apart from humanity; that nothing I may feel, think, perceive, experience, despise, desire, or despair of is really unknowable to any other man."[11]

In stating this truth, the artist negates the negation of reality. If community of feeling or thought exists, it must be expressed in the intercourse of people. It must have a logic that can be trusted, arising from causes and events that are observed and tested in the realm of actuality.

Creators of nonrealist films feel, of course, that communication is possible; if they despaired of communicating, they would stop making films. Many would say that contact between people is obstructed in their society, and that they are trying to restore forms of perception, sensibility or emotion which enable men to know each other better. The critical view of contemporary society and the desire to see and feel more deeply are valid and important—this accounts for the passion of these artists, their creative élan, their faith in themselves, their unwillingness to compromise.

If they did not possess these qualities and if they did not on occasions communicate them in their work, their theories would not demand this extended consideration. Their production is more significant—closer to reality, more responsive to human perceptions and sensibilities—than the "realism" of Hollywood.

Their rejection of the commercial story-film is a rejection of the society that sponsors these mendacious narratives. This is a moral judgment because it implies an idea of what constitutes a good society. It is an aesthetic judgment because it implies standards of aesthetic value.

The abstractionists isolate the aesthetic component from the whole context of external experience. They refuse to deal with social or moral issues on the ground that these issues are objective, while they themselves are concerned only with subjective processes. But this separation is artificial and negates their own activity: by making films, they enter the social milieu which they have endeavored to exclude from their consciousness.

The attack on bourgeois society is implicit in the work of all these artists and explicit in the declarations of many of them. But they are bourgeois intellectuals—this is the profound paradox in their position—and they cannot see beyond the specific system of class relationships which is so repugnant to them. They identify this system, its juridical and moral assumptions, its lies and illusions, with the real world, because it is the only reality they know or are able to imagine. Their rejection of capitalism is unrealistic, because they do not see it in its historical perspective, as a phase of human development that has run its course and must now give way to a higher form of social organization. They reject the collective experience of capitalistic society, which is an experience of class struggle, of growth and change and human aspiration. They negate the achievements of the past three hundred years, the industrial organization, the rational thought and scientific method, which are the bourgeoisie's permanent contribution to the progress of civilization.

Thus the artist is in a void between two worlds. He cannot go back to the bourgeois past and he cannot go forward to the socialist future. But his agonized solitude is an aspect of actuality. The past and the future are real enough, and his "rejection" does not change the fact. He develops techniques to express his feeling that reality has lost its stability and meaning.

Jonas Mekas writes that in making his film, *Guns in the Trees,* he used "single disconnected scenes as parts of an accumulative fresco—like an action painter uses his splashes of paint. The film abandons realism and attempts to reach into the poetic."[12]

Stanley Brakhage, whose films, *The Dead* and *Prelude,* won the Fourth Independent Film Award in 1962,[13] calls on us to "Abandon aesthetics . . . negate techniques, for film, like America, has not been discovered yet." Brakhage is engaged in a voyage of discovery; he is enchanted by the camera's possibilities:

> One may hand-hold the camera and inherit worlds of space. One may over- or under-expose film. One may use the filters of the world, fog, downpours, unbalanced lights, neons with neurotic color temperatures, glass which was never designed for a camera.

Brakhage combines this delight in the physical world with a deep sense of alienation: "It seems to me that the entire society of man is bent on destroying that which is alive within its individuals. . . ."[14]

"Pure cinema" is a cry of anger and despair; the anger is desperate because it is directed against "the entire society of man." At the same time, the artist is engaged in a search for personal consciousness, which necessarily brings him back to the reality he has rejected. His technique is largely a matter of "pure" sensibility, fragmentary moments of beauty and delight, obscure contrasts, brilliant insights that are rejected or distorted because they cannot become part of a rational design.

The technical achievements are noteworthy. The insistence on a direct relationship between the film-maker and process of film-making releases cinema from its bondage to the stultifying methods of industrial production. A fresh consciousness of reality is inherent in the confusion and fervor of the young film-makers.

The advocates of "pure cinema" are driven by the contradictions in their theory and practice to seek some solution. They cannot be content with a static opposition between the subjective withdrawal from reality and the constant attraction of sight and sound. They cannot make images out of blank space: they must either attempt to make sense out of their surroundings or find ways of giving form and substance to their inner consciousness. This is the classic dilemma illustrated in the contrasting careers of Buñuel and Cocteau from the early thirties to the present.

Cocteau carries us into the realm of the unconscious or subconscious, but what he finds there are clouded reflections of objective experience. In *Le Sang d'un Poète* (1932), Cocteau introduces us to a poet's universe, but it is inhabited by images of flesh and blood. There are various sexual episodes, but the core of meaning lies in the return to childhood. The poet-child suffers a symbolic wound and dies a symbolic death; by meeting these conditions of life—pain and the imminence of death—in symbolic form, the poet wins his temporary freedom from the horror of reality. The concept is obscure, but it is developed more clearly in *La Belle et la Bête* (1945). Cocteau has said that in this film he wished to plunge into the "lustral bath of childhood."

Neal Oxenhandler observes that "the persistent aspect of evasion of responsibility, flight from involvement or engagement in all his work suggests that there is something almost childlike in his conception of poetry."[15]

In *Orphée* (1949) there is the clearest allegory of flight into death: in order to escape reality, the poet must journey to the nether regions. But the dark ruins through which he passes on his journey are actually the ruins of St. Cyr near Paris, where the picture was filmed at night. Reality is unconquerable, and Cocteau's poetic power lies in his awareness of the truth. He acknowledges that the retreat into the subconscious is equivalent to dying. Yet the conditions of life are so intolerable that he must accept the alternative. In accepting death the poet is ironically triumphing over life, for he sees death as the basic condition of existence.

The idea of death is given a sort of allegorical universality in Cocteau's work. But it is related to the view that we are encompassed by blood and violence. This concept of reality has exerted a dominant influence on the development of film thought.

Notes

[1] Richter, "Film as an Original Art Form," *Film Culture* (New York), January, 1955.

[2] *Ibid.*

[3] *Film Quarterly* (Berkeley, California), Spring, 1961.

[4] *Op. cit.*

[5] *Little Review,* Winter, 1926.

[6] "Declamation on Film," *Film Culture* (New York), Summer, 1961.

[7] *Film Culture* (New York), Spring, 1962.

[8] Maya Deren, "A Statement of Principles," *Film Culture* (New York), Winter, 1961.

[9] Richter, *op. cit.*

[10] *Ibid.*

[11] *Op. cit.*

[12] "Notes on the New American Cinema," *Film Culture* (New York), Spring, 1962.

[13] The award is given annually by the magazine *Film Culture.*

[14] "Notes on the New American Cinema," *Film Culture* (New York), Spring, 1962.

[15] Neal Oxenhandler, "Poetry in Three Films of Jean Cocteau," Yale French Studies, *Art of the Cinema* (New Haven, 1956), p. 18.

7 Obscenity as an Esthetic Category

Abraham Kaplan

The philosophy of art, which Lewis has approached as a critic and Lawson has faced as an artist, is most germane to Kaplan's understanding of the meaning of obscenity. Like the censorship it so often provokes, at times with justice, obscenity is an incorrigibly plural concept. A master of methodology, Kaplan neatly dissects the various meanings of obscenity and assigns each meaning to a relevant context. As the reader will see, there is a passion for order in the following essay, but the passion arises from intelligence, not partisanship.

Reprinted, with permission, from a symposium, "Obscenity and the Arts," appearing in *Law and Contemporary Problems* (Vol. 20, No. 4, Autumn 1955), published by the Duke University School of Law, Durham, North Carolina.

DR. KAPLAN has served as chairman of the U.C.L.A. philosophy department, has been a consultant of the Rand Corporation, and has been visiting professor of philosophy at New York University, Columbia, Harvard, and at other colleges and universities. A frequent contributor to proceedings and symposia, Dr. Kaplan has written a perceptive critique of social science methodology, *The Conduct of Inquiry*.

My problem is not what to do about obscenity, but what to make of it. Control over the arts in this country—whether by official power or by unofficial influence—rests largely on allegations of obscenity. But patterns of social control cannot reasonably be appraised without some conception of what it is that is being controlled. Accordingly, I ask what constitutes obscenity in relation to the arts: Can a work of art be obscene and still be esthetic in status and function? What part, if any, does the obscene play in the esthetic experience? What characteristics of the art object mark its occurrence?

These questions are meant as belonging to the philosophy of art, not to its psychology or sociology. To answer them is not to assert matters of fact, but to clarify relations of ideas. Such a clarification must take facts into account, of course—but its outcome, if successful, is a clear conception rather than a true proposition. Still less does an answer to these questions entail a social policy or a procedure for implementing policy. I do not pretend that the distinctions to be drawn in this essay can be directly applied in a court of law. I shall be content if they throw light on the problem of obscenity for the artist, his audience, and the critic who interprets each to the other.

I

Many people anxious to defend freedom of expression in the arts attack the suppression of obscenity on the grounds that obscenity has no objective existence, but it is to be found only in the mind of the censor. I share the conclusion which this argument is intended to bolster—namely, that censorship is to be condemned; but the argument itself appears to me to be fallacious. Its premise is the undeniable proposition that judgments of the obscene vary with time and place. But from this true premise, the invalid inference is made to a subjectivist conclusion: All that can be common to such varying judgments is simply a subjective emotion of disapproval. "Obscenity exists only in the minds and emotions of those who believe in it, and is not a quality of a book or picture."[1] To think otherwise, so this logic runs, is to be guilty of a superstition which is "the modern counterpart of ancient witchcraft."[2]

Now those exercised over obscenity do perhaps resemble the old prosecutors of witchcraft in their fanaticism and irrationality.[3] The emphasis on the relativism of obscenity thus exposes the narrowness and rigidity of traditionalist morality. But the belief in witchcraft was simply false. The belief in obscenity is false only if its rational character is overlooked. What is superstitious is an absolutist conception,[4] alleged to apply universally whether it be recognized or no. The alternative to absolutism is not subjectivism, but an insistence on objectivity *relative to a specified context.* The rationality of a belief is similarly relative to the evidence available for it. But this relation is not only compatible with objectivity, but even defines it. Such a standpoint has come to be known as *objective relativism* or *contextualism.*[5]

Judgments of obscenity vary because they are contextual. I mean more than that "dirt" is misplaced matter, *i.e.*, that propriety varies with circumstances. I mean that obscenity is to be found in words or pictures only in so far as these can be interpreted to have a certain meaning; and meaning itself is contextual. D. H. Lawrence has protested against objectivism that "it is the mind which is the Augean stables, not language."[6] But language has no content at all, obscene or otherwise, without mind. It means what it does only because it is interpreted as it is in definite contexts, and it is in just such contexts of interpretation that its obscenity is to be localized. So far as the facts of relativity are concerned, obscenity is no more subjective than is any esthetic quality whatever.

What is sound in the relativist position is preserved in the recognition of the difference between an art *object* and the *work* of art which results when the object is responded to in an esthetic context. The art experience is not a passive one, but requires the active participation of the respondent. And obscenity is a property of the resultant work and not of the object out of context. When people disagree whether something is obscene, they are likely to be judging different works of art (constructed, as it were, from the same object), rather than reacting differently to the same work. The important problem posed by relativism is, then, *which* work we are to judge when confronted with a particular art object: it is the problem of interpretation. Of course, standards of propriety may differ, just as there are differences in, say, what would amuse us and the Greeks. But when we read the comedies of Aristophanes, these differences either enter into the interpretation we give to the plays (the art objects), and so give rise to different works of art for us than for his contemporaries, or else the differences are not esthetically relevant at all. Once such differences are explicitly brought into the context, the relativism is objectified.

Now all art is essentially ambiguous, in the sense that the interpretation it calls for is an imaginative one. The object cannot be so fully specified as to leave no room in its reading for our own creative activity.[7] But what allows for an imaginative reading also makes possible a reading which is wholly our own projection. It is this danger, and not subjectivism, which is the point of the truism that "to the pure all things are pure." But not all interpretations *are* merely projective. The qualifications of the reader may make all the difference. A pure mind is just as likely to miss an entendre in Shakespeare as an ignorant one is to misread his Elizabethan usages. A proper judgment of obscenity in the arts can only be made by an informed and sensitive reader—not necessarily because only he can decide whether a work *is* obscene, but because only he can decide *what* work it is that is being judged.

I say a "proper" judgment, but more accurate is: a judgment made in the *ideal* context—ideal, that is, from the standpoint of esthetic appreciation and criticism. But there are other sorts of contexts in which a judgment might be made. There is the *personal* context, constituted by the judger himself. And there are various *standard* contexts (specified statistically or in other ways) which also occur and have their uses. Which context is to be chosen depends on the purpose for which the judgment is being made. I know of no principle of selection or evaluation apart from such purposes. To the question "Who is to judge whether a work is obscene?" we can reply only with the counter-questions, "What is to be done with the judgment when it is made? And why is it being made at all?"

Yet, I do not mean to pretend that the principle of contextualism leaves us with no difficulties in practice. On the contrary, it allows us to become clearly aware of just how serious the difficulties are. Competent critics disagree sharply among themselves. The ideal context is as difficult to achieve as ideals usually are. But it is not true that from the nature of the case the ideal is a hopeless one. Beauty and obscenity alike are in the eye of the beholder. But if—as artists, critics, and lovers of the arts, not as censors—we are prepared to enter into interpretation and evaluation in the one case, why not in the other?

II

Contextualism has brought us to the position that obscenity may be an objective property of a work of art, provided that the work itself be recognized as being relative to some context of response to the art object. Now many people deny that obscenity is an attribute even of the work of art, localizing it instead in the mind of the artist, by way of his "intention." But what are we to understand by artistic "intention"? Are there not different *sorts* of answers appropriate to the question why a particular art object was created?

We may answer, first, in terms of the artist's *motive:* money or glory or whatever ends external to his efforts he expected to be served by them. The legal judgment of obscenity sometimes considers motive—apparently, a work is more likely to be obscene if the artist expected to make money from his labors. But plainly, motive as such is completely irrelevant esthetically. A poet may write to pay for his mother's funeral (Johnson's *Rasselas*) or to seduce a woman who reminds him of his mother, but neither motive has much to do with *what* he writes.

Second, artistic "intention" may be construed as *purpose:* a specification in terms of the artist's medium of how his motive is expressed. The purpose may be to satirize the clergy, to expose the madness of chivalric romance, or to proclaim the rights of woman. Unquestionably, purpose must be conceded an esthetic relevance—it is what the artist tried to do *in* his work, not *by* it. Many artists accused of obscenity have defended themselves by insisting on their moral purpose.

But more important than what the artist tried to do is what in fact he *did* do, and this may be taken as a third sense of "intention"—the *intent* of the work itself. A specification of purpose may define an esthetic genre, but never a particular work of art. Every work has its own unique intent: the purpose as embodied in its own specific substance. When Judge Woolsey speaks of Joyce's not "exploiting" obscenity, he is referring to Joyce's artistic purpose, perhaps also to his lack of a monetary motive.[8] But when he refers to the absence of "the leer of the sensualist," it is intent which is involved.[9] What is at question is as much an experienced quality of the work as is the "ring" of sincerity, which is to be contrasted with sincerity itself—the latter being a matter of motive and purpose but not of intent.

Motive, then, helps localize obscenity only in so far as it determines purpose, and the latter, in turn, only as it is embodied in intent. But this brings us back once more from the mind of the artist to the perceived characters of the work of art itself.

The alternative remains to be considered of localizing obscenity in the mind of the audience, *i.e.*, in the effect of the work. The obscene, in the classical legal conception, is what tends to corrupt. This criterion is thought to be more "objective" than reference to the artist's intention. But such reference, at least in the sense of intent, is inescapably involved in the criterion. For the effect might otherwise have been the result of a purely projective interpretation, in which case it is not *that* work which is being judged to be obscene. To resort to the effect of the work is to commit oneself to distinguishing between its causal agency and its operation as a trigger mechanism, *i.e.*, as providing an occasion for projecting onto itself a corruption already present in the reader.

Plainly, which context is selected becomes crucial. The courts may choose as standard context Judge Woolsey's *"l'homme moyen sensuel,"*[10] but unless this standard is carefully specified (by Dr. Kinsey?), there is the serious danger that it will be replaced unwittingly by the personal context of the man passing judgment. To compare it with the standard of "the reasonable man" in the law of torts is to overlook the fact that "reasonableness" can, in principle, be intersubjectively specified (at least in part)—in terms of probabilities and their logical consequences. But where is the logic of sexual sensitivity that corresponds to the "reasonableness" of inductive and deductive inference? This question is especially embarrassing in view of the claim sometimes made that "familiarity with obscenity blunts the sensibilities,"[11] so that on the criterion of effect, the standard context invites a circular argument: the work is obscene because it *would* produce the effect if only it were not such familiar obscenity!

In the ideal context, the test of effect is wholly inapplicable. For the esthetic experience requires a kind of disinterest or detachment, a "psychic distance," which is incompatible with the corruption in question. Only when we hold the work of art at arm's length is it artistic at all. The work brings emotions to mind or presents them for contemplation. When they are actually felt, we have overstepped the bounds of art. Sad music does not make us literally sad. On the contrary, the more vividly and clearly we apprehend the specific quality of "sadness" of the music, the less sorrowful our own emotions. Of course, art evokes feeling; but it is *imagined* feeling, not what is actually felt as a quality of what we do and undergo. And art works against the translation of imagined feeling into action. It does so partly by providing us insight into feeling, and so allowing us to subject passion to the control of the understanding, as was urged by Spinoza;[12] and partly by providing a catharsis or sublimation of feeling, as in the conceptions of Aristotle and Freud.[13] In short, "there is a high breathlessness about beauty that cancels lust," as Santayana put it.[14] To be sure, the extreme of psychic distance is also incompatible with esthetic experience, as in the case of the intellectual or—what is more to the point—the philistine. But to ignore altogether the role of distance is to confuse art with promotion—advertising or propaganda.

Now *pornography* is promotional: it is the obscene responded to with minimal psychic distance. Fundamentally, therefore, it is a category of effect. To say that a work is pornographic is to say something about the feelings and actions which it produces in its respondents. We may, of course, identify it by its purpose rather than by direct observation of effect. Its motive—monetary or sexual or whatever—it is likely to share with most art. But as to esthetic intent, this is lacking altogether in so far as the object is being read as pornographic. For in this case, it is not itself the *object* of an experience, esthetic or any other, but rather a stimulus *to* an experience not focussed on it. It serves to elicit not the imaginative contemplation of an expressive substance, but rather the release in fantasy of a compelling impulse.

Pornography as such, therefore, is no more esthetic than is an object of sentiment, which has no intrinsic interest but is responded to by way of associations external to its own substance, though not external to the references it contains (as in the words "Souvenir of San Francisco" on the bottom of the tasteless ashtray). But though the poronographic as such is never artistic, contextualism warns us that an art object in a particular context—like that of the schoolboy with the Venus—may serve pornographically rather than as a basis for cooperation with the artist in creating a work of art. Indeed, the converse is also possible: a Pompeian wall-painting or a Central American sculpture may have been deliberately produced as pornographic but may constitute for us a work of art. In our culture, pornography masquerades as art with sufficient frequency to deserve a special designation—I suggest *erotica.* It is a species of what artists call "kitch": the vulgarities that hide behind a label of Art with a capital "A." Erotica consists of works that lack even the decency of being *honestly* pornographic.

The distinctions among these categories, however, have been made here on only the conceptual level. As a matter of fact, little is known concerning the actual effects—either stimulation or sublimation—which can be produced by words and pictures. But when obscenity is distinguished from pornography by reference to effect, it follows that art as such is never pornographic (though it may be obscene and in several senses is very likely to be). The effect of art on life is not so specific and immediate as is comprised in the concept of pornography. Action flows from impulses, habits, and predispositions which are not so easily changed as puritans both fear and hope. At most, an art object might trigger a process already primed. But in so far as this is its manner of working, it ceases to be art.

Obscenity, then, so far as it relates to art, can be localized neither in intention nor in effect, but only in the expressive substance of the work of art itself. Ultimately, to be sure, the content of a work of art, as of any vehicle of communication, is an abstraction from both intention and effect. Whether a word is insulting depends, at bottom, on its being used in order to convey an insult and its being responded to as conveying one. Yet, when this usage is established, the word is insulting even when spoken in innocence or to an insensible hearer; it has been misused or misunderstood, that is all. The question is one of the ideal context of its occurrence, not the personal context, nor yet a standard context selected to serve some extraneous interest.

I do not mean to say that obscenity is a matter of the occurrence of "dirty words." On the contrary! It is the work as a whole which must be considered. For it is an important characteristic of a work of art that it cannot be interpreted piece-meal. Each element affects the content of all the others. The work is an integrated, coherent whole whose expressive quality cannot be additively constructed from what is expressed by its isolated parts. Judge Woolsey's position is esthetically unassailable when he says of *Ulysses* that, although it contains "many words usually considered dirty. . . . Each word of the book contributes like a bit of mosaic to the detail of the picture which Joyce is seeking to construct for his readers."[15] Indeed, isolated words may easily lose their expressiveness by mechanical repetition, to be restored to artistic potency only by skillful exploitation of a fresh setting in a complex work. The obscenity that occurs in a work of art may be as shocking to some as army talk; but it is wholly different in quality. The one is expressive; the other marks both the failure of expression and the lack of something to express.

It is a further consequence of this conception that obscenity in art not only does not lie in a baldness of sexual reference, but is, in fact, incompatible with wholly explicit statement. Explicitness may be pornographic, but it has no place in art. Where nothing is left to the imagination, the reading of the art object may stimulate an experience but does not itself constitute one. No opportunity is provided for that sharing in the act of creation which alone makes an experience esthetic. Nothing is a work of art for *me* unless I have been able to put something of my deeper self into it. The art object invites me to express something of that self and guides me in my efforts to do so; but the effort must be mine. Hence the popularity of the merely pornographic; it makes so few demands. Genuine expression is replaced by a spurious consummation.

As an esthetic category, obscenity is, by contrast, of the very stuff of imagination. In one etymology, "obscene" is from "obscurus"—what is concealed. Now expression is concealment as well as revelation. Art speaks in symbols, and at the core of every symbol is a secret which only imagination can fathom. The symbol itself thus takes on the mysterious quality of what it hides. It is experienced as charged with feeling and produces tension by at once inviting and resisting penetration. Both art and obscenity have a single genetic root: the infantile capacity to endow a mere sign with the effect that belongs properly to what it signifies.[16] A creature incapable of obscenity is also incapable of art. Magic, too, avails itself of the same capacity: words themselves, imbued with mysterious powers over other things. Psychologically, obscenity stands between art and magic—neither wholly make believe like the one, nor yet wholly believing like the other. In many cultures, obscenity has an important role in magical rituals. In our own, its magical character is betrayed in the puritan's supposition that words alone can work evil, and that evil will be averted if only the words are not uttered.

III

Because there is, after all, a difference between a symbol and what it symbolizes, obscenity is a matter, not of what the work *refers* to, but rather of the *expressive* substance of the work. Puritans may condemn a work for presenting certain aspects of life; artists may defend it because what is presented are certain aspects of *life.* Truth is used both as a mark of obscenity and as a mark of its absence. In fact, it can serve as neither. The question whether the world *is* as art (referentially) presents it to be is irrelevant to esthetic quality in general, and to the quality of obscenity in particular. Art is not obscene by virtue merely of its subject, nor does it cease to be obscene merely because its subject is virtuous. A verse attributed to D. H. Lawrence complains, "Tell me what's wrong with words or with you, that the thing is all right but the word is taboo!" But there is nothing wrong with recognizing that words and things are different, and that properties of the one cannot necessarily be imputed to the other. Words are public, for instance, and easy to produce, and can occur in contexts where the things they refer to would not be appropriate and could not occur. The Stoics argued that "there being nothing dishonest in the conjugal duty, it could not be denoted by any dishonest word, and that therefore the word used by clowns to denote it is as good as any other."[17] The question is, however, whether clowning is not different from conjugal life as the Stoics themselves conceived it, and whether the language used is not in fact part of the clowning.

In short, obscenity, like art itself, is not a matter of referential, but of expressive meaning. What is relevant is not subject, but substance; not an isolable message, but an embodied content. The artist does not bodily translate a subject into the work, but transforms it—he selects from it and gives it form. Thereby the work becomes more than merely an instrument of communication; it commands intrinsic interest because of its own inherent qualities. No subject as such can be obscene (one can always talk about it in Latin!). To be sure, the subject of a work of art contributes to its substance—reference enters into the service of expression—and so has an indirect relevance.[18] But the indirectness is crucial. A sexual subject (or similar reference) is a necessary condition for obscenity but not a sufficient one; only for pornography, as for propaganda, does the referential message suffice.

Thus, though censorship may extend to themes as well as treatments, obscenity does not. The immorality of the actual characters and conduct which provides the novelist with his material is alike irrelevant to the charge of obscenity and to the defense against it. For words are not the things they mean; art is not life. Art supplements life and does not merely duplicate it. The question of obscenity is a question of what the novelist is bringing on the scene, and the first answer to that question must be "a novel"; a sequence of incidents *with form and expression.* The qualities of the work are not determined by the traits of its subject matter. Truth, therefore, in the sense of depicting life as it is, neither produces nor precludes obscenity.

IV

Obscenity, then, is an experienced quality of the work of art and can no more be localized in the subject matter of the work than in its intention or effect. But *what* quality is it? There are, in fact, several species of the obscene, which must be distinguished from one another because they differ so widely in their esthetic status and function.

First, is what I call *conventional obscenity:* the quality of any work which attacks established sexual patterns and practices. In essence, it is the presentation of a sexual heterodoxy, a rejection of accepted standards of sexual behavior. Zola, Ibsen, and Shaw provide familiar examples. The accusations of obscenity directed against them can be seen clearly—in retrospect!—to have been social rather than moral. The guilt with which they were charged was not sin, but a violation of good taste and, even more, of sound judgment. For sexual heterodoxy is frequently generalized, by the writer and his readers alike, to an over-all radicalism. To attack established morality in any respect is to undermine the authority of every established pattern. It surprises no one that the author of *Nana* also wrote *J'Accuse;* of *Ghosts, An Enemy of the*

People; and of *Mrs. Warren's Profession, Saint Joan.* It is a commonplace that mores tend everywhere to be moralized, so that unconventionality of any kind is condemned as immoral, and if sexual, as obscene.

The dual vocabulary for sexual subject-matters, to be found in many cultures besides our own, is a device to preserve the conventions. The four-letter word is a scapegoat which allows the rest of the language to be free of sin.[19] The use of a foreign language (especially Latin) for questionable passages conveys a detached point of view which leaves the conventions undisturbed. More important, the foreignness restricts the work to a well-educated elite, whose conformity is not in doubt or who may, indeed, feel privileged to stand above the mores altogether. Conventional obscenity is not too good for the masses. It is too dangerous for them. If they begin by attacking accepted standards of sexual behavior, so the theory runs, they will end by rejecting all social constraints in an orgy of anarchic egoism.

Accordingly, it is conventional obscenity which is the main concern of the censor—not, say, the pornography of night-club entertainment. From the viewpoint of the censor, the tired businessman may call "time-out," but he mustn't change the rules of the game. It is one thing for him to declare a moratorium on his debt to society, but quite another for him to repudiate his honorable obligations. In short, he may be wicked but not scandalous; and scandal consists in open revolt against sexual constraints rather than covert evasion of them. Pope Paul IV was consistent in expurgating Boccaccio by retaining the episodes but transforming the erring nuns and monks into laymen:[20] thereby scandal was averted.

Now it might appear that conventional obscenity has nothing to do with art as such, but only with propaganda. For a work is usually identified as conventionally obscene on the basis of its message, not its expressive content; and art does not convey messages. As Sidney long ago pointed out in his defense of poesie,[21] the poet does not lie because he asserts nothing. He therefore does not assert that sexual conventions must be changed, but at most presents for imaginative contemplation the workings of our or other conventions. Some artists, however, consciously adopt a propagandistic stance. Yet, conventional obscenity does not depend upon a literalistic approach to art by way of subject, reference, and message rather than substance, expression, and embodied meaning. Both puritan and propagandist overlook the more subtle morality in the content of a work of art, in terms of which conventional obscenity is not limited to a reformist purpose, but plays an important role in all artistic intent.

The artist's integrity requires that he present the world as he sees it; his creativity, that he sees it afresh, in his own terms. The new vision is bound to be different, and as different, as judged to be wicked by the conformist morality of the old. The Hays production code requires that "correct standards of life" be presented, "subject only to the requirements of drama and entertainment"! But if they are subjected also to the requirements of honest and creative art, their "correctness" is likely to be challenged. Again and again in the history of art, the creative artist has had to take his stand against the Academy, as the repository of tradition not merely in art, but in life as well. Clive Bell is scarcely exaggerating when he warns that "of all the enemies of art, culture is perhaps the most dangerous."[22] The academic artist is likely to be free of conventional obscenity, but also to be innocent of esthetic quality. The artist who creates new forms and exploits new techniques—who develops, in a word, a new style—does so because he has something new to say; and in art, whatever is said needs its own language. The very newness is then felt as an attack on established patterns. The hostility to "modern art" evinced by the pillars of church, state, and society is not a product of insensitivity. On the contrary, it displays a realistic awareness of the threat which art has always posed to sheer conformity. The charge of obscenity directed against the arts is strictly comparable to the moral depravity regularly ascribed to heretical religious sects. "Thou shalt have no other Gods before me!" and a new vision of God—so says the priesthood—can only be a visitation of the Devil.

Art, in short, is a matter of inspiration as well as of skill. And inspiration—from the standpoint of the conventional—is a demonic corruption of the old rather than a new revelation of the divine. The "genius" is one who is possessed and hence dangerous. Mann's *Faustus* embodies a recurrent myth of the artist: he has sold his soul to the Devil to enjoy the fruits of the sin of *hubris* committed in imitating the Creator. A vicious circle is thus engendered. The philistine distrust of the artist leads to his rejection by established society, which provokes a counter-attack that in turn is taken to justify the initial reaction. The situation, then, is not that we can generalize from sexual heterodoxy to a wholesale radicalism. It is rather that we can particularize from the artist's rejection of convention—because for him it is stale, flat, and unprofitable—to a sexual heterodoxy, and thus to conventional obscenity. The representation of pubic hair, for instance, is commonly regarded as obscene. But this is largely because it did not appear in the classic nude; and it did not appear there because the prevailing custom was to remove the hair from the body.[23] This is not our custom; but it is the custom in our art, and to depart from it is, therefore, to be obscene.

Now it is easy to exaggerate the danger to established patterns from art. We have already seen that there is no ground for supposing the effect of art on life to be immediate and direct. On the other hand, it is easy to exaggerate also the contribution to society which conventional obscenity makes. Traditional morality may be sound even if conformist, and in many respects surely *is* sound. Society needs stability as well as change; some changes *are* for the worse. Stability cannot be identified with stagnation and death, as Herbert Read has rashly claimed in defense of the artists as *advocati diaboli.*[24] The part of reason, it seems to me, is to reject both the sterile conformism which condemns art for its conventional obscenity and the destructive individualism which takes pride in standing above "the law of the herd."

V

A second type of obscenity I call *Dionysian obscenity.* It consists in what society regards as "excessive" sexualism. Familiar examples are provided by Aristophanes, Boccaccio, Rabelais, and the Elizabethans. As a quality of the work of art, it is an expression of an exuberant delight in life. Dionysian obscenity is present in its clearest form in the old Greek comedy where its connection with fertility rites and phallic ceremonies is obvious. It has played a part in such rites and ceremonies in many cultures.

Its occurrence in art forms is equally widespread. For art rests above all on a delight in color, sound, texture, and shape. The appeal of art is first sensuous; and between the sensous and sensual the difference is only in the suffix not the root. The art object presents for enjoyment an esthetic surface in which formal and expressive values are present, to be sure, but only as fused with an immediate sensory appeal. The work of art may lead us, as Plato and Plotinus hoped,[25] to the world beyond sense; but it can do so only *through* sense. And sense must delight us in the passage. This fact was at the bottom of the iconoclastic controversy and has led some strict puritans to condemn all art as essentially immoral. The premise from which the condemnation springs is a sound one, even if the conclusion is not. We cannot consistently worship beauty and despise the pleasures which the bodily senses can afford. Matthew Arnold was distressed at the "vulgarity" of some of Keats' letters to Fanny Brawne; but more realistic critics have recognized that if he were incapable of such letters, he would not have written *The Eve of St. Agnes.*[26]

Dionysian obscenity in art is of a piece with the enthusiasm which the artist displays over the delightful qualities of his medium.

But the artist is not merely celebrating the joys of esthetic perception. He is also providing a symbolic consummation for the entire range of human desire. It is the artist who can truly say, that, being human, nothing human is alien to him. He is forever drawing the circle which takes in what man and nature reject. He himself is wounded by such rejection, and in comforting himself he pleases everyone. It is scarcely accidental that so much art, in all cultures and in all media, has to do with love. The human interest of love, in all its phases and manifestations, is the inexhaustible riches from which art unceasingly draws beauty. Can anyone doubt that if the human mammal gave birth in litters, painters and sculptors would find in multiple breasts the exquisite forms that the female nude now provides them? Whatever art touches it transfigures. But though the poet makes of love the divine passion, it remains *passion.* And when he presents it for what it is, in its full-bodied vigor, we call him obscene.

Whatever else art may be, it is an intensification of emotion. And when the emotion is a sexual one, the result is Dionysian obscenity. It cannot be pretended that the poetry, paintings, sculpture, and even music of love owe nothing and repay nothing to our sexuality. We may recognize this debt without reducing beauty altogether to an effusion of sex. But art is not confined to the bare surface of human feeling. It enriches experiences only because its roots penetrate to the depths of feeling and so bring our emotional life to flower.

The consummations of art, however, are symbolic. It is for this reason that "excessive" sexuality so often finds a place in art: there is no other place for it to go. The symbol is possible when the reality is not. Dionysian obscenity is a symbolic release of impulses thwarted in fact. It compensates us for the frustrations imposed by rigid conventions. It is not merely a device to elude external repression; it is a mechanism whereby we can admit our feelings to ourselves. Sex becomes permissible when it is esthetically symbolized. We condemn it as obscene only when being brought face to face with our own impulses overwhelms us with anxiety and guilt.

On this basis, Dionysian obscenity not only need not be immoral, but may even serve as a moral agent. By providing a catharsis or sublimation, art may act as a safety-valve without which libidinal pressures become explosive. This is especially suggested by the comic quality so characteristic of Dionysian obscenity. Modern burlesque, from a historical viewpoint is a pathetic attempt to recapture this quality. Comedy releases in laughter tensions which might otherwise prove no laughing matter. The comic spirit detaches us from our impulses and their frustration to allow a satisfaction on another level .

It is for this reason, too, that Dionysian obscenity is so seldom pornographic. Pornography is grim and earnest and feeds only on frustration. In art, sexual energies are not gathered up for a desperate assault on social restraints, but are canalized so as to structure an esthetic experience which is in itself deeply satisfying.

The protest against Dionysian obscenity is essentially a protest against sexuality as such. It is a denunciation of the innate depravity of human nature, which finds satisfaction in "the lure of the senses and the evils of the flesh." The Dionysian, on the other hand, refuses to regard the act of love as inherently sinful. On the contrary, for him it is the supreme manifestation of what is good in life: the indomitable creative impulse. This same impulse finds expression in art. In Dionysian obscenity, art and life join in vigorous, unrestrained laughter.

VI

Completely different in quality is a third kind of obscenity, which I call *the obscenity of the perverse.* Unlike conventional obscenity, it is not an attack on accepted standards, nor is it, like Dionysian obscenity, an affirmation of impulse despite restraints. It is rather a rebellion against convention which at the same time acknowledges the authority of received standards. In the obscenity of the perverse, the artist "accepts the common code only to flout it; conscious of sin, he makes sin attractive; his theme is 'the flowers of evil.' "[27] Baudelaire himself, as he claimed, does make sin hideous. The truly perverse finds sin attractive *because* it is sin (*e.g.*, Huysmans, de Sade). His obscenity lacks the naïveté of the Dionysian; it is likely to be lewd in a sophisticated fashion. The effect is that of calculated indecency.

Dionysian obscenity celebrates sex; conventional obscenity is neutral toward sex, being concerned primarily with the social evils of particular sex patterns; for perverse obscenity, sex is dirty, and it occupies itself with sex for the sake of the dirt. In viewing all obscenity as "smut" and "filth," the puritan only betrays his own perversion. There is here a profound ambivalence, a rebellion which is also a submission. Satan is not a free spirit, but a rebel divided against himself. In freedom, there is a vigor and forthrightness, an enlargement of the soul, which is the antithesis of evil. In perverse obscenity, we have the pathetic spectacle of the Black Mass—worshippers without a God, seeking in hatred and rejection what they are incapable of accepting in love.

At bottom, the obscenity of the perverse is sheer hypocrisy: it is not so black as it paints itself. While pretending to rise above morality, it abjectly submits to it and only thereby becomes truly immoral, in playing false to its own dignity and freedom. While pretending to delight in sex, in fact it abhors sexuality, being convinced of its sinfulness and seeking it out only for the sin. For the perverse, sex is desirable only because it is forbidden; but it remains in the end a bitter fruit. Paradoxically, it is the puritan who creates such obscenity. For its foundation is secrecy and shame. The obscene is what is off the scene, hidden, covered. And shame, as ethnologists have long recognized, is not merely the cause of covering, but the effect.[28] The secret becomes shameful because of its secrecy. To be perverse is to uncover it merely because it is hidden. This is the obscenity of the leer and innuendo. The asterisks and dashes of the supposed puritan serve in fact to convey unambiguously the perverse content.

Basically, what perverse obscenity expresses is fear—fear of the great power of the sexual impulses. It is because of this power that prohibitions and constraints have been imposed upon it in all societies. But just because it is hidden it looms larger and more threatening. What is perverse is not the concern with being overwhelmed by brute desire; it is the part of reason to look to the defenses of rationality. The perversion consists in purchasing freedom from anxiety by assuming a burden of guilt, selling one's soul to the Devil for fear of being rejected by God. Perverse obscenity tries to cope with the forces of sexuality by a symbolic denial of their potency. It plays with fire in a childish effort to convince itself it cannot be burned. But what is most manifest in it is only the futility and the fear. By contrast, Dionysian obscenity triumphs over impulse by freely yielding to it, while conventional obscenity resolutely sets itself to canalize impulse more effectively than custom permits.

There is thus a close connection between the obscenity of the perverse and blasphemy. Historically, indeed, it was only on the basis of this connection that the early strictures against obscenity proceeded.[29] The obscenity of the perverse simultaneously makes too much of sex and too little; just as the blasphemer acknowledges God by denying Him, profanes the holy to damn himself. Diabolism, after all, is just another religion. Perverse obscenity does not wish to profane love in order to remove the taboo from it. Just the contrary: it pretends to ignore the taboo so as to destroy what is, for it, the fearful holiness of love. It is perverse obscenity, not the Dionysian, which is likely to be exploited in pornography; for pornography, as D. H. Lawrence has noted, is "the attempt to insult sex, to do dirt on it."[30] In the obscenity of the perverse, sex is no more than a disgusting necessity; the perversion lies in finding pleasure in the disgust.

Such an attitude is plainly foreign to art and could enter into esthetic experience only to drain it completely of esthetic quality. It is approximated, however, by a type of obscenity which lies between the Dionysian and the perverse—what might be called *romantic obscenity*. This is the category, exemplified in Swinburne and the "fleshly" school, which preserves the sense of sin yet celebrates sexuality in spite of it. It lacks the pagan innocence of the Dionysian but also the lust for evil of the perverse. It is romantic, as expressing a felt need to cover the nakedness of sex with sentiment and estheticism. This need is nowhere more apparent than in the strident insistence on being unashamedly sensual. The art in which romantic obscenity is to be found has something of the pathos of adolescent bravado.

VII

In one of its etymologies, the word "obscene" is given the sense of inauspicious and ill-omened.[31] This is the sense appropriate to the obscenity of the perverse, for its content is hate, not love. It seeks in sexuality only what is life-denying, finding in sinfulness the great Nay which it struggles to express. Its impulse is to destroy itself, though it contents itself with a stylized gesture towards the self-castration which some fathers of the church performed in fact. Obscenity may thus become linked with symbols of violence.

Aggression is as much repressed and controlled by society as are libidinal impulses. Murder is as universally condemned as incest, hostility as rigidly patterned as sexuality. Aggressive impulses, therefore, also seek expression in the symbols of art. Corresponding to the sexuality of Dionysian comedy is the violence of Greek tragedy. The impulses of love and hate may become confused and intertwined and sex patterned into sado-masochistic perversion. In the expression of this content, psychic distance can no longer be maintained, but is submerged in empathic identifications both with brutality and with its victims. A new category of the obscene emerges: the *pornography of violence.*

In this type of obscenity, sexual desires find symbolic release only as transformed into acts of aggression.[32] A phenomenally popular series of novels is constructed according to a rigid pattern of alternation of violence and sex which coincide only at the climax when the virile hero is allowed to shoot the wicked beauty. More sophisticated in style and structure, but essentially the same in substance, is the work of the "realistic" school sometimes associated with the name of Hemingway. Death in the afternoon prepares for love at midnight. There is no question that writing of this genre is effective; the question is only whether the effect is esthetic—an abattoir can also provide a moving experience. Esthetic or not, this genre is enormously successful; taking into account the "detective" story and the crime "comic," the pornography of violence is more widespread in our culture than all the other categories of obscenity put together.

It is, perhaps, banal to associate this fact with the role of violence in our culture, as a source even of recreation for the spectator. Yet, Henry Miller's denunciation must be taken seriously: "Fear, guilt and murder—these constitute the real triumvirate which rules our lives. *What is obscene then?* The whole fabric of life as we know it today."[33] It is easy to dismiss so sweeping a judgment. Yet, it remains true that the pornography of violence enjoys an immunity denied altogether not only to Dionysian obscenity, but even to the fundamentally respectable conventional obscenity. A noteworthy exception is the action of the British Board of Film Censors in prohibiting the showing of Disney's *Snow White* to children, on the ground that it might frighten them, at a time when all the children in London were being taught how to wear gas-masks.[34]

VIII

Moral issues, as such, fall outside the scope of this essay. Yet, esthetics cannot ignore the moral content of art, and the esthetics of obscenity must finally face the question of how obscenity, in its various species, affects that content.

The moral content of art is plainly not a matter of doctrinaire messages but something more fundamental. As I conceive it, it is nothing less than the affirmation of life, a great yea-saying to the human condition. In mastering its medium and imposing form on its materials, art creates a microcosm in which everything is significant and everything is of value, the perfection of what experience in the macrocosm might be made to provide. In this capacity, art may serve as the voice of prophecy and, like all prophets, go unheard or be stoned when its teaching is at variance with a law no longer alive to the demands of life. If, as in literature, human life itself is the subject to be artistically transformed, art insists on seeing it whole, for only thus can it understand and revitalize it; but when art uncovers what men wish to keep hidden, it is despised and condemned. And always, art remains a challenge to evil and death, forcing enduring human value out of the sadly deficient and evanescent material of experience.

In this conception, conventional and Dionysian obscenity, and perhaps also romantic obscenity, all play their part in the performance of the esthetic function; but not pornography, not the obscenity of the perverse, and especially not the pornography of violence. For these are in the service of death, not of life. They belong to that monstrous morality and taste of the burial-ground where death is glorified and the sculpture of Michelangelo is given a fig leaf. The god of such obscenity is not Eros, but Thanatos. Not the wages of sin, but sin itself, is death.

Notes

[1] Theodore Schroeder, *Freedom of the Press and "Obscene" Literature* 42 (1906); and *"Obscene" Literature and Constitutional Law* 13–14 (1911).

[2] Morris L. Ernst and William Seagle, *To the Pure . . . a Study of Obscenity and the Censor* x (1928).

[3] See 2 Vilfredo Pareto, *The Mind and Society* 1010 (Livingston ed. 1935).

[4] See Mortimer J. Adler, *Art and Prudence* 126 (1937).

[5] See John Dewey, *Art as Experience* (1934).

[6] D. H. Lawrence, *Sex Literature and Censorship* 59 (1953).

[7] See Kaplan and Kris, "Esthetic Ambiguity," in Ernest Kris, *Psychoanalytic Explorations in Art* c. 10 (1952).

[8] United States v. One Book Called "Ulysses," 5 F. Supp. 182, 183, (S.D.N.Y. 1933), *aff'd,* 72 F. 2d 705 (2d Cir. 1934) (the court's decision is reprinted as a preface in James Joyce, *Ulysses* (Random House ed. 1934)).

[9] *Id.* at 183.

[10] *Id.* at 184.

[11] United States v. Harmon, 45 Fed. 414, 423 (D. Kan. 1891).

[12] See Benedictus Spinoza, *Ethics, passim.*

[13] See *The Poetics of Aristotle, passim;* Sigmund Freud, *A General Introduction to Psychoanalysis* 327–28 (1938).

[14] George Santayana, *Reason in Art* 171 (1934).

[15] United States v. One Book Called "Ulysses," 2 F. Supp. 182, 184 (S.D.N.Y. 1933), *aff'd,* 72 F. 2d 705 (2d Cir. 1934). See also James T. Farrell, "Testimony on Censorship," in *Reflections at Fifty* 212 (1954).

[16] See Sandor Ferenczi, "On Obscene Words," in *Sex in Psychoanalysis* c. 4 (1950).

[17] Pierre Bayle, *The Dictionary Historical and Critical* 850 (1837).

[18] See Kaplan, "Referential Meaning in the Arts," 12 J. *Aesthetics and Art Criticism* (1954).

[19] See Read, "An Obscenity Symbol," 9 *American Speech* 264, 267 (1934).

[20] See A. L. Haight, *Banned Books* 8 (1935).

[21] Philip Sidney, *The Defence of Poesie.*

[22] Clive Bell, *Art* 267 (1927).

[23] See 4 Havelock Ellis, *Studies in the Psychology of Sex* 94 (1936).

[24] See Marjorie Bowen, *Ethics in Modern Art* ix (1939).

[25] See *The Symposium of Plato, passim;* Plotinus, *On the One and Good, Being the Treatises of the Sixth Ennead, passim.*

[26] *E.g.*, Bell, *op. cit., supra* note 22, at 271–72.

[27] Albert Guérard, *Art for Art's Sake* 189–90 (1936).

[28] See, *e.g.*, Edward Westermarck, *The History of Human Marriage* 211 (3d ed. 1901).

[29] See, *e.g.*, Alpert, *Judicial Censorship of Obscene Literature*, 52 Harv. L. Rev. 40, 43–44 (1938).

[30] D. H. Lawrence, *op. cit. supra* note 6, at 74.

[31] See Havelock Ellis, "The Revaluation of Obscenity," in *More Essays of Love and Virtue* 99 (1931).

[32] See generally Gershon Legman, *Love and Death* (1949); George Orwell, "Raffles and Miss Blandish," in *Critical Essays* 142 (1946).

[33] Miller, *Obscenity and the Law of Reflection*, Tricolor, Feb. 1945, p. 48, reprinted in Henry Miller, *The Air-Conditioned Nightmare* (vol. 2, *Remember to Remember*) 274, 286 (1947).

[34] See H. L. Mencken, *The American Language Supplement One* 644 (1948).

CENSORSHIP
AND CONFLICT

8 Polemic and the Word

Walter J. Ong, S.J.

Ong's essay aptly introduces the final section of this reader. Censorship is most readily identified with conflict. In time of war the American government increases its censorship powers over information to protect our military programs and over free debate of political ideas to diminish the danger of internal dissension.

"Polemic and the Word" is a small selection from Ong's book adaptation, *The Presence of the Word,* of his 1966 Terry Lectures at Yale University. A scholar's scholar, Ong brings his formidable scholarship to bear on the cultural and religious differences between oral-aural man and print-oriented man, a distinction made popular by McLuhan, with whom Ong was associated at St. Louis University in the forties.

The reason for the inclusion of Ong's work in this collection, and at this point in the collection, is that he shows the intimate relationship between the use of language and the need for self-protection and defense against others. He also sees language as a bridge between men for peace. Between these poles, the social control of communication exercises an ambiguous function, at times lessening tensions, at times exacerbating them.

Reprinted by permission of the publishers from Walter J. Ong, *The Presence of the Word* (New Haven: Yale University Press, 1967),

Father Ong is professor of English at St. Louis University. He has

been visiting professor at New York University and is the author of hundreds of articles and several books, among them *The Barbarian Within* and *In the Human Grain.*

Note

The term 'fliting' as used by Ong means: "the concerted exchange of personal abuse, combined often with boast and challenge, which forms a staple of oral performance especially but not exclusively, in the epic from the *Iliad* through *Beowulf* and beyond."—*The Presence of the Word,* p. 207.

Central to the history of the word, both secular and religious, is a vexing group of phenomena and questions involving the relationship of the word and peace. In some of the perspectives earlier suggested here, it would appear that the word is an assault or a threatened assault on another person and, to that extent at least, a warlike manifestation. And in the following pages it will be seen that oral cultures in certain ways do in fact foster a polemic world view. This is all the more puzzling because of the way in which the word is ordered essentially, if somewhat mysteriously, to peace.

The word moves toward peace because the word mediates between person and person. No matter how much it gets caught up in currents of hostility, the word can never be turned into a totally warlike instrument. So long as two persons keep talking, despite themselves they are not totally hostile. This is one of the things that makes hateful talk hurt so much: you are punishing someone with whom you are somehow still at one by reason of the fact that you are maintaining verbal contact with an individual who is obviously to a degree at one with you if he replies. Hostile talk is hate in the midst of love *manqué,* or perhaps of wounded love.

All verbal abuse attests some attraction between interlocutors as well as their hostility. Even in the formalized all-out verbal hostility of standard epic fliting, as a Homer or *Beowulf* or the medieval *Disputisoun between the Body and the Soul* or *The Owl and the Nightingale,* through all their contention the disputants manifest simultaneously some reluctant or wry attraction, even admiration, and thereby attest to a strange pacific undertow in their streams of verbal abuse. In these instances the contestants are distanced from each other not only by contention but also by nature or status or profession or culture, and the irenic pull in speech can be relatively unnoticed. Verbal abuse carried on between those more closely attached to each other produces greater tension still. Hence the nerve-racking effects of the domestic fliting in Edward Albee's *Who's Afraid of Virginia Woolf?* By making the contestants husband and wife, Albee maximizes the attraction of his hostile characters for each other and thereby the love-hostility tension which the fliting itself suggests and which the title of the play, whatever its actual immediate source, clearly sets forth: Virginia (young girl, innocent, lovable, winsome) Woolf (savage beast, malevolent, hateful, repulsive), plus the attraction-repulsion stance of "Who's afraid?"

When hostility becomes total, the most vicious name-calling is inadequate: speech is simply broken off entirely. One assaults another physically or at least "cuts" him by passing him in total silence. Or one goes to court, where, significantly, the parties do not speak directly to each other but only to the judge, whose decision, if accepted as just by both parties, at least in theory and intent brings them to resume normal conversation with each other once more. The use of advocates or lawyers as intermediaries shows further how the courtroom situation registers the breakdown of ordinary verbal exchange. Mediation is here three-deep: between the parties there intervene the accuser's lawyer, the judge, and the defendant's lawyer. In a similar way, the breakdown to total hostility in international relations is commonly signaled by withdrawal of diplomatic representatives. The hostile nations cease talking directly. For a while, they may resort to intermediaries for diplomatic business. Should matters worsen, the next step is physical attack, war. If noncommunication persists without physical attack, we have a "cold war," which is indeed war, for without communication there is no peace.

But granted all this, that speech as such in some way both signals and fosters accord, the fact is that the history of the word, at least in the West, is intimately tied up with the history of certain kinds of polemic. Indeed, the main line in the history of verbal communication can be significantly plotted by studying changes in the uses of hostility. Changes here relate directly to the movement from primitive oral culture to our present communications situation. The changes have simultaneously secular relevance and, especially in the Hebrew-Christian tradition, religious relevance as well. In brief, the movement from oral through typographic culture, as we shall see, corresponds in great part in a shift from a more polemically textured culture to a less polemically textured one, from a culture in which personality structures are expressly organized quite typically for combat, real or imaginary, to one in which hostilities are less publicly exploited and personality structures become expressly organized for greater "objectivity" and, ultimately, for decision making under maximally quantified, neutralized control (decision making based on massive command of data such as computers implement).

The Polemic Texture of Verbomotor Culture

Any student of earlier periods of Western culture from classical antiquity through the Middle Ages and the Renaissance soon becomes aware that he is dealing with cultures in which overt personal hostilities are exhibited and even flaunted far more than in the ordinary technological style of existence. It may sound quaint to say this in a society so unfortunately given to wars as our technological society still is, but, despite the potential for mass destruction in an atomic age, the evidence is overpowering that earlier man commonly accepted hostility as part of the manifest fabric of life to a degree beyond that typical of technological man.

The point here has to do not with hostilities connected with out-and-out wars, or even with cold wars, but rather with the way in which the individual experienced himself in his environment, human and natural. It is not that individuals in technologized cultures necessarily feel fewer hostilities than did earlier man, but only that earlier cultures on the whole (for these cultures differed much among themselves) displayed hostilities more overtly as an expected response to the environment. In *Man and the Sacred,* Roger Caillois contrasts primitive society, where war commonly (though of course not in every instance) constitutes "a permanent state that forms the fabric of basic existence," with modern society, which takes peace to be the permanent or normally expected state, at least psychologically (p. 177). In primitive society even festivals are often defined by their relationship to war. They are allied to war in that both "inaugurate a period of vigorous socialization and share instruments, resources, and powers in common" (p. 166). The festival, however, interrupts the normal flow of hostilities, "temporarily reconciles the worst enemies, causing them to fraternize," but "in the same effervescence" characterizing the state of war, as when the Olympic Games suspended Greek quarrels. In modern society, Caillois goes on to explain, "the opposite occurs," for it is not festivals but wars which stop everything. The football game is not the interruption that the Olympic Games were; it is rather more of the regular cloth of life. Modern man's festivals are less urgent than primitive man's because modern man, even when he wars, does not regard war as being necessarily of the fabric of basic existence.

All primitive societies are not of course equally warlike, but there are or have been enough that are or were of the cast Caillois describes to give his generalization real substance. One thinks not only of the ancient Greeks or Romans but also of the world of the Old Testament Hebrews, where individuals took for granted that their surroundings were swarming with active, enterprising foes. "Behold my enemies are many and hate me violently" (Psalm 24[25]:19) is a constant Old Testament theme, recurring not only in the many Psalms of malediction but elsewhere, too, from Genesis through Maccabees. Play, which in the past, as today, could work off aggressiveness in harmless and even constructive fashion, was more likely to be itself martial play; and grimmer contests, such as dueling, publicly advertised hostilities in the fabric of real life, as of course did also the common custom of bearing arms.

The nonhuman environment, too, was often felt as the object of combat. Disease, which technological man has learned to view and work against objectively, easily became a "foe." A work, for example, such as *Bulleins Bulwarke of Defence against All Sicknes, Sornes, and Woundes* (London, 1562) perpetuates a long-standing outlook, of which technological man is not entirely free when he describes his "battles" against disease. The sea and the mountains and the weather were equally hostile—until the Romantic era, which, as will shortly be seen, marks the end of the old oral polemic culture on other scores, too. The awful brutality of punishment is widely known.

It is a common complaint today that literature is filled with violence, but much earlier literature, as the oral performance which lay behind it, not only was filled with violence but institutionalized it. The great verbal art form coming out of the heroic age, the epic, took the martial as its central theme. It celebrated verbal as well as physical combat. Epic poetry formalizes verbal polemic in fliting, the systematic exchange of savage recriminations between opposed characters.

The reasons for the overt hostilities of early man's life-world were of course complex. One evident reason was the lack of mastery over environment. An economy of scarcity prevailed everywhere, as it still prevails over much of our globe. With a limited supply even of necessities, abundance for one automatically spelled scarcity for others or—what came to the same thing—was thought to do so. Life was physically more of a struggle than it is for those living in a technologized economy of abundance under the auspices of modern medicine. Death struck often far earlier than today and more unexpectedly, unless one concedes that it was actually expected all the time. Infant and child mortality was high, as Philippe Ariès circumstantially reports in *Centuries of Childhood* (pp. 38–41). "All mine die in infancy," wrote Montaigne of his children with a resignation that strikes us as distressingly offhand and impersonal.

The individual in such cultures rightly felt himself physically beset by his environment, and his hostilities were understandably more likely to show. Part of this environment was his fellow men. As we know from urban conditions today, overcrowding and the resulting lack of privacy can develop hostilities to the point of explosion. Earlier societies lacked privacy almost everywhere, as Aries has documented in detail. Even in Europe of the sixteenth century and later, the most privileged classes lived in houses swarming with as many as sixty or eighty occupants, houses where even bedrooms formed regular avenues for traffic from one part of the house to the other, day and night (the curtains on the four-poster beds were not merely for decoration; there were besides the itinerants, often several beds in one room). Lower classes lived in even more exacerbating proximity to their fellows. Privacy is pretty well a modern invention. In earlier tribal societies, the individual found life a texture of inescapable personal contacts, many of which are a torture sure to nourish hostilities.

In such societies, the individual is, it is true, protected and given a sense of identity by the in-group or in-groups with which he is associated. But it is a commonplace that in tribal societies, as for example among early American Indians, in-group identity is achieved all too often by feeding on hostilities toward out-groups. Murder, intolerable within the clan, is negligible or even admirable if the victim is an outsider. Tribal structures generated feuding on a large scale, extramural and intramural, from that in King David's family in the Book of Kings through that in Homer and on down to the Hatfields and the McCoys celebrated in the ballads of the hill country in the eastern and central United States.

Little wonder that social institutions were interpreted in polemic or quasipolemic terms with an insistence that strikes us as bizarre. Renaissance treatises for educating the courtier, for example, such as Castiglione's *Il Cortegiano* or Sir Thomas Elyot's *The Book Named the Governor,* are likely to trace governmental failures deriving as we now know, from complex economic, social, political, and psychological "forces," to enemies among the king's advisors—"bad guys." Book prefaces and dedications, curiously enough, provide an excellent sampling of how man felt his life-world as late as the age immediately following the development of print. Hostility here manifests itself not merely in the excoriation of various persons (often enough including the printer) but also in praising patrons or other dedicatees, for the writer of dedications commonly pictures the dedicatee as surrounded by hosts of enemies from whom the author and his friends gallantly propose to defend him. Of the one hundred and twenty pieces in Clara Gebert's *Anthology of Elizabethan Dedications and Prefaces,* I find only twenty which do not mention or clearly deal with enmity, hostility, protest, or fear, and all but two of these twenty are so fulsome in their praise as to suggest that their dedicatees are actually under threat from others. In *The Professional Writer in Elizabethan England* (p. 44), Edwin Haviland Miller has noted similar quarrelsomeness or sycophancy in writers' relations to readers. This polemic is all highly conventional, to be sure, but one wonders about the texture of the soil on which such conventions could ever have been made to stand in such massive and bizarre array.

The polemic stance which came so naturally to earlier man of course manifests itself in many ways in close association with his use of the word. Education in ancient Greece and Rome was predominantly rhetorical, for combat in the law courts or legislative bodies or elsewhere—even when rhetoric took a purely epideictic turn and became the showy use of words, it never lost its combative cast entirely. The medieval universities erected dialectical jousting into the sole and prescribed way of intellectual life, unable to find a way to truth except by cutting through whole phalanxes of adversaries, real or imaginary.

Explanations of the overt hostilities of earlier cultures based on economic conditions and social structures are certainly valid enough so far as they go, and nothing that we have found here would minimize them. The history of the word, however, suggests that there are still further dimensions to the situation beyond those which the socioeconomic explanations account for. Not merely external conditions but also interior psychological structures (themselves both cause and effect of the external conditions) were at work to produce the polemic bias in early society. Habits of auditory synthesis charged man's life-world with dynamism and threat which visual syntheses would later minimize. The spoken word itself is dynamic in implication, as has been seen, and, moreover, the modes of information storage demanded by oral culture and persisting long after writing and print, as has also been seen, encouraged a world view in which even nonhuman actuality was assimilated to a struggle polarized around good and evil, virtue and vice. In such a view, polemic becomes a major constituent of actuality, an accepted element of existence of a magnitude no longer appealing to modern technological man.

Here lies much of the explanation for an overwhelmingly assertive phenomenon which is massively present, thoroughly researched in some of its details, and yet so little accounted for as a whole: the extraordinary quantity of literature welling out of antiquity through the Middle Ages and well past the Renaissance which is self-consciously and explicitly concerned with praise and blame, virtue and vice. Superficially, preoccupation with virtue and vice can be interpreted as an index of the religiosity of a culture, and it is frequently so interpreted, particularly in studies of the European Middle Ages. But from what we have seen it should be apparent that the tendency to reduce all of human existence, including patently nonmoral areas such as the incidence of disease or of physical cataclysm to strongly outlined virtue-vice or praise-blame categories can be due in great part to the tendency in oral or residually oral cultures to cast up accounts of actuality in terms of contests between individuals. Virtue and vice polarities thus enter deeply into knowledge-storing systems, as Frances A. Yates makes clear in *The Art of Memory* (pp. 84, etc.). This is not to say that virtue and vice are not themselves actualities, for they certainly are. But the reality of virtues and vices does not of itself justify the abandon with which early nontechnological societies have tended to polarize in virtue-vice categories not merely moral matters as such but also a great deal of essentially nonmoral actuality, seeing, for example, the operation of what we know today to be economic or social or political or even purely physical forces as essentially naked struggles between moral good and evil.

We have enough scholarly studies of virtue-vice polarity in early literature to make it evident how widespread and weighty a cultural phenomenon we are dealing with here. Much of the study has been focused on the Middle Ages, where the preoccupation with virtue and vice reaches one of its peaks. Johan Huizinga provides a good deal of material in *The Waning of the Middle Ages* and we have many special studies such as Morton Bloomfield's on *The Seven Deadly Sins*, or other studies on the tradition of the four "cardinal" virtues of prudence, justice, temperance, and fortitude, on the twelve moral virtues (which furnished Spenser with the schema for his epic), on the dance of death, the morality plays exemplified by *Everyman* which erect virtues and vices into dramatic personifications, and the incalculably numerous and massive collections of *exempla*, stories about men or beasts, including bestiaries proper, ranged often under headings of various virtues or vices. These last well illustrate the moral torque given to much nonmoral material. For example, as Florence McCulloch reports in *Medieval Latin and French Bestiaries* (pp. 91–92), in the bestiaries the whale's habit of sounding makes him a symbol of deceit, for he thereby drowns the innocent picnickers or shipwrecked sailors who, with surprising regularity, mistake his back for an island, beach a boat there, and, predictably, light a fire. (To a less moralizing age the ignited whale would appear to be practicing not the vice of deceit but simply the virtue of self-preservation.) This reduction of irrelevant material to virtue-vice polarities is well known in medieval scholarship, although it is not ordinarily viewed in the perspectives suggested here as residual oralism. In *The Enduring Monument*, O. B. Hardison has shown how strongly the virtue-vice preoccupation persisted through the sixteenth and seventeenth centuries. The way in which the commonplace tradition, itself a product and later a persistent relic of oral culture, drifted into almost exclusive concern with virtue and vice has been discussed in chapter 2 above.

The deeper roots of this preoccupation with virtue and vice trace in part to a polemic spirit connected with the oral cultural institutions tied in so intimately with what has long been called the "heroic age." In chapter 2 we drew on Eric Havelock's *Preface to Plato* to show how the processing of knowledge for retention, recall, and use in an oral culture tends to develop characters which are more or less types. Here we can turn again to Havelock's analysis of the oral culture of Homeric Greece to show further how the economy of knowledge demanded by oral society readily generates a quite overtly hostile context for human life.

In an oral culture knowledge cannot be stored in abstract, categorized forms. This is not because oral-aural peoples for some inscrutable or even perverse reasons elect to be "imaginative" or "concrete" or "oriental" rather than abstract or scientific. The large-scale accumulation of exact knowledge which makes possible elaborate and dispassionate causal analyses and sharp abstract categorization depends absolutely on writing. Astronomy, mathematics, physics, grammar, logic, metaphysics, and all other abstract knowledges remain mere potentials of the human mind until some use can be made of script. Without script, knowledge is best stored not in abstract categories but in terms of events, happenings, *res gestae*—things done or goings-on. Such events are preserved in the minds of men not by being classified and listed but by being clustered into the stories told about a relatively small number of heroic figures. This economy of storage determines what sort of knowledge is stored. "The psychology of oral memorization and oral record," writes Havelock (p. 171), "required the content of what is memorized to be a set of doings." An oral culture has great difficulty in formulating abstractions, because they are not the kind of knowledge it can readily recall.

Doings imply actors or agents. In the oral conceptual economy, all phenomena, even nonhuman ones, must in some manner be translated into the doings of such agents or made to cluster around their doings. Otherwise they are lost. Thus Homer's famous catalogue of ships in the second book of the *Iliad*, which interests us today largely as a kind of list conveying demographic information of the sort one finds in a gazetteer, is in Homer made a part of the panoply of epic battle.

In oral cultures virtually all conceptualization, including what will later be reshaped into abstract sciences, is thus kept close to the human life-world. Moreover, since public law and custom are of major importance for social survival but cannot be put on record, they must constantly be talked about or sung about, else they vanish from consciousness. Hence the figures around whom knowledge is made to cluster, those about whom stories are told or sung, must be made into conspicuous personages, foci of common attention, individuals embodying open public concerns, as written laws would later be matters of open public concern. In other words, the figures around whom knowledge is made to cluster must be heroes, culturally "large" or "heavy" figures like Odysseus or Achilles or Oedipus. Such figures are absolutely essential for oral culture in order to anchor the float of detail which literate cultures fix in script. These figures, moreover, cannot be too numerous or attention will be dissipated and focus blurred. The familiar practice sets in of attributing actions which historically were accomplished by various individuals to a limited number of major figures (Rome's complex early history is seen as the biography of Aeneas or as the story of Romulus and Remus); only with writing and print could the number of characters in a modern history book or in fiction such as *Finnegans Wake* be possible at all.

Thus the epic hero, from one point of view, appears as an answer to the problem of knowledge storage and communication in oral-aural cultures (where indeed storage and communication are virtually the same thing). Homer, it will be remembered from what was said in chapter 2 above, was not merely a verbal entertainer, but concurrently a knowledge storer and repeater, the best his oral culture could produce. His heroes were not only entertaining but also highly serviceable. With writing and print, heroic figures decline on both these scores. The decline is observable in literature, but it is equally observable in political life. Bureaucracy is based on written storage of records, as its name hints (*bureau,* desk), and as bureaucracy becomes a more and more effective way to successful government (Machiavelli was a clerk), the heroic figure of the king is no longer needed as a rallying point for political organization. Loyalties can be otherwise mobilized.

When manuscript and print cultures gradually replace the old oral institutions, the hero operates less and less effectively and convincingly as the oral residue in such cultures shrinks more and more. By the beginning of our present electronic age, when the possibility of storing detailed verbalized knowledge becomes virtually infinite, the hero has almost vanished as a major conservator of culture. He is replaced by his opposite, the antihero who, instead of storing knowledge, comes ultimately to reflect wryly on the vast quantities of it which are stored and on the storage media themselves, as do Samuel Beckett's typical technological-age antiheroes Murphy or Malone or, more particularly, Krapp, mulling over the hopeless electronic reproduction of his own earlier voice in *Krapp's Last Tape.*

The older method of knowledge storage, in terms of actions attributed to heroes, establishes a world view in which even the physical forces at work are seen in terms of interactions involving men and/or highly anthropomorphized gods. Such a world view automatically generates a high quotient of hostility. Events are typically seen as resulting not from natural forces but from personal decisions. When something undesirable happens, one surmises that it is the work of an enemy, a malevolent will. Disaster, of which there is always a surfeit, implies the existence of a foe. Habits of auditory synthesis support this polemic outlook by representing the world not as a float of objects strung out before one's eyes but rather as a happening or event, something going on.

Unable to control or even to assemble massive causal detail, oral-aural man thus tends to believe or to make out that matters stand the way they do because some*body* had *done* something, made some sort of decision, perhaps out of caprice, ill will, or perversity. It is often said that proximate physical causes do not interest oral-aural man. This of course is nonsense. Proximate physical causes interest him intensely, but he has limited access to their operations, which he can conceptualize only with difficulty if at all. Human motivation and decision, on the other hand, are familiar to him, and he is prone to design his explanations so that he can ascribe to personal action what otherwise eludes his understanding. Unable, for example, to identify the physical causes for meteorological phenomena, he tends to account for them in terms of motivation and resulting decisions in the lives of living beings, ordinarily the gods: Zeus has a bad day and shows it by making thunder. As convenient sources of explanation, gods are multiplied. Havelock (pp. 169–70) points out how an oral culture thus favors polytheism and animism. A pantheon should not be too large, just as an epic cast of characters must not be so large as to overburden oral storage devices (the inflated pantheons of late Greece and Rome are known to be synthetic developments of fairly literate cultures). But a decently populous pantheon, like a decently full cast of epic characters, provides the set of personal tensions, hostilities, and hence acceptable motivations for what is going on in heaven and on earth. In striking contrast to the plausible motivations of such a pantheon, the will of a single omnipotent God remains essentially inscrutable. Monotheism goes not so much with myth as with science.

Havelock thus indirectly suggests the importance of literacy in the economy of Hebrew revelation. It should be a bit easier for literates to stay on a monotheistic track. Nevertheless, since the ancient Hebrews were so oral and unscientific despite the alphabet, it is strange that they could maintain the monotheistic tradition so effectively as they did. More thoroughly alphabetized cultures like that of the Greeks have normally a far worse record of entrenched polytheism.

9 Anglo-Saxon Law Against Seditious Libel

Edward G. Hudon

The legal history of control of speech and print in early England and America shows the concrete means men devised to meet the needs of social order as they were then perceived. The deeper roots of these measures can be found in the analysis of Ong and the thesis of Innis, which the reader may wish to read again in conjunction with the last article.

Here we see censorship with its gloves removed. Hudon's brief survey also serves as an historical orientation for the legal suppression of our own century that Chafee describes in the subsequent, and final, article of this reader.

Reprinted by permission of the publishers from Edward G. Hudon, *Freedom of Speech and Press in America* (Washington, D.C.: Public Affairs Press, 1963).

Hudon's contribution is taken from the second chapter of his book, *Freedom of Speech and Press in America*. Dr. Hudon has served in the United States Supreme Court Library since 1947 as Assistant Librarian.

Historical Trends

The law of speech and press as it existed in England and America at the time of the American Revolution was the result of a historical development of long duration. From the beginning concern for the security of the state and the preservation of the public peace motivated whatever measures were adopted, whether by legislative enactment or by judicial interpretation, however oppressive the measures happened to be. Any self-expression, even though honest and sincere, which expressed dissatisfaction with the government or with the conduct of its affairs by its officials was considered a threat to law and order and therefore intolerable. Such self-expression was presumed to harbor a malicious intent which did not necessarily mean an evil or spiteful intent, but rather a foreseeable tendency to create public mischief that was translated into constructive or presumptive intent. In his discussion of criminal libel Sir William Russell illustrated the temper of the body of law which ensued: "The ground of the criminal proceedings is the *public mischief*, which libels are calculated to create in alienating the minds of the people from religion and good morals, rendering them hostile to the government and magistry of the country; and, where particular individuals are attacked, in causing such irritation in their minds as may induce them to commit a breach of the public peace."[1]

The era in which this development took place was turbulent. During much of it neither organized police nor standing armies existed and private war was not unknown. To a considerable extent, severity of law and of punishment were relied on for the preservation of the public peace.

Freedom of the Press in England

To trace the history of this body of law in England the starting point is the statute *De Scandalis Magnatum* enacted in 1275[2] which was political in nature and had as its object the preservation of the realm rather than the redress of private wrong. It provided for imprisonment of anyone who should disseminate false news or "tales" from which discord might result between the king and his people. The statute was re-enacted in 1378 to include peers, prelates, justices, and various other officials,[3] and again in 1388 with the provision for the punishment of offenders "by the advice of the said council."[4] The re-enactments of 1554,[5] and 1559,[6] added "seditious words" to the statute. With this new provision, vague or general words that could not support an action at common law could support such an action under the statute if spoken of a "magnate." The truth could not be pleaded as a defense.

The statute *De Scandalis Magnatum* is significant. It was a criminal law which punished political scandal. It was administered by the Court of Star Chamber once its administration by the Common Law Courts was considered ineffectual.

The Court of Star Chamber was originally that part of the King's Council which sat in the "starred chambre" at Westminster to handle administrative and judicial matters, as distinguished from that part of the Council which followed the King, the "Council at Court" that later became the Privy Council. Henry VII included in its jurisdiction wrongs not immediately within the reach of the Common Law Courts.[7] Prior to the time of Elizabeth the Common Law Courts provided practically no remedy for defamation. To a great extent the Star Chamber was responsible for the evolution of censorship and the law of seditious libel. Its intervention was largely due to the invention of printing, and it was to preserve order that it undertook to suppress defamation likely to endanger the safety of the government. Furthermore, it was well suited to cope with the increasing prominence of the press as a means of expressing public opinion which had its start during the reign of Henry VIII. As a royal court that enjoyed the royal prerogative it was unhampered by rules of evidence and it had no regard for form; it heard only its own counsel and it sat whenever it desired.

To supplement the statute *De Scandalis Magnatum* the Star Chamber incorporated into English law the Roman law of *injuria* and *libellus famosus*. The latter treated verbal insults as criminal or quasi criminal,[8] and it provided an additional basis for the jurisdiction exercised by the Star Chamber.

During the reign of Elizabeth the Star Chamber effectively controlled printing and publishing by censorship, a measure that was thought essential for the peace and security of the state. Its ordinance of 1585 required a special license to print a book and it established a monopoly of printing in the Stationers' Company composed of ninety-seven London stationers. This company was empowered to seize all publications by outsiders; offenders were brought before the Star Chamber. In 1637 printing was further regulated by another ordinance which limited the number of printers, presses, and apprentices. This one required a fresh license to reprint a book once examined and licensed, and it regulated the importation of books from abroad.

As the law was administered by the Court of Star Chamber the security of the state was regarded as imperilled by seditious libel against the rulers of the state. Moreover, the maintenance of peace was considered threatened by libels on individuals, especially if they were influential. Furthermore, the Star Chamber sought to put down duelling, generally provoked by libels. Some measure of control was necessary. "*If it be against a private man it deserves a severe punishment*, for although the libel be made against one, yet it incites all those of the same family, kindred, or society to revenge, and so tends *per consequens* to quarrels and breach of the peace, and may be the cause of shedding of blood, and of great inconvenience: *if it be against a magistrate, or other public person, it is a greater offence*; for it concerns not only the breach of the peace, but also the scandal of government; for what greater scandal of government can there be than to have corrupt or wicked magistrates to be appointed and constituted by the King to govern his subjects under him? And greater imputation to the state cannot be, than to suffer such corrupt men to sit in the sacred seat of justice, or to have any meddling in or concerning the administration of justice."[9]

A libel was punishable although it pertained to a dead person. If it was of a dead private individual revenge was still possible by his family and that could cause a breach of the peace; if it was of a dead magistrate or public person it was a scandal on the government which does not die. Furthermore, it did not matter whether the libel was true or false, whether it was of a person of good or of ill repute. A libel might take the form of an epigram or rhyme in writing or sung and repeated in the presence of others; it might also take the form of an ignominious or shameful painting or sign. If it was against a private person a finder might either destroy it or deliver it to a magistrate; but if it was against a magistrate or public person the finder was admonished to deliver it to a magistrate so that its author might be found and punished.

The Star Chamber was so efficient in its prosecution of libels that in one case an author was fined £10,000, given a sentence of life imprisonment, branded on the forehead, his nose slit and his ears cut off. His crime consisted of having expressed a dislike for actors and acting in a book. This was looked upon as directed against the Queen who had recently taken part in a play, and therefore against the government.[10]

Although the Long Parliament abolished the Star Chamber in 1641 it continued the licensing system by its orders of 1642 and 1643. After the Restoration the licensing statute was revived by the Licensing Act of 1662, a temporary statute which was kept in force until 1679. In 1685, during the reign of James II, the act was renewed; it did not finally lapse until years later. But even during the interim from 1679 to 1685 licensing was no less effective. When Chief Justice Scroggs was summoned by the King to render an opinion on what could be done to regulate the press, he announced the opinion of the court that it was criminal to publish any public news without first having obtained a license. Whether the news was true or false, of praise or censure, was immaterial.

While the licensing system was in force, "authors and printers of obnoxious works were hung, quartered, mutilated, exposed in the pillory, flogged, or simply fined and imprisoned, according to the temper of the judges; and the works themselves were burned by the common hangman."[11] With its expiration in 1695, newspapers multiplied and immediately became an instrument for party warfare. As a result strong opposition to the press developed among governing classes. A revival of the licensing act was suggested but rejected. Instead in 1711, during the reign of Queen Anne, a Stamp Act was enacted that levied a duty on all newspapers and advertisements.[12] The objective was to restrain the press and crush small newspapers.

Although it was partially taken care of by the Stamp Act, the vacuum left in 1695 by the expiration of the licensing act was largely filled by the Common Law Courts. Not to be outdone by the Star Chamber, these had already incorporated within their jurisdiction the principles developed by the latter, and as early as 1606 the case *De Libellis Famosis*[13] had established that seditious writing was punishable either by indictment at common law or by the Star Chamber. With the abolition of the Star Chamber in 1641 the Common Law Courts assumed or inherited the position of *custos moram* of the realm and absorbed the entire jurisdiction over defamation. At first, these courts were hampered by the necessity of establishing a malicious intent, a finding of fact by a jury. But seditious libels affected the state and it became accepted that the intentional publication of a document, seditious or defamatory in character, constituted the offense. The jury merely determined the fact of intentional publication, the court decided as a question of law whether or not the publication was seditious or defamatory.[14]

When it is realized that during this era it was treason to so much as imagine the King's death,[15] it can readily be understood why political libels were the order of the day. And these were carried to such limits that in 1684 Sir Samuel Barnardiston was tried, convicted, and fined for expressing political opinions in a private letter written to a friend.[16] He had done no more than repeat the current political rumors, some of which favored the Whigs. One of his remarks was directed at Sir George Jeffreys who presided over the trial and charged the jury.

On another occasion the jury that tried John Tutchin was told in part by the presiding judge: "To say that corrupt officers are appointed to administer affairs, is certainly a reflection on the government. If people should not be called to account for possessing the people with an ill opinion of the government, no government can subsist. For it is very necessary for all governments that the people should have a good opinion of it. And nothing can be worse to any government, than to endeavor to procure animosities, as to the management of it; this has always been looked upon as a crime, and no government can be safe without it be punished."[17] Tutchin had published articles in which he had alleged mismanagement of the navy and corruption in the ministry. The seditious character of the matter printed having been determined as a matter of law, he was found guilty of composing and publishing.

In 1731 Richard Franklin was tried for publishing "A letter from the Hague" in his newspaper, *The Craftsman.*[18] This was an opposition paper and the letter was critical of the government's foreign policy. An offer to prove the truth of the matter published was rejected by Lord Chief Justice Raymond. He said, "It is my opinion, that it is not material whether the facts charged in a libel be true or false, if the prosecution is by indictment or information." The Chief Justice then pointed out the serious nature of libels against private individuals, and the even more serious nature of libels against public officials. These were said "to sow sedition, and disturb the peace of the kingdom." Any who thought this wrong were advised to "apply to the Court, and they will do you justice." The jury was instructed to determine the question of publication and also to determine if the letter referred to the ministers of Great Britain. Whether or not the matter published was a libel was reserved for the court. The usual conviction together with punishment by fine and imprisonment followed.

The law of the press as it existed in England at the end of the eighteenth century was probably best summarized by Blackstone as follows: "The liberty of the press is indeed essential to the nature of a free state; but this consists in laying no *previous* restraints upon publications, and not in freedom from censure for criminal matter when published. Every freeman has an undoubted right to lay what sentiments he pleases before the public; to forbid this, is to destroy the freedom of the press: but if he publishes what is improper, mischievous, or illegal, he must take the consequences of his own temerity."[19]

Although Blackstone's *Commentaries* has been dismissed by an English court as "an elementary text book for students and must be judged as such,"[20] ample judicial support for Blackstone's view is found in Lord Mansfield's instructions to the jury in the case of *H. S. Woodfall:* "As for the liberty of the press, I will tell you what it is; the liberty of the press is, that a man may print what he pleases without a licenser: so long as it remains so, the liberty of the press is not restrained."[21]

In the denial of the motion for a new trial in the *Dean of St. Asaph's Case,* Mansfield again defined liberty of the press. This time as follows: "To be free, is to live under a government by law. The *liberty of the press* consists in printing without any previous license, subject to the consequences of law. The *licentiousness* of the press is *Pandora's* box, the source of every evil."[22]

At common law, unfavorable criticism of the King's conduct, the constitution, the laws, or of men in public office was absolutely forbidden. Such criticism was considered to bring disrepute on the government and to weaken its authority. It was no defense to show that the purpose of the criticism was to bring about orderly reform in government and not to stir up disorder. It was according to this principle of law that John Wilkes, a member of the House of Commons, was convicted. He had published an attack on the King's message to Parliament in his newspaper.[23]

The criminality of an act in an indictment for libel was a question of law for the court and not for the jury to decide. Truth or falsity was immaterial and again not for the jury to decide; the crime consisted merely of publishing a libel. Criminal intent charged to the defendant was merely a matter of form. It was not a part of the definition of libel, it required no proof on the part of the prosecutor, and it admitted no proof in rebuttal on the part of the defendant.[24] This was the unanimous answer of the judges on the occasion of the consideration of the Fox Libel Act[25] when seven questions were submitted to them by the House of Lords to determine the state of the law as to the function of juries in cases of libel.[26] That was the law as it had already been expounded in the *Trial of Woodfall*[27] and the *Dean of St. Asaph.*[28]

Only after the Constitution of the United States and its First Amendment had been adopted did the Fox Libel Act[29] become law in England. Based largely on Erskine's argument for a general verdict in the defense of the Dean of St. Asaph,[30] this act of 1792 enlarged the scope of the jury's function in libel cases and authorized a general verdict of guilty or not guilty upon the whole matter put in issue. The jury could no longer be directed by the presiding judge to find the defendant guilty merely upon proof of publication.[31]

But even after the passage of the Fox Libel Act, trials for political and seditious libel continued. Indeed, they were as common as before, if not more so. In fact, on December 18, 1792, subsequent to the passage of the act, the prosecution of Thomas Paine for publishing *The Rights of Man* took place.[32] As soon as the defense had been presented in the case, Paine was convicted by a jury that expressed the desire to hear neither reply nor summing-up. In effect, the Fox Libel Act substituted the jury for the judge and as late as 1914 Dicey could assert that "Freedom of discussion is then, in England, little else than the right to write or say anything which a jury, consisting of twelve shopkeepers, think it expedient should be said or written."[33]

In 1843, fifty years after the Constitution of the United States had been adopted, freedom of the press became a reality in England. The event which brought this about was the enactment of Lord Campbell's Act, a law which made truth a defense to an indictment for libel.[34] But it was not until 1855 that the Stamp and Advertising Tax was finally rejected.

Freedom of Speech in England

At the time of the adoption of the American Constitution, the only guarantee of freedom of speech that existed in England was that of freedom of speech and debate in Parliament. But even this was established only after a long struggle between the Crown and Parliament which culminated in the Bill of Rights, a condition imposed on William and Mary when they accepted the crown after the banishment of the Stuarts in 1688.

During the Middle Ages the Speaker of the House of Commons claimed freedom of speech alone as Prolocutor of the House. However, as early as 1523 a claim was made by Sir Thomas More, the Speaker, for this freedom for all of the members of Commons. The claim was made again in 1541, and it has since become an established practice but not without a struggle. The need for such freedom is illustrated by the conviction of Haxey, a member of Commons, as a traitor in 1396 because he had submitted a bill to reduce the excessive charges of the Royal household. It is also illustrated by the imprisonment of Richard Strode in 1512, also a member of Commons, because he had proposed a bill for the regulation of tin-mining. Haxey's conviction was later reversed as "against the law and custom which had been before in Parliament."

In her speech at the dissolution of Parliament in 1566, Queen Elizabeth expressed her resentment at the discussion in Parliament and at the petition that had been presented to her on the question of succession. In 1571, in reply to the Speaker's petition for privileges at the opening of the Parliament, the Queen warned Commons "to meddle with no matters of state, but such as should be propounded unto them."[35] At the opening of the Parliament of 1593 the request for liberty of speech met with an even cooler reception. This time the Queen asserted that the "Privilege of speech is granted, but you must know what privilege you have; not to speak every one what he listeth, or what cometh in his brain to utter that; but your privilege is *Aye* or *No*."[36] In 1576 and 1587 Peter Wentworth was bold enough to speak in resistance to the Queen's interference with liberty of speech in Parliament. His efforts in both instances were rewarded with imprisonment.

James I got along no better with his Parliaments than did Elizabeth when the question was freedom of speech. His answer to a petition which expressed hope for a marriage of the Prince of Wales to a Protestant princess, instead of the Infanta of Catholic Spain, was a letter to the Speaker forbidding Commons from meddling with the mysteries of state. They were told not to speak of the proposed match.[37] Although Commons considered this a threat to freedom of speech, an "ancient and undoubted right, and an inheritance received from (their) ancestors,"[38] the King did not see it that way. By way of reply he remarked, "Although we cannot allow of the style, calling it your ancient and undoubted right and inheritance; but would rather have wished, that ye had said, that your privileges were derived from the grace and permission of our ancestors and us; (for most of them grow from precedents, which shews rather a toleration than inheritance) yet we are pleased to give you our royal assurance, that so long as you contain yourself within the limits of your duty, we will be as careful to maintain and preserve your lawful liberties and privileges as ever any of our predecessors were, nay, as to preserve our own royal prerogative. So as your house shall only have need to beware to trench upon the prerogative of the crown; which would enforce us, or any just king, to retrench them of their privileges, that would pare his prerogative and the flowers of the crown: but of this, we hope, there shall never be cause given."[39]

Charles I followed the example of his predecessors. During his second Parliament, he committed to the Tower two of the members for alleged insolent speech. They were not released until the King had been assured that the two had not spoken the words imputed to them. Following the dissolution of his third Parliament (1629), the King proceeded against those who had been active against him. Some were committed to the Tower and others were prosecuted before the King's Bench where judgment was rendered against them. The convicted were fined and ordered imprisoned during the King's pleasure, not to be released until they had given surety of good behavior. One, Sir John Elliot, refused to give surety and he died in prison.[40]

The question was resolved with the banishment of the Stuarts in 1688. William and Mary took the throne, but only after they had agreed to the conditions under which they could reign. They had to subscribe to the Bill of Rights which declared "that the freedom of speech and debate or proceedings in Parliament ought not to be impeached or questioned in any court or place out of Parliament."[41]

Freedom of Press in the American Colonies

In the colonies, as in England, licensing and censorship followed very close the introduction of printing.[42]

The first book to be published in the colonies was one published by Steevan Days in Massachusetts in 1639; in 1656 Samuel Green established a press in Massachusetts, the second in the colonies. The efforts of both were rewarded by the General Court with 300-acre land grants, but this tolerance was short-lived. It seems that religious books which were thought to be dangerous had appeared and in 1662 two licensors were appointed without whose permission nothing could be published. Early in 1663 the General Court repealed the licensing act, only to reimpose a similar one the following year. The act of 1664 followed the pattern set in England: no printing press could be established elsewhere than in Cambridge and nothing could be printed without the permission of the licensors. Violations were punished by forfeiture of equipment and the right to engage in the occupation. In one instance, in 1668, approval already granted by the licensors was revoked by the General Court. The author of the book questioned was thought to be a "popish minister."

From this early beginning, a license continued to be a prerequisite to publication in Massachusetts until 1719, twenty-four years later than in England. As in the mother country after the expiration of the licensing act, freedom of the press meant nothing more in this colony than freedom from prior restraint. In 1768 the Chief Justice of the colony probably best summarized the colonial law of the press in an instruction to a grand jury as follows: "Formerly, no Man could print his Thoughts, ever so modestly and calmly, or with ever so much candour and Ingenuousness, upon any subject whatever, without a License. When this restraint was taken off, then was the true Liberty of the Press. Every Man who prints, prints at his Peril; as every

Man who speaks, speaks at his Peril. It was in this Manner I treated this Subject at the last Term, yet the Liberty of the Press and the Danger of an *Imprimatur* was canted about, as if the Press was going under some new and illegal Restraint. No Gentlemen of the Bar, I am sure, could have so misunderstood me. This Restraint of the Press, in the Prevention of Libels, is the only Thing which will preserve your Liberty. To suffer the licentious Abuse of Government is the most likely Way to destroy its Freedom."[43]

The story was repeated in Pennsylvania. At the solicitation of William Penn, William Bradford brought a press to that colony in 1682. No sooner had the advance sheets to his first publication been seen by the Secretary of the Council than Bradford was in trouble. He was ordered not to print anything without a license from the Council. To add to his troubles, Bradford was ordered by the Society of Friends to submit to censorship by four of its members. Finally, in 1691 he was prosecuted for seditious libel. At his trial he argued that it was for the jury to decide the seditious character of the publication as well as the fact of printing. This argument was rejected then as it was one hundred years later when it was again advanced by Thomas Erskine in England. Bradford was released when the jury disagreed. He then moved his establishment to New York City where his talents were better appreciated. The Council of that city provided an inducement of a yearly salary of £40 and a promise of the public printing.

The southern colonies lagged behind those of the north in the development of printing. However, this did not displease the authorities. Indeed, in 1671 Governor Berkeley expressed his pleasure at this lack of progress in Virginia in the following manner: "But, I thank God, we have no free schools nor printing; and I hope we shall not have these hundred years; for learning has brought disobedience and heresy and sects into the world; and printing has devulged them, and libels against the government. God keep us from both."[44]

Even the laws of the colony could not be printed without a license. John Bucknew was made aware of this in 1682 when he was arrested for printing the laws of Virginia without one. The advice of the King was sought in the matter and his instructions were quite simple: no printing press on any occasion whatever. Thereafter printing was not allowed in Virginia from 1683 to 1729. From 1729 until 1765, one press which was largely controlled by the governor existed in the colony.

The first newspaper to be published in the American colonies did not survive its first issue. Known as "Public Occurrences" from the words that appeared on its first page, it was published in Boston by Richard Pierce in 1690 but it was immediately suppressed because it mentioned the Indian Wars and commented on local affairs.[45]

In Pennsylvania James Franklin was imprisoned in 1722 because of a letter in the form of a satire which appeared in his newspaper, the *New England Courant.* The letter criticized the government of the colony for its lack of promptness in dealing with pirates off the coast. Because of his efforts at public discussion, Franklin was ordered to submit to censorship. When he did not do so and the next issue of the newspaper appeared with another satire on the government, he was ordered to cease publication. But this proved not to be too great an obstacle. Publication was continued in the name of Benjamin Franklin. Even earlier, James Franklin had encountered another type of difficulty when his newspaper had been condemned as an "inspiration of the devil" by the clergy.[46]

The first newspaper to be published in Virginia, the *Virginia Gazette,* appeared in 1736. It expired with its owner in 1750, but in 1751 it was revived and it continued until 1778. The value of this enterprise is reported to have been described by Jefferson as follows: "Till the beginning of our revolutionary disputes we had but one press; and that having the whole business of the government, and no competition for public favor, nothing disagreeable to the governor could find its way into it."[47]

Of all the prosecutions against newspapers and their publishers that took place in colonial America, without a doubt the most celebrated was that of Peter Zenger in New York.[48] This arose from satirical ballads reflecting on the Governor and his Council which Zenger published in his newspaper, *The New York Weekly Journal*. The issues objected to were described "as having in them many things tending to raise factions and tumults among the people of this province, inflaming their minds with contempt for his majesty's government, and greatly disturbing the peace thereof." 17 Howell's State Trials 675,682 (1735). These particular issues were ordered by the Council to be publicly burned by the common hangman, but when this officer refused to carry out the order they were burned by the sheriff's Negro slave. This Grand Jury failed to indict Zenger and the General Assembly refused to take action. Therefore, an information was filed by the Attorney General who acted under the orders of the Governor.

To add to Zenger's dilemma, counsel retained by him were disbarred from practice when they had the temerity to question the right of the Chief Justice of the colony to sit at the trial. However, Andrew Hamilton, a Quaker lawyer from Philadelphia who was Speaker of the Pennsylvania Assembly, appeared unsolicited and defended Zenger. At the trial, Hamilton admitted publication by Zenger, but he offered to prove that the matter published was true. This was rejected as follows: "You cannot be admitted, Mr. Hamilton, to give the truth of a libel in evidence. A libel is not to be justified; for it is nevertheless a libel that it is true."[49]

When Hamilton pressed for a general verdict he was told: "No, Mr. Hamilton; the jury may find that Mr. Zenger printed and published these papers, and leave it to the Court to judge whether they are libellous. You know this is very common: it is in the nature of a Special Verdict where the jury leave the matter of law to the court."[50] Hamilton appealed to the personal knowledge of the jury and won an acquittal. His feat was without fee or reward other than to be awarded the freedom of the City of New York. It was, however, acclaimed as a "generous defense of the rights of mankind, and the liberty of the press."[51] Furthermore, it provided excellent script for present-day radio and television writers.

Notes

[1] Russell, *A Treatise on Crimes and Misdemeanors* (2nd ed., 1826), v. 1, p. 211.

[2] 3 Edward I, c. 34 (1274).

[3] 2 Richard II, stat. 1, c. 5 (1378).

[4] 12 Richard II, c. 11 (1388).

[5] 1 and 2 Philip and Mary, c. 3 (1554).

[6] I Elizabeth, c. 6 (1559).

[7] 3 Henry VII, c. 1 (1478). See Hallam, *Constitutional History of England* (5th ed., 1841), v. 1, pp. 35–40, v. 2, pp. 22–26.

[8] The early Roman law treated verbal insults as criminal or quasi-criminal. A private action was granted in all cases of insult. Redress was by means of a fine proportionate to the insult. By the law of the Twelve Tables the public singing of ribald songs was a breach of the public order and was punished with death as the penalty. See *Sohm's Institutes of Roman Law*, trans. by Ledlie, 3rd ed. (1907), p. 422.

[9] *De Libellis Famosis,* 3 Coke's Reports 254, 255 (Pt. 5, pp. 125a 125b), (1605).

[10] *Trial of Wm. Prynn,* 3 Howell's State Trials 561 (1632).

[11] Taswell-Langmead, *English Constitutional History* (2nd ed., 1880), p. 759.

[12] 10 Anne, c. 19 (1711). In one form or another the stamp tax lasted until 1861.

[13] 3 Coke's Reports 254 (1606); Stephen, *History of Criminal Law in England, op. cit.*, v. 2, pp. 304, 305.

[14] *Trial of John Udall,* 1 Howell's State Trials 1271 (1590); *Bushell's Case,* Vaughan, 135 (1670); *Trial of Richard Francklin,* 17 Howell's State Trials 625 (1731).

[15] 25 Edw. 3 c. 2 (1350); 26 Hen. 8, c. 13 (1534). See also *Trial of Robert Earl of Essex,* 1 Howell's State Trials 1333 (1600).

[16] 9 Howell's State Trials 1334 (1684).

[17] 14 Howell's State Trials 1095, 1127 (1704).

[18] 17 Howell's State Trials 625 (1731). The quotations appear at pages 658, 659. See also, *Trial of Benjamin Harris*, 7 Howell's State Trials 925 (1680); *Trial of Frances Smith*, 7 Howell's State Trials 933 (1680); *Trial of Henry Carr*, 7 Howell's State Trials 1111 (1680); *Trial of William Owen*, 18 Howell's State Trials 1203 (1752); *Case of H. S. Woodfall*, 20 Howell's State Trials 895 (1770).

[19] 4 Blackstone's *Commentaries* 151, 152 (published in 1759).

[20] *Rex v. Joyce*, All England Reports (1945–2), pp. 673, 675. The court quoted from the Earl of Birkenhead's short life of Blackstone in *Fourteen English Judges* (1926), p. 203.

[21] 20 Howell's State Trials 895, 903 (1770).

[22] 21 Howell's State Trials 847, 1040 (1783–84).

[23] *Trial of John Wilkes*, 19 Howell's State Trials 1075 (1770).

[24] *Trial of John Stockdale*, 22 Howell's State Trials 238, 294–304 (1789); *Trial of John Almon*, 20 Howell's State Trials 803 (1770); *Trial of Woodfall*, 20 Howell's State Trials 895 (1770); *Dean of St. Asaph's Case*, 21 Howell's State Trials 847 (1783–84).

[25] 32 George III, c. 60 (1791).

[26] 22 Howell's State Trials 294–304 (1789).

[27] *Rex v. Woodfall*, 20 Howell's State Trials 895 (1770). See also Stephen, v. 2, pp. 324, 325.

[28] *Rex v. Shipley*, 21 Howell's State Trials 847 (1783). See again Stephen, v. 2, p. 330, *et seq.*

[29] 32 George III, c. 60 (1792).

[30] Among other things Erskine had argued that when a plea of not guilty is entered to a bill of indictment or to an information charging a crime, the jury is entitled to enter a general verdict of guilty or not guilty and is not limited to a special verdict on the facts, the commission of which the indictment or information charges the crime to consist. 21 Howell's State Trials 847, 961, 962 (1784).

[31] "the jury sworn to try the issue may give a general verdict of guilty or not guilty upon the whole matter put to issue upon such indictment or information; and shall not be required or directed, by the court or judge before whom such indictment or information shall be tried, to find the defendant or defendants guilty, merely upon the proof of the publication by such defendant or defendants of the paper charged to be a libel, and of the sense ascribed to the same in such indictment or information."

[32] 22 Howell's State Trials 357 (1792).

[33] Dicey, *Introduction to the Study of the Law of the Constitution* (10th ed., 1959), p. 246.

[34] 6 & 7 Vict., c. 96 (1843). "And be it enacted, That on the trial of an

Indictment or Information for a defamatory libel, the Defendant having pleaded such Plea as herein-after mentioned, the Truth of the Matters charged may be inquired into, but shall not amount to a defense, unless it was for the Public Benefit that the said Matters charged shall be punished."

[35] Tanner, *Tudor Constitutional Documents* (1930), p. 563; Taswell-Langmead, *English Constitutional History*, 10th ed. by Plucknett (1960), p. 316.

[36] Hansard, *Parliamentary History of England* (1806–20), v. 1, p. 862; Taswell-Langmead, p. 316.

[37] Hansard, v. 1, pp. 1326, 1327 (1621).

[38] Hansard, v. 1, pp. 1334, 1335 (19 James I, 1621); Taswell-Langmead, pp. 356–357; Hallam, v. 1, pp. 267–270.

[39] Hansard, v. 1, p. 1344 (19 James I, 1621).

[40] May, *The Law, Privileges, Proceedings and Usage of Parliament* (16th ed., 1957), p. 51.

[41] 1 William and Mary, sess. 2, c. 2 (1689). See Taswell-Langmead, pp. 449, 454, for the full text of the Bill of Rights.

[42] Michael, "Freedom of the Press Under Our Constitution," 33 *West Virginia Law Quarterly* 29, 36 (1926–27); Schuyler, *Liberty of the Press in the American Colonies Before the Revolutionary War* (1905), p. 7; Duniway, *The Development of Freedom of the Press in Massachusetts* (1906), p. 16.

[43] Quincy's Massachusetts Reports, 1761–1772, p. 266.

[44] 2 Hennings Statutes at Large [Virginia], 1619–1792 (1819–23) 517; 1 *Virginia Colonial Decisions*, edited by Barton (1909), p. 137. See also Cooley's *Constitutional Limitations* (8th ed., 1927), v. 2, p. 822; Michael, p. 36.

[45] Schuyler, p. 9; Michael, p. 37; Hudson, *Journalism in the United States from 1690 to 1872* (1873), pp. 44–49.

[46] Hudson, p. 67.

[47] 1 *Virginia Colonial Decisions* 145, 146 (Quoting from Thomas' *History of Printing*, p. 321).

[48] 17 Howell's State Trials 675 (1735).

[49] 17 Howell's State Trials 675, 699.

[50] *Ibid.*, p. 706.

[51] *Ibid.*, pp. 724, 725.

10 The Espionage Act And The Abrams Case

Zechariah Chafee, Jr.

While this reader was being prepared, the conviction of Dr. Spock and Yale Chaplain William Sloane Coffin was being appealed to the Supreme Court by Arthur Goldberg and other lawyers. Spock, Coffin, and three others had been indicted for criminal conspiracy to obstruct the administration of the 1967 Selective Service Act. Their offenses were the public words they spoke and the rallies they attended, and petitions they signed critical of the draft being used to support the war in Vietnam.

Chafee chronicles another war and another case. The selection you are about to read is taken from Chafee's authoritative and classic *Free Speech in the United States*, an abundantly documented study of constitutional law and legal protection for free expression of ideas in a democracy. At a time when free speech is both outrageously abused and severely, if selectively, repressed, it is up to the reader to draw whatever parallels he can from this case of the First World War to our own troubled times of demonstrations, racist conflicts, police power, black power, and student power—to say nothing of the overwhelming Pentagon power.

Holder of the Langdell Professor of Law Chair at Harvard University, CHAFEE has been widely praised for his *Government and Mass Communications*.

First of all, . . . it must be a peace without victory. . . . Victory would mean peace forced upon the loser, a victor's terms imposed upon the vanquished. It would be accepted in humiliation, under duress, at an intolerable sacrifice, and would leave a sting, a resentment, a bitter memory upon which terms of peace would rest, not permanently, but only as upon quicksand. Only a peace between equals can last. Only a peace the very principle of which is equality and a common participation in a common benefit. The right state of mind, the right feeling between nations, is as necessary for a lasting peace as is the just settlement of vexed questions of territory or of racial and national allegiance.

WOODROW WILSON,
Address to the Senate, January 22, 1917.

On April 6, 1917, Congress declared war against Germany. On May 18 it enacted the Selective Service Act for raising a National Army. The people, by an overwhelming majority, believed conscription to be a necessary and just method of waging an unavoidable war, and the machinery for enforcing the draft by civilian aid was admirably planned. "The result," says Attorney General Gregory,[1] "was that the ultimate opposition to the draft by those liable was surprisingly small, considering the persistent propaganda carried on against the policy of the law and against its constitutionality." And his Assistant, Mr. John Lord O'Brian, adds, "No anti-draft propaganda had the slightest chance of success." The decision of the Supreme Court sustaining the validity of the statute[2] merely fulfilled the general expectation.

Besides the military and civilian organization for reaching the men who were liable to registration and subsequently called into service, the government had at its disposal several criminal statutes enacted during the Civil War. These it could and did use to punish conspiracies by Emma Goldman and others aiming to resist recruiting and conscription by riots and other forcible means, or seeking by speeches and publications to induce men to evade the draft.[3] In some respects, however, these statutes were felt by the Department of Justice to be incomplete. (1) It was not a crime to persuade a man not to enlist voluntarily. (2) Inasmuch as one man cannot make a conspiracy all by himself, a deliberate attempt by an isolated individual to obstruct the draft, if unsuccessful, was beyond the reach of the law, except when his conduct was sufficiently serious to amount to treason. The treason statute, the only law on the books affecting the conduct of the individual, was of little service,[4] since there was considerable doubt whether it applied to utterance. Therefore, although it is probable that under the circumstances the existing conspiracy statutes would have taken care of any serious danger to the prosecution of the war, new legislation was demanded.

If the government had been content to limit itself to meeting the tangible needs just mentioned, the effect on discussion of the war would probably have been very slight, for treason, conspiracies, and actual attempts constitute a direct and dangerous interference with the war, outside the protection of freedom of speech as defined in the preceding chapter. Two additional factors, however, influenced the terms of the new statutes, and even more the spirit in which they were enforced. First came the recollection of the opposition during the Civil War, which was handled under martial law in so far as it was suppressed at all. Some persons, full of old tales of Copperheads were eager to treat all opponents of this war as spies and traitors. A bill was actually introduced into the Senate which made the whole United States "a part of the zone of operations conducted by the enemy," and declared that any person who published anything endangering the successful operation of our forces could be tried as a spy by a military tribunal and put to death. President Wilson wished to head off such legislation as unwise and unconstitutional.[5] A turmoil would arise if army officers could thus dispose of the liberties and lives of civilians. Any control of the government over civilians outside actual war areas ought to be exercised through judges and juries.

And yet the legal advisers of the administration felt that the conspiracy statutes were not enough to enable the ordinary courts to handle on a large scale dangerous activities short of treason. So it would be easier to resist pressure to take matters away from judges and juries, if a new criminal statute gave judges and juries wider and stiffer powers. The second factor was the fear of German propaganda, and the knowledge of legislation and administrative regulations guarding against it in Great Britain and Canada.[6] Although we did not adopt the British administrative control, which combined flexibility with possibilities of despotism, it was easy to forget our own policy of non-interference with minorities and put the United States also in a position to deal severely with written and spoken opposition to the war.

I. *The Espionage Acts of 1917 and 1918*

I approve of this legislation but . . . I shall not expect or permit any part of this law to apply to me or any of my official acts, or in any way to be used as a shield against criticism.

WOODROW WILSON, letter of April 25, 1917.

The result of these various influences was the third section of Title I of the Espionage Act. As originally enacted on June 15, 1917 (and still in force in 1940), this section established three new offenses:

(1) Whoever, when the United States is at war, shall willfully make or convey false reports or false statements with intent to interfere with the operation or success of the military or naval forces of the United States, or to promote the success of its enemies (2) and whoever, when the United States is at war, shall willfully cause or attempt to cause insubordination, disloyalty, mutiny, or refusal of duty, in the military or naval forces of the United States, (3) or shall willfully obstruct the recruiting or enlistment service of the United States, to the injury of the service or of the United States, shall be

punished by a fine of not more than $10,000 or imprisonment for not more than twenty years, or both.[7]

Although most of the Espionage Act deals with entirely different subjects like actual espionage, the protection of military secrets, and the enforcement of neutrality in future conflicts between other nations, the section just quoted is buttressed by several provisions. Section 4 of the same Title (50 U. S. C. A. § 34) punishes persons conspiring to violate section 3, if any one of them does any act to effect the object of the conspiracy. Title XI (18 U. S. C. A. §§ 611–633) authorizes the issue of search warrants for the seizure of property used as the means of committing a felony, which would include violations of the section just quoted. It was under this provision that the moving-picture film was confiscated in the *Spirit of '76* case,[8] and raids were made on the offices of anti-war organizations. Finally, Title XII (18 U. S. C. A. §§ 343,344) makes non-mailable any matter violating the Act, or advocating treason, insurrection, or forcible resistance to any law of the United States, directs that it shall not be conveyed or delivered, and imposes heavy penalties for attempting to use the mails for its transmission.

Eleven months later the Episonage Act was greatly expanded by a second statute. Attorney General Gregory thought the original 1917 Act did not go far enough in some respects. He stated that although it had proved an effective instrumentality against deliberate or organized disloyal propaganda, it did not reach the individual casual or impulsive disloyal utterances. Also some District Courts gave what he considered a narrow construction of the word "obstruct" in clause 3, so that, as he described it, "most of the teeth which we tried to put in were taken out."[9]

These individual disloyal utterances, however, occurring with considerable frequency throughout the country, naturally irritated and angered the communities in which they occurred, resulting sometimes in unfortunate violence and lawlessness and everywhere in dissatisfaction with the inadequacy of the Federal law to reach such cases. Consequently there was a popular demand for such an amendment as would cover these cases.[10]

The history of subsequent events shows what is likely to happen in times of panic, when sedate lawyers ask for "just a wee drappie mair of suppression, and where's the harm in that." The Attorney General requested only a brief amendment of the Espionage Act by the addition of attempts to obstruct the recruiting service, and the punishment of efforts intentionally made to discredit and interfere with the flotation of war loans. The Senate Committee on the Judiciary, being thus stirred up, took the bit in its teeth, and decided to stamp on all utterances of a disloyal character. It went for a model of legislation affecting freedom of discussion to a recent sweeping sedition statute of the state of Montana, and inserted most of its clauses into the new federal law.

This amendment of May 16, 1918 (repealed in 1921),[11] which is sometimes called the Sedition Act, inserted "attempts to obstruct" in the third of the original offenses, and added nine more offenses, as follows: (4) saying or doing anything with intent to obstruct the sale of United States bonds, except by way of bona fide and not disloyal advice; (5) uttering, printing, writing, or publishing any disloyal, profane, scurrilous, or abusive language, or language intended to cause contempt, scorn, contumely or disrepute as regards the form of government of the United States; (6) or the Constitution; (7) or the flag; (8) or the uniform of the Army or Navy; (9) or any language intended to incite resistance to the United States or promote the cause of its enemies; (10) urging any curtailment of production of any things necessary to the prosecution of the war with intent to hinder its prosecution; (11) advocating, teaching, defending, or suggesting the doing of any of these acts; and (12) words or acts supporting or favoring the cause of any country at war with us, or opposing the cause of the United States therein. Whoever committed any one of these offenses during the war was liable to the maximum penalty of the original Act, $10,000 fine or twenty years' imprisonment, or both.

The 1918 amendment was fortunately repealed on March 3, 1921.

The Abrams Case

The expedition [to North Russia] was nonsense from the beginning.
SECRETARY OF WAR NEWTON D. BAKER.[1]
I was in command of the United States troops sent to Siberia and, I must admit, I do not know what the United States was trying to accomplish by military intervention.
GENERAL WILLIAM S. GRAVES.[2]

Unlike the other Supreme Court decisions, which arose under the original Espionage Act of 1917, the Abrams case involved the more sweeping provisions of the 1918 amendment.[3] The defendants were not prosecuted for pacifist or pro-German utterances, as in the general run of Espionage Act cases, but for agitation against the government's policy in despatching American troops to Vladivostok and Murmansk in the summer of 1918. The case deserves extensive presentation because it brings out the serious difficulties of trying political offenses satisfactorily in our courts.

In the early morning of August 23, 1918, loiterers at the corner of Houston and Crosby streets in New York were surprised to see the air full of leaflets thrown from a window of a manufacturing building close by. One set of leaflets was in English, as follows:[4]

THE
HYPOCRISY
OF THE
UNITED STATES
AND HER ALLIES

"Our" President Wilson, with his beautiful phraseology, has hypnotized the people of America to such an extent that they do not see his hypocrisy.

Know, you people of America, that a frank enemy is always preferable to a concealed friend. When we say the people of America, we do not mean the few Kaisers of America, we mean the "People of America." You people of America were deceived by the wonderful speeches of the masked President Wilson. His shameful, cowardly silence about the intervention in Russia reveals the hypocrisy of the plutocratic gang in Washington and vicinity.

The President was afraid to announce to the American people the intervention in Russia. He is too much of a coward to come out openly and say: "We capitalistic nations cannot afford to have a proletarian republic in Russia." Instead, he uttered beautiful phrases about Russia, which, as you see, he did not mean, and secretly, cowardly, sent troops to crush the Russian Revolution. Do you see how German militarism combined with allied capitalism to crush the Russian Revolution?

This is not new. The tyrants of the world fight each other until they see a common enemy—WORKING CLASS—ENLIGHTMENT as soon as they find a common enemy, they combine to crush it.

In 1815 monarchic nations combined under the name of the "Holy Alliance" to crush the French Revolution. Now militarism and capitalism combined, though not openly, to crush the Russian Revolution.

What have you to say about it?

Will you allow the Russian Revolution to be crushed? You: Yes, we mean YOU the people of America!

THE RUSSIAN REVOLUTION CALLS TO THE WORKERS OF THE WORLD FOR HELP.

The Russian Revolution cries: "WORKERS OF THE WORLD! AWAKE! RISE! PUT DOWN YOUR ENEMY AND MINE!"

Yes friends, there is only one enemy of the workers of the world and that is CAPITALISM.

It is a crime, that workers of America, workers of Germany, workers of Japan, etc., to fight the WORKERS' REPUBLIC OF RUSSIA.

AWAKE! AWAKE, YOU
WORKERS OF THE WORLD!
REVOLUTIONISTS

P.S. It is absurd to call us pro-German. We hate and despise German militarism more than do your hypocritical tyrants. We have more reasons for denouncing German militarism than has the coward of the White House.

The other leaflet was in Yiddish, and was thus translated:

WORKERS—WAKE UP

The preparatory work for Russia's emancipation is brought to an end by his Majesty, Mr. Wilson, and the rest of the gang; dogs of all colors!

America, together with the Allies, will march to Russia, not, "God Forbid," to interfere with the Russian affairs, but to help the Czecho-Slovaks in their struggle against the Bolsheviki.

Oh, ugly hypocrites; this time they shall not succeed in fooling the Russian emigrants and the friends of Russia in America. Too visible is their audacious move.

Workers, Russian emigrants, you who had the least belief in the honesty of our government must now throw away all confidence, must spit in the face the false, hypocritic, military propaganda which has fooled you so relentlessly, calling forth your sympathy, your help, to the prosecution of the war. With the money which you have loaned or are going to loan them, they will make bullets not only for the Germans but also for the Workers Soviets of Russia. Workers in the ammunition factories, you are producing bullets, bayonets, cannon, to murder not only the Germans, but also your dearest, best, who are in Russia and are fighting for freedom.

You who emigrated from Russia, you who are friends of Russia, will you carry on your conscience in cold blood the shame spot as a helper to choke the Workers Soviets. Will you give your consent to the inquisitionary expedition to Russia? Will you be calm spectators to the fleecing blood from the hearts of the best sons of Russia?

America and her Allies have betrayed (the workers). Their robberish aims are clear to all men. The destruction of the Russian Revolution, that is the politics of the march to Russia.

Workers, our reply to the barbaric intervention has to be a general strike! An open challenge only will let the government know that not only the Russian Worker fights for freedom, but also here in America lives the spirit of revolution.

Do not let the government scare you with their wild punishment in prisons, hanging and shooting. We must not and will not betray the splendid fighters of Russia. Workers, up to fight.

Three hundred years had the Romanoff dynasty taught us how to fight. Let all rulers remember this, from the smallest to the biggest despot, that the hand of the revolution will not shiver in a fight.

Woe unto those who will be in the way of progress. Let solidarity live!

THE REBELS.

The Military Intelligence Police sent two army sergeants, who climbed from floor to floor of the building asking questions until at a hat factory on the fourth story they arrested Rosansky, a young Russian, who eventually confessed that he had thrown out the leaflets. The Military Police with his aid captured six other Russians, five men and a girl. The oldest man, Abrams, was twenty-nine; the youngest, Lipman, twenty-one, the same age as the girl, Molly Steimer. The group lived in a bare apartment three flights up a rear staircase on East 104th Street. A police instructor examined the prisoners in the presence of several army sergeants. They refused to tell where the pamphlets were printed, but the Military Police discovered that they had a motor-driven press and a small hand press in the basement of 1582 Madison Avenue, where misprinted pamphlets and corrected proof lay crumpled upon the floor.

The prisoners, one of whom died before trial, were indicted for conspiracy to violate four clauses of the Espionage Act of 1918.[5] The Department of Justice had prevented several other prosecutions of so-called Bolshevists for opposition to the government's Russian policy, inasmuch as no war had been declared against Russia. However, the appeal of the Abrams group to munitions workers for a general strike was regarded as more serious.

1. *The District Court*

SCOTCH POLITICAL PRISONER: All great men have been reformers, even our Savior himself.

LORD BRAXFIELD: Muckle he made o'that, he was hanget.

The trial of Abrams and his associates, except Schwartz, began on October 10, 1918, in the United States Court House in New York City, before Judge Clayton of the Northern and Middle Districts of Alabama. Henry De Lamar Clayton was then sixty-one years of age. Belonging to a distinguished Alabama family, he had graduated from the State University and practised law in Montgomery. For eighteen years he represented Alabama in Congress, serving eventually as Chairman of the Judiciary Committee of the House and giving his name to the well-known Clayton Act. In 1914 he was appointed to the United States bench. This was his first prominent Espionage Act case.

There were in the Southern District of New York three judges with extensive experience in the difficulties of war legislation—Mayer, and Learned and Augustus Hand.[6] In the Abrams trial, six persons risked the best part of their lives upon the decision of the perplexing problems of freedom of speech. The position of the defendants could hardly be understood without some acquaintance with the immigrant population of a great city, some knowledge of the ardent thirst of the East Side Jew for the discussion of international affairs. Yet because the New York dockets were crowded the Abrams case was assigned to a judge who had tried no important Espionage Act case, who was called in from a remote district where people were of one mind about the war, where the working class is more conspicuous for a submissive respect for law and order than for the criticism of higher officials, where Russians are scarce and Bolshevists unknown.

The government was represented by Francis G. Caffey, United States Attorney, with John M. Ryan and S. L. Miller, Assistant United States Attorneys, of counsel. Harry Weinberger of New York appeared for the defendants. The jury was duly empaneled and sworn on Monday, October 14, and the trial ended on Wednesday, October 23.

The overt acts were proved without contradiction. Soon after United States troops were ordered to Vladivostock in the first week of August, 1918, the group had begun meeting in their bare "third-floor back," and decided to protest against the attack on the Russian Revolution, with which as anarchists or socialists they strongly sympathized. After printing five thousand copies of each leaflet they stopped for lack of funds. They had distributed about nine thousand leaflets, throwing them in the streets where there were the most working people or passing them around at radical meetings. There was no evidence that one person was led to stop any kind of war work or even that the leaflets reached a single munitions worker.

The defense, besides contending that the Espionage Act was unconstitutional, maintained that it was not violated, and in particular that the criminal intent required by express terms of the statute of 1918 did not exist. Each count of the indictment covered a conspiracy to violate one clause of the Act as italicized below, as follows, according to the language of the statute. Certain phrases in the indictment which are not in the Act are enclosed in brackets.

Whoever, when the United States is at war, . . . shall willfully utter, print write, or publish

(Count 1) any disloyal, . . . scurrilous, or abusive language about the form of government of the United States, . . .

(Count 2) or any language intended to bring the form of government of the United States . . . into contempt, scorn, contumely, or disrepute, . . .

(Count 3) or . . . any language *intended to incite, provoke, or encourage resistance to the United States* [*in said war with the German Imperial Government*], ...

(Count 4) or shall willfully by utterance, writing, printing, publication, . . . urge, incite, or advocate any curtailment of production in this country of any thing or things, product or products, [to wit, ordnance and ammunition necessary or essential to the prosecution of the war in which the United States may be engaged [to wit, *said war with the Imperial German Government*], *with intent* by such curtailment *to cripple or hinder the United States in the prosecution of the war*, . . . shall be punished by a fine of not more than $10,000 or imprisonment for not more than twenty years or both.

The first[7] and second counts may be dismissed from further discussion. The Supreme Court refused to pass on their constitutionality; but this did not benefit the prisoners, because twenty-year sentences could be sustained if they were properly convicted under either the third or fourth count.[8] Justice Clarke contented himself with suggesting that the distinction between abusing our form of government and abusing the President and Congress, the agencies through which it must function in time of war, might be only "technical." If so, these sections of the Espionage Act must have been more frequently violated in Wall Street than in Harlem.

Since most of the controversy about this case revolves around the fourth count of the indictment, we can confine ourselves to that. Aside from questions of constitutionality, the government had to establish the specific criminal intent required by the indictment and the Espionage Act. (1) It had to prove intention to publish the pamphlets. This the government undoubtedly did. (2) Under the fourth count it had to prove intention to produce curtailment of munitions because the words "urge, incite, advocate" create an offense analogous to criminal solicitation, which involves a specific intent to bring about the overt act. There are a few sentences in the Yiddish leaflet which show such an intention, although it is open to question whether an incidental portion of a general protest which is not shown to have come dangerously near success really constitutes criminal solicitation or amounts to advocating. (3) Anyhow, the main task of the government was to establish an additional *intention to interfere with the war with Germany*. The question whether it proved anything more than an intention to obstruct operations in Russia is the vital issue of fact in the case.

Since we had not declared war upon Russia, protests against our action there could not be criminal unless they were also in opposition to the war with Germany. There are two conceivable theories of guilt, which might connect the leaflets with the war. The first theory is that the despatch of troops to Siberia was "a strategic operation against the Germans on the eastern battle front," so that any interference with that expedition hindered the whole war. The second theory is that the circulars intended to cause armed revolts and strikes and thus diminish the supply of troops and munitions available against Germany on the regular battle front.

Clearly the second theory is the only legitimate basis for conviction. The alternative argument, that opposition to the armed occupation of neutral territory and assertions of its illegality, are *per se* criminal, is clearly a travesty on the defense of Belgium and a violation of the right of freedom of speech. Hence this first theory has been rejected by the majority Supreme Court opinion in the Abrams case, by the government's brief, and by writers[9] who support the decision. They have adopted the second theory of guilt and have taken it for granted that the jury followed the same course. If so, the convictions represent a finding of fact by the jury that the defendants intended to interfere with operations against Germany itself. Nevertheless, the record of the trial makes it highly probable that these defendants were convicted on just the other theory—for trying to hinder the Russian expedition.

As a state trial, this case cannot be understood without reference to the atmosphere in which the defendants wrote the circulars and the jury reached their verdict. I have no desire to venture into the Serbonian bog of the Russian Revolution, but a few undisputed facts must be recalled.[10] On January 8, 1918, two months after the establishment of the Soviet Government, President Wilson declared as the sixth of his Fourteen Points that Russia must have "an unhampered and unembarrassed opportunity for the independent determination of her own political development," and that the treatment accorded her by her sister nations during the months to come would be "the acid test of their good-will." On March 11 he telegraphed the Pan-Soviet Congress, promising that Russia would be secured "complete sovereignty and independence in her own affairs." Four months later a small body of American marines joined in the occupation of Murmansk, and shortly afterwards American troops were sent to Vladivostok. On August 3, an official statement from Washington announced that military intervention in Russia would only add to the confusion there and dissipate our forces on the western front. Consequently, we would not interfere with the political sovereignty of Russia or intervene in her local affairs, but would merely send a few thousand men to Vladivostok in cooperation with Japan and other Allies, who would be asked to give similar assurance.

A few days later Abrams and his friends wrote and printed the leaflet headed, "The Hypocrisy of the United States and her Allies."

The Soviet government failed to distinguish between military intervention and the arrival of foreign troops on Russian soil. The diplomatic breach was complete. Soon afterwards the newspapers were filled with accounts of Bolshevist atrocities. In September the United States recognized the Czechoslovaks as a belligerent government warring against Germany and Austria, with their capital in Washington and their chief army in Siberia, so that the seacoast of Bohemia was evidently the Pacific Ocean. On September 15 the United States Committee on Public Information published nation-wide in the press the documents[11] collected by its representative, Mr. Edgar Sisson, which were stated to show that the present heads of the Bolshevist government were merely hired German agents. No one who recalls the widespread popular identification of the Soviet government with Germany in the summer and early autumn of 1918 can doubt that an October jury would inevitably regard pro-Bolshevist activities as pro-German, and consequently apply the first or Russian theory of guilt, besides having a prejudice against the defendants as sympathizers with the Russian Revolution. This prejudice could only be overcome by an exposition of the Russian situation from sources which had as yet found no expression in the newspapers.

Early on Friday, October 18, the fifth day of the actual trial, the government rested. Mr. Weinberger opened the case to the jury on behalf of the defendants, and called to the witness stand Colonel Raymond Robins, who had recently spent six months in Russia with the Red Cross and knew the Bolshevist leaders intimately. After a dozen introductory questions, the United States attorney objected to further examination and the witness thereafter was obliged to remain silent while the defendants' counsel ran through a series of thirty unanswered questions in order to get them on the record. This was repeated with Albert Rhys Williams who had also been in Russia in 1917–1918 and acted for the Soviets in foreign affairs. It was not considered worth while to call Edgar Sisson at all. The admissibility of the evidence of these three witnesses raises problems that go to the heart of the case.

The first theory of guilt raised the complex question whether the Russian expedition was a part of the war. If this was a political question which must be answered in the affirmative on the mere *ipse dixit* of the government, the existence of a war enables the government to withdraw the most remote and questionable policies from the scope of ordinary discussion simply by labeling them a war matter. The annexation of Mexico to prevent its becoming a base for German operations, the use of American troops to put down strikes in England or Sinn Fein in Ireland, were no more remotely connected with the war with Germany than the Russian affair. On the other hand, if the relation of such an expedition to the war was put in issue to be decided by the jury, the defense ought to have been allowed to call witnesses to disprove it. On this account, in the Abrams case, Raymond Robins and other eyewitnesses of Russian affairs were summoned to prove that the Bolshevist and Czechoslovak situation was such that our intervention was not anti-German; but this testimony and all questions of the constitutionality of intervention were excluded by Judge Clayton with the remark, "The flowers that bloom in the spring, tra la, have nothing to do with the case."

This phase of the trial is very important for its demonstration of the enormous difficulties of proof into which we have brought ourselves in the United States by creating political crimes. Before the Espionage Act our criminal law punished men almost entirely for acts which take place in the tangible world and are proved by the evidence of our five senses. This Act punishes men for fords which cause no injury, but have a supposedly bad tendency to harm the state, and also for intentions which are regarded as evil. Now, bad tendency and bad intention cannot be seen or heard or touched or tasted or smelled. They are, as we have seen, a matter of inference from the complex and obscure background of general conditions. Consequently, that background becomes, whether we admit witnesses or not, an issue in the case. The rules of evidence for the trial of overt criminal acts prove almost useless. Common sense makes it plain that a knowledge of Russian affairs was essential to a jury with the attitude of that moment, obliged to interpret the repeated references to Russia in the circulars, and as we shall see, told often by the judge that the defendants were guilty if their pamphlets were issued for the purpose of preventing the government from carrying on its operations in Russia.

All prosecutions for words will involve us in the same awkward dilemma that was suggested in connection with the "false statements" clause in the Pierce case.[12] If we follow the logical course just indicated and allow the alleged promoter of sedition to bring in a mass of evidence from Russia or other dark and distant regions to show that neither he nor his utterances are liable to cause even remote injury to the national welfare, the prosecution is justly entitled to call other witnesses to establish the evil character of the agitation. Every sedition trial will be a rag-bag proceeding like the 1919 hearings about Bolshevism before the Overman Committee of the Senate.[13] As Judge Clayton pointed out in the Abrams trial, the admission of Raymond Robins' testimony would open up a Pandora's box. The district attorney would offer on his side to prove that Trotsky had been bought by the German Government.

> To use a vulgar expression, it would be "swiping" them on the other hand, and we would forget all about the issues in this case, and we would find ourselves trying Lenine and Trotsky, which is something I do not intend to do. I have enough trouble trying these people here in the United States, and God knows I am not going into Russia to try anybody there.

On the other hand, if for the sake of speed and convenience we adopt the policy of Judge Clayton and exclude general testimony as to bad tendency, pinning the evidence down to the facts of publication and the precise intention of the defendants, we shall often do a grave injustice to the prisoners. The jury and even the judge may bring to the trial preconceived views of the bad tendency and evil purposes of utterances opposed to the existing economic and social order or to war policies supported by the great mass of the population. If no counterevidence to show that the opinions of the defendants may be reasonable or honest is admitted from third persons like Raymond Robins, these presuppositions must inevitably remain. Even if a defendant is allowed a wide scope in testifying in his own behalf, he is often the sort of man whose arguments carry little weight. In other words, in spite of the judge's desire to exclude outside evidence on either side as to bad tendency and bad intention from the case, such evidence in favor of a bad tendency and a bad intention is often automatically admitted the moment that the jury enter the box, and no system of challenges can avoid it. During a war they have for months been supplied with evidence by the government and the loyal press, diametrically opposed to the utterances for which the prosecution is brought. Unless something is done to tear the tribunal out of the fabric of public sentiment, a conviction is almost certain to result in prosecutions for political crimes, where the ordinary tests of the five senses play no part and men are forced to judge of the opinions and character of the prisoners by their own opinions and character as formed in the furnace of war. What Mr. Robins has since said and written makes it clear that his evidence would have been highly valuable to the defense.

Despite the practical inconveniences of such testimony as his in political prosecutions, it is the method pursued in countries where political crimes have existed when unknown in the United States. France, for instance, allows a "free defense," as in the *Affaire Dreyfus*. The defendant is not only allowed to say anything in his own favor, but may bring forward any witnesses he pleases, who express themselves fully and unhindered. Strange as it seems to us, the results are said to be very satisfactory.[14] Consequently, if we are going to continue to prosecute men for the bad political tendency of their disloyal or anarchistic utterances, we may have to adopt a similar wide-open policy in justice to the defendants.

Better far to reject both horns of the dilemma and refuse altogether to make tendency a test of criminality. If we are not willing to allow the free defense, we ought to abolish political crimes by the repeal of the Espionage Act and all other sedition statutes.

In the absence of any established technique for political crimes in this country, the exclusion of the Robins testimony is understandable, especially as it did not bear directly on the only legitimate theory of guilt but this only made it all the more imperative that Judge Clayton should repeatedly during the trial and in his charge insist to the jury that opposition to our Russian policy was not in itself a crime. He ought to have cleared Russia and Bolshevism out of the case for good and all, and pounded home the proposition that the only issue under the third and fourth counts (which alone should have gone to the jury, if anything went at all) was whether the defendants intended by inducing strikes in munition factories and other forms of protest to interfere with the supply of munitions *for use against Germany.* No one who will put himself back into the atmosphere of October, 1918, can doubt that the jury would naturally regard pro-Bolshivist activities as pro-German, and that it was the duty of Judge Clayton to warn them explicitly against the Russian theory of guilt, and confine their attention to the pro-German theory. There is no adequate warning on this in the record.[15] Instead, Judge Clayton himself repeatedly proclaimed the unsound theory of guilt, that if the defendants intended to oppose the government's Russian policy, they had *ipso facto* violated the law.

Before the defendants had put in any material testimony, he said:

> Now the charge in this case is, in its very nature, that these defendants, by what they have done, conspired to go and incite a revolt; in fact, one of the very papers is signed "Revolutionists," and it was for the purpose of avoiding—a purpose expressed in the paper itself—the purposes of the Government and raising a state of public opinion in this country of hostility to the Government of the United States, so as to prevent the Government from carrying on its operations and prevent the Government from recognizing that faction of the Government of Russia, which the Government has recognized, and to force the Government of the United States to recognize that faction of the Government in Russia to which these people were friendly.

Now, they cannot do that. No man can do that, and that is the theory that I have of this case, and we might as well have it out in the beginning.

The court did tell the jury that this statement was not part of the evidence and should be disregarded in passing on the issues of fact, but the harm was done and he took no steps to present any concrete alternative view. The second and legitimate theory of guilt was never stated by him, and it is doubtful if he himself ever realized the distinction or what really was in issue. Instead, he continued to apply the Russian theory in his cross-examination of Lipman, for it is one of the remarkable features of this case that most of the cross-examination of the prisoners was not by the district attorney, but by the court, who sometimes broke in upon the direct examination before half a dozen questions had been asked.[16] Lipman was testifying in response to his counsel that he had written the English pamphlet because the President after sending the telegram of sympathy to the Soviets had a few weeks later despatched a military expedition to Russia. Judge Clayton took over the witness:

"The President, you thought, and all that he was doing ought to be stopped and broken up?" "I thought when I know he is elected by the people they should protest against intervention. . . . I did not want to break up. I called for a protest, which as I understand it, from my knowledge of the Constitution, the people of America had a right to protest." . . .

"Did you intend to incite or provoke or encourage resistance to the Government of the United States?" "Not to the Government—never did."

"Who was acting for the Government if the President was not?"

"I thought it was the Congress and Senate that was supposed to represent the people of America."

"The President is the executive head. . . . You intended to incite opposition to what the President did?" "I did not. I intended to enlighten the people about the subject, for, as I stated, the papers were afraid to state it, and I thought it was the right time."

". . . The Government acts through the President, and you intended to incite opposition to what he was doing?" "I intended to incite opposition to every wrong act I understood to be wrong."

"You had the specific intention to make public opinion and arouse public opinion against intervention in Russia?" "Yes."

When the judge also kept saying that the defendants' opinion of the legality of the President's action could not justify them in breaking the law, he made their anti-interventionist propaganda seem a crime in itself, and there was no need for the jury to consider whether they had any intention to prevent the shipment of munitions to the western front. There is nothing in the charge about such an intention, nothing to exclude Russian operations from the scope of the war. Therefore, it is very probable that the defendants were convicted on an erroneous theory of guilt, simply because they protested against the despatch of armed forces to Russia.

However, it is maintained that the defendants did intend to hinder the fighting against Germany and so were properly convicted on the second theory of guilt. There are three classes of evidence in the case bearing on their intention.

First, the two pamphlets speak for themselves. Both plainly protest against our Russian policy and not against the war. The English circular emphatically repudiates the charge of pro-Germanism. It is nearly all expository, but throws in a few general exhortations which have been tossed about in every socialistic hall and street-meeting since the Communist Manifesto in 1848. Military imagery ought not to be taken literally in radical propaganda, any more than in church hymns. The Yiddish leaflet is more specific and has a few sentences calling for a general strike, which can no more be kept out of a radical pamphlet than King Charles' head could be barred from Mr. Dick's Memorial. We ought to hesitate a long while before we decide that Congress made such shopworn exuberance criminal. Very likely, as Justice Clarke says, "This is not an attempt to bring about a change of administration by candid discussion,"[17]—but how much political discussion is candid? If nothing but candid discussion is protected by the First Amendment, its value for safeguarding popular review of official acts is *nil.* And even if words like "fight" and "revolution" indicate violence, though often used in a grandiose vein, the advocacy of strikes and violence is not a crime under this indictment unless intended to resist and hinder the war with Germany.

Second, as subsidiary evidence of evil intention Justice Clarke relied on a yellow paper with handwriting taken from Lipman when arrested, and some typewritten sheets found in a closet in Abrams' rooms. In these long discussions wholly concerned with the wrongs suffered by Russia at the hands of Germany and ourselves, he pounced on a few sentences about keeping the allied armies busy at home so that there would be no armies to spare for Russia, or saying that if arms are used against the Russian people, "so we will use arms, and they shall never see the ruin of the Russian revolution."[18] Justice Clarke then commented:

> These excerpts sufficiently show, that while the immediate occasion for this particular outbreak of lawlessness, on the part of the defendant alien anarchists, may have been resentment caused by our government sending troops into Russia as a strategic operation against the Germans on the eastern battle front, yet the plain purpose of their propaganda was to excite, at the supreme crisis of the war, disaffection, sedition, riots, and, as they hoped, revolution, in this country for the purpose of embarrassing and if possible defeating the military plans of the government in Europe.

Thus the defendants entered prison with the prospect of staying fifteen or twenty years largely because of scattered passages in manuscripts for which they were not indicted, and which they had neither printed nor distributed. There is not the slightest testimony that Lipman ever showed them to anybody after dashing them off. Moreover, the typewritten sheets were plainly a first draft for the English leaflet, and in revision all Justice Clarke's objectionable passages vanished. It is going pretty far to condemn an author for what he leaves out.

Thirdly, we have the testimony of the defendants on the vital issue, whether they intend to defend the Russian Revolution by the methods of impulsive youth or intended to hinder us in our war against German militarism. All were born in Russia and had remained citizens of that country during their few years in the United States. All were anarchists except Lipman, and he was a socialist. Nothing in the case rebuts the natural inference that such persons were devoted to Russian radicalism and bitterly hostile to Imperial Germany.

Abrams said that he had offered his services to the President to go to Russia and fight Germany, but permission had been refused; that he would help send propaganda from Russia to Germany to start a revolution there, as he had done on the border of Austria and was sent to Siberia for it. As to the appeal for strikes, he called upon the workers here not to produce bayonets to be used against the workers in Russia.

"I say it is absurd I should be called a pro-German, because in my heart I feel it is about time the black spot of Europe should be wiped out."

"You are opposed to German militarism in every form?" "Absolutely."

"You would overthrow it and help overthrow it if you could?" "First chance."

The other defendants testified to the same effect, even Molly Steimer, the most inflexible, whose creed was that any human being should be free to live anywhere on earth that he or she desired. There is not a word in the whole *Record* to show that any prisoner was opposed to the war with Germany or desired Germany to win it or had any intention except an absorbing desire to protest against intervention in Russia.

It is hard to see how the jury could have convicted on this evidence if they had been instructed that a specific intent to hinder the war with Germany was necessary, but the judge did virtually nothing except repeat the words of the statute. He gave no explanation of the importance of this specific intent. He did not distinguish it from a general intention to publish the leaflets. Instead, the judge charged, "People who have circulars to distribute, and they intend no wrong, go up and down the streets circulating them." During the trial, although the defendants' counsel reminded him that Russian meetings in New York had been broken up, Judge Clayton said he would leave it to the jury whether throwing pamphlets out of windows squared with good, honest intention, and whether being anarchists and wanting to break up all government squared with honesty and sincerity of purpose. Soon afterward he stated:

> If it were a case where the defendant was indicted for homicide, and he was charged with having taken a pistol and put it to the head of another man and fired the pistol and killed the man, you might say that he did not intend to do that.
>
> But I would have very little respect for a jury that would come in with a verdict that he didn't have any intent.

Plainly these rulings of Judge Clayton ignored the specific intent to oppose or hinder the war with Germany, as demanded by the statute; he authorized the jury to convict the defendants for intention to publish the pamphlets and a generally bad mind.

The verdict against Abrams, three other men, and Molly Steimer was guilty on all four counts. The sixth prisoner was acquitted, for insufficient evidence of connection with the leaflets. The district attorney's office, which thought he had distributed leaflets at radical meetings, cites his acquittal as evidence of the fairness of the jury.

One more feature of the trial demands attention. Legal historians have always taken interest in the criminal judge who jests with the lives of men.[19]

"You keep talking about producers," said Judge Clayton to Abrams. "Now may I ask why you don't go out and do some producing? There is plenty of untilled land needing attention in this country."

. . . The witness said that he was an anarchist and added that Christ was an anarchist.

"Our Lord is not on trial here. You are . . ."[20]

"When our forefathers of the American Revolution" the witness began, but that was as far as he got.

"Your what?" asked Judge Clayton.

"My forefathers," replied the defendant.

"Do you mean to refer to the fathers of this nation as your forefathers? Well, I guess we can leave that out, too, for Washington and the others are not on trial here."

Abrams explained he called them that because, "I have respect for them. We all are a big human family, and I say 'our forefathers.' . . . Those that stand for the people, I call them father."

The day after conviction the prisoners were called before Judge Clayton for sentence. The court said:

"I am not going to permit anybody to start anything today. The only matter before this court is the sentencing of these persons. There will be no propaganda started in this court, the purpose of which is to give aid and comfort to soap-box orators and to such as these miserable defendants who stand convicted before the bar of justice."

When Lipman, the socialist, stepped forward to address the court and started to harangue about democracy, "You don't know anything about democracy," said Judge Clayton, "and the only thing you understand is the hellishness of anarchy." . . .

"These defendants took the stand. They talked about capitalists and producers, and I tried to figure out what a capitalist and what a producer is as contemplated by them. After listening carefully to all they had to say, I came to the conclusion that a capitalist is a man with a decent suit of clothes, a minimum of $1.25 in his pocket, and a good character.

"And when I tried to find out what the prisoners had produced, I was unable to find out anything at all. So far as I can learn, not one of them ever produced so much as a single potato.[21] The only thing they know how to raise is hell, and to direct it against the government of the United States. . . .

"But we are not going to help carry out the plans mapped out by the Imperial German Government, and which are being carried out by Lenine and Trotsky. I have heard of the reported fate of the poor little daughters of the Czar, but I won't talk about that now. I might get mad. I will now sentence the prisoners."

Rosansky was given three years in prison, Molly Steimer fifteen years and $500 fine, Lipman, Lachowsky, and Abrams twenty years (the maximum), and $1,000 on each count. If they had actually conspired to tie up every munitions plant in the country, and succeeded, the punishment could not have been more.[22]

"I did not expect anything better," said Lipman.

"And may I add," replied the judge, "that you do not deserve anything better."

2. *The Supreme Court*

In this case sentences of twenty years imprisonment have been imposed for the publishing of two leaflets that I believe the defendants had as much right to publish as the Government has to publish the Constitution of the United States now vainly invoked by them.

JUSTICE HOLMES

Seven judges of the Supreme Court were for affirmance of these convictions, Justice Clarke delivering the majority opinion. Justice Holmes read the dissenting opinion, in which Justice Brandeis concurred. The Supreme Court had only a limited power to correct any errors that may have occurred at the trial.[23] It could not revise the sentence. It could not set aside the verdict merely because its judges would have found differently on the facts themselves. Only two questions were clearly before the court: (1) the existence of the requisite evidence of specific intent under the third and fourth counts (the others being disregarded); (2) whether the two corresponding clauses of the Espionage Act could constitutionally be interpreted to apply to the publication of these leaflets.

Enough will be said if I limit myself mainly to the fourth count,[24] for urging by printing and publication curtailment of production of ordinance and ammunition necessary or essential to the prosecution of the war against Germany, "*with intent by such curtailment to cripple or hinder the United States in the prosecution of the war.*"

The required specific intent to hinder the war with Germany is worked out by Justice Clarke in this way:

> It will not do to say . . . that the only intent of these defendants was to prevent injury to the Russian cause. Men must be held to have intended, and to be accountable for, the effects which their acts were likely to produce. Even if their primary purpose and intent was to aid the cause of the Russian Revolution, the plan of action which they adopted *necessarily* involved, before it could be realized, defeat of the war program of the United States, for the obvious effect of this appeal, if it should become effective, as they hoped it might, would be to persuade persons . . . not to aid government loans and not to work in ammunition factories . . .[25]

In order to analyze this reasoning about intent, let us block out three different types of situations. First, A for a joke yelled "Fire!"

in a crowded theater. Many of the audience rushed for the doors in panic and a girl was trampled to death. Undoubtedly A is liable for manslaughter. When A protests that he intended no harm to anybody and least of all a fatality, the judge might reply in a hackneyed legal phrase. "The prisoner must be taken to have intended the natural and probable consequences of his acts."[26] Now, this statement is obviously a roundabout and fictitious way of stating the correct proposition that a man is often responsible for the natural and probable consequences of his act, whether or not he intended those consequences. His intention, as to what happened after his act, is immaterial. The defendant would be properly convicted, but the judge's reasoning would be wrong.

The Abrams case cannot be classified in this first situation, although Justice Clarke's second sentence hints in that direction. Why not? Because although in manslaughter and several other crimes any real intention of the defendant to do the resulting harm may be ignored where there is recklessness, this is not true when the offense charged is created by a statute which expressly requires an intent to cause a specific kind of injury. In such crimes, a man is not punished for the probable consequences of his act unless the tribunal finds that he really did have those consequences in mind.[27] Or, to put the matter another way, it is not enough for the defendant to do an act which is considered objectionable unless he actually has the mental state described in the statute.

My second situation illustrates the principles just stated. B is indicted under a federal statute providing that "If any person intending to devise any scheme to defraud, to be effected by correspondence with any person, shall, in and for executing such schemes," use the mails he shall be punishable on conviction. B, who is not a physician, has operated under the name of Boston Medical Institute, an establishment carrying on extensive correspondence about the treatment of alleged diseases. The testimony of medical experts shows that his course of treatment is not helpful, and may cause serious nervous conditions, so that it is clear that his patrons have paid their money without any adequate return. The trial judge charges: "The law presumes that every man intends the natural and legitimate and necessary consequences of his acts. Wrongful acts, knowingly or intentionally committed, can neither be justified nor excused on the ground of innocent intent. The intent to injure or defraud may be presumed upon an unlawful act which results in loss of injury, if proved to have been knowingly committed." B's conviction must be reversed on appeal, because no such rule as the trial judge stated is applicable to this type of case. B cannot be properly convicted unless he really intends to defraud his patrons. If he is just a muddle-headed person who ignorantly and obstinately believes in the value of his treatment then he is not guilty of the statutory crime, however harmful his conduct appears to the court and the public.[28]

As between the first and second situations, it is clear that the Abrams case is much more like the second. But before we decide to place it in the second situation, which will necessarily make the prisoners innocent, we must give our attention to a third situation. C throws a brick at a man behind a plate-glass window, which is of course broken. He is indicted for intentional destruction of property. He defends himself by saying that he merely intended to hit the man, and did not want to break the window. This defense is clearly bad. C's principal desire may have been to hit the man, but that necessarily involved smashing the window; and if he knows this fact he has a secondary intention to break the glass even though he would much rather not have done so.[29] Similarly, when a man was indicted for assault on another with intent to disfigure him by biting off his ear, it was useless for him to argue that he intended only to injure but not to disfigure. The disfigurement was a necessary and obviously a known consequence of the intended act.[30] These cases differ from those in the second group, because there the harmful results were only probable and perhaps unknown to the accused, while here the harmful results are inevitable, as the accused realizes.

The majority opinion in the Abrams case substantially takes the position that the defendants were like C and the ear-biter. Thus the first sentence quoted from Justice Clarke urges that aiding Russia was not the only intent of these defendants. It is argued that they had two intents: (1) to curtail production of munitions in order to help Russia, (2) to bring about interference with the war against Germany, which they knew would inevitably result from such curtailment during the process of accomplishing the first object; that it is immaterial which intent was principal and which was subordinate so long as both intentions were in their minds when they distributed the leaflets.

There are several answers to this argument that one who intends a curtailment of munitions for any purpose must know that fewer munitions will hinder the war and therefore must *ipso facto* intend to hinder the war. First, the analogy of the stone-throwing and biting cases just stated is too simple to have a proper application to free speech situations like the Abrams case. There is no such obvious and mechanical chain of cause and effect in complex social conditions, and the obscure factors involved are entirely beyond the capacity of a jury to decide. The argument supposes (1) that the hindrance of the war was inevitable, (2) that this inevitable consequence must have been in the defendants' minds. Both steps are very questionable, and the opinion of a jury on either step should have no weight with an appellate court. As to the first step, Justice Clarke's assumption that the defendants' plan "necessarily involved the defeat of the war program" merely states his own opinion on an issue which cannot be proved by legal evidence and as to which reasonable men might well think differently. Justice Holmes says, "An intent to prevent interference with the Revolution in Russia might have been satisfied without any hindrance to carrying on the war in which we were engaged." Thus a very short strike that stopped intervention would have caused a very small loss in munitions for shipment to France, which would have been enormously offset by the release of troops and equipment previously diverted to Russia; and a different Russian policy might have created great liberal enthusiasm in this country and elsewhere for the President's war aims.[31] The second step ignores the defendants' belief that a friendly Soviet government would render valuable aid in attacking Imperial Germany by war, or at least by propaganda, which was proved effective by the German collapse within a fortnight after the conviction of Abrams and his friends.

Secondly, if every curtailment of munitions, whatever its purpose, is necessarily criminal under this Act, because of its alleged obvious and inevitable effect on the war, why does the Espionage Act take pains to limit the crime to "curtailment" . . . *with intent . . . to cripple or hinder the United States in the prosecution of the war*?"[32] This clause is superfluous and meaningless, if every advocacy of curtailment involves such an intent. This clause about intent in a very severe criminal statute, and especially a statute limiting popular discussion, must mean what any layman who wished to urge a strike in war time lawfully would assume it to mean, that interference with the war must not be the object of his exhortation, the purpose at which he aims. Such a man would be entrapped if "intent" means an incidental, undesired, and at the most a vaguely considered consequence of his utterances.[33] Strikes are not ordinarily illegal, and it would be startling if Congress in 1918 intended to prohibit all incitement to them during the war. Naturally the statute confined itself to strikes and similar measures that were specifically planned to interfere with the war.

This is not, as has been charged, a confusion of intent and motive.[34] The distinction which I have drawn is between intent in its broadest sense (including both results desired and results known to be the necessary concomitants of the desired results), on the one hand; and, on the other hand, intent in the more narrow sense, limited to results actually desired. Even if we concede the dubious contention of the majority that the aims of the Abrams group "*necessarily* involved defeat of the war program of the United States," still the strong reasons set out by Holmes should limit "intent" in a statute affecting freedom of speech so as to mean only desired results. In other words, if we let our decision as to guilt depend on speculations as to what unwanted consequences are necessarily caused by the accomplishment of a purpose legitimate in itself, we are far from provable facts and our conclusions about punishable utterances are sure to be much swayed by our own fears and beliefs. Hence it is much wiser to group these free speech cases requiring a specific intent with the second situation described above (the Medical Institute case), although they are not exactly the same.

To return to the facts of the Abrams case. The primary intent of the defendants, as Justice Clarke expressly recognizes, was to help Russia. The defendants desired to produce certain tangible results, notably protest meetings, which in turn were desired to produce another tangible result, the end of intervention. Their motive was love for Russia. They also desired as a part of their machinery of protest to produce a general strike. They may properly be said to have intended all these results. But interference with the war was at the most an incidental consequence of the strikes, entirely subordinate to the longed-for consequence of all this agitation, withdrawal from Russia. And such incidental consequences should not be the main basis for punishment restricting open discussion.

In other words, this argument of inevitable hindrance proves too much. If these defendants were guilty under the fourth count, so was every other person who advocated curtailment in the production of war essentials, no matter what his purpose. The machinists in Bridgeport who struck in defiance of the arbitration of the National War Labor Board violated the Espionage Act, although they intended to obtain higher wages. The Smith and Wesson Company violated it in refusing to continue to manufacture pistols under another arbitration, although they intended to retain an open shop.[35] The coal miners in the autumn of 1919 violated that Act in calling a srtike. The government should have threatened all these people with the twenty-year penalty of the Espionage Act instead of acting under its general war statutes or imposing the milder rigors of the Lever Act and an injunction.[36]

To sum up, the Supreme Court was construing not only a criminal statute which must be applied in a fashion which the laymen who are menaced by it will understand, but also a statute limiting discussion and hence to be carefully interpreted in the light of the First Amendment. It ought not to be assumed that Congress meant to make all discussion of any governmental measure criminal in war time simply because of an incidental interference with the war. As Justice Holmes says, "Congress certainly cannot forbid all effort to change the mind of the country." The danger of the majority view is that it allows the government, once there is a war, to embark on the most dubious enterprises, and gag all but very discreet protests against such enterprises. To give extreme concrete examples: Irish munition workers could not have been urged to strike had our government been sending arms to Dublin Castle, because this would have lessened munitions for France, since a machinist could not be sure that any particular shell or gun was going to Ireland. Incitement to armed resistance to an executive edict nationalizing women would be opposition that might paralyze the war, and therefore easily suppressed under this Act.

The majority opinion dismisses this matter of constitutionality in two sentences, citing decisions on the Espionage Act of 1917 to establish the validity of the far more objectionable provisions of the Act of 1918.[37] Furthermore, the Court did not have to declare the clauses involved in the third and fourth counts void. Indeed, they are probably constitutional when construed in accordance with the First Amendment. It is the same situation that Judge Hand pointed out in *Masses v. Patten*;[38] it is a question of giving valid legislation a construction which will permit discussion outside the precise terms of the Act. These leaflets were political agitation on matters not directly related to the war with Germany,[39] and about the invasion of a country against which Congress had not declared war. The specific intent clause of the statute punishes agitation against the war. Therefore, the Act should not have been stretched to cover the leaflets. The First Amendment requires doubts to be resolved in favor of innocence, especially in the absence of "clear and present danger." Discussion of public matters should be left as wide as possible, when not expressly forbidden by Congress. Hence it was erroneous for the Court to construe the Act so as to make the remote bad tendency and possible incidental consequences of these pamphlets a valid basis for conviction.

The decision of the majority worked injustice to the defendants, but its effect on the national ideal of freedom of speech should be temporary in view of its meager discussion and the enduring qualities of the reasoning of Justice Holmes. Although a dissenting opinion, it must carry great weight as an interpretation of the First Amendment, because it is only an elaboration of the principle of "clear and present danger" laid down by him with the backing of a unanimous court in *Schenck v. United States.* This principle is greatly strengthened since the Abrams case by Justice Holmes's magnificent exposition of the philosophic basis of this article of our Constitution:

Persecution for the expression of opinions seems to me perfectly logical. If you have no doubt of your premises or your power and want a certain result with all your heart you naturally express your wishes in law and sweep away all opposition. To allow opposition by speech seems to indicate that you think the speech impotent, as when a man says that he has squared the circle, or that you do not care whole-heartedly for the result, or that you doubt either your power or your premises. But when men have realized that time has upset many fighting faiths, they may come to believe even more than they believe the very foundations of their own conduct that the ultimate good desired is better reached by free trade in ideas—that the best test of truth is the power of the thought to get itself accepted in the competition of the market, and that truth is the only ground upon which their wishes safely can be carried out. That at any rate is the theory of our Constitution. It is an experiment, as all life is an experiment. Every year if not every day we have to wager our salvation upon some prophecy based upon imperfect knowledge. While that experiment is part of our system I think that we should be eternally vigilant against attempts to check the expression of opinion that we loathe and believe to be fraught with death, unless they so imminently threaten immediate interference with the lawful and pressing purposes of the law that an immediate check is required to save the country. . . . Only the emergency that makes it immediately dangerous to leave the correction of evil counsels to time warrants making an exception to the sweeping command, "Congress shall make no law abridging the freedom of speech." Of course I am speaking only of expressions of opinion and exhortations, which were all that were uttered here, but I regret that I cannot put into more impressive words my belief that in their conviction upon this indictment the defendants were deprived of their rights under the Constitution of the United States.

The preceding chapters have been written in support of this danger-test as marking the true limit of governmental interference with speech and writing under our constitutions, but an able and thoughtful criticism of Justice Holmes's dissent[40] makes it imperative to say something more on the subject. In the first place, the First Amendment is very much more than "an expression of political faith." It was demanded by several states as a condition of their ratification of the Federal Constitution, and is as definitely a prohibition upon Congress as any other article in the Bill of Rights. The policy behind it is the attainment and spread of truth, not merely as an abstraction, but as the basis of political and social progress. "Freedom of speech and of the press" is to be unabridged because it is the only means of testing out the truth. The Constitution does not pare down this freedom to political affairs only, or to the opinions which are held by a majority of the people in opposition to the government. A freedom which does not extend to a minority, however small, and which affords them no protection when the majority are on the side of the government, would be a very partial affair, enabling the majority to dig themselves in for an indefinite future. The narrow view that the amendment does not protect a few of the people against the force of public opinion throws us back to the English trials during the French Revolution, and the Sedition Law of 1798, for which the United States through many years showed its repentance by pardoning all prisoners and repaying to them the fines imposed. These were none the less injurious to the cause of truth because they had the sanction of the majority.

Undoubtedly, although we are not infallible, we must assume certain opinions to be true for purposes of action; but this does not make it right or desirable to assume that they are true for the purpose of crushing those who hold a contrary doctrine.

> There is the greatest difference between presuming an opinion to be true, because, with every opportunity for contesting it, it has not been refuted, and assuming its truth for the purpose of not permitting its refutation.[41]

The vote of the majority of the electorate or the legislature is the best way to decide what beliefs shall be translated into immediate action, and the government must resist if its opponents begin to carry on the conflict of opinions by breaking heads instead of counting them. But it is equally inadvisable for the government to seek to end a contest of ideas by imposing or exiling its intellectual adversaries. Force seems like force to its victims, whether or not it has the sanction of law. No one will question that the government must resist a revolt, however Utopian in purpose, but the inference that logically it must also condemn all utterances "aimed at such subversion or tending solely thither" ignores the difference of degree emphasized by the First Amendment. It is the unfailing argument of persecutors. The opinions to which they object are always conceived to aim at revolution, violence, and nothing else, although such utterances are usually in large part the exposition of political and economic views. The advocates of parliamentary reform in England were condemned on just such reasoning. To throw overboard the danger-test and permit "the suppression, whenever reasonably necessary, of utterances whose aims render them a menace to the existence of the state," inevitably substitutes jail for argument, since the determination of the vague test of "menace" depends on the tribunal's abhorrence of the defendant's views. It is no answer that this tribunal (outside of the crushing powers of the post office and of the immigration officials in deportation cases) is a jury. A fitness to apply a common-sense standard to alleged criminal acts bears no resemblance to a capacity to appraise the bad political and social tendency of unfamiliar economic doctrines during panic. The Abrams case shows the capacity of a judge to decide such a question. The only tribunal which can pass properly on the menace of ideas is time.

We must fight for some of our beliefs, but there are many ways of fighting. The state must meet violence with violence, since there is no other method, but against opinions, agitation, bombastic threats it has another weapon—language. Words as such should be fought with their own kind, and force called in against them only to head off violence when that is sure to follow the utterances before there is a chance for counterargument. To justify the suppression of the Abrams agitation because the government could not trust truth to win out against "the monstrous and debauching power of the organized lie" overlooks the possibility that in the absence of free discussion organized lies may have bred unchecked among those who upheld the course of the government in Russia.

The lesson of *United States v. Abrams* is that Congress alone can effectively safeguard minority opinion in times of excitement. Once a sedition statute is on the books, bad tendency becomes the test of criminality. Trial judges will be found to adopt a free construction of the act so as to reach objectionable doctrines, and the Supreme Court will probably be unable to afford relief.

Most of the discussion of the Abrams case has turned on the question whether the decision of the United States Supreme Court affirming these convictions was right or wrong. It seems to me much more important to consider the case as a whole, and ask how the trial and its outcome accord with a just administration of the criminal law.

The systematic arrest of civilians by soldiers on the streets of New York City was unprecedented, and the seizure of papers without a warrant was illegal. The trial judge ignored the fundamental issues of fact, took charge of the cross-examination of the prisoners, and allowed the jury to convict them for their Russian sympathies and their anarchistic views. The maximum sentence available against a formidable pro-German plot was meted out by him to the silly, futile circulars of five obscure and isolated young aliens, misguided by their loyalty to their endangered country and ideals, who hatched their wild scheme in a garret, and carried it out in a cellar. "The most nominal punishment" was all that could possibly be inflicted, in Justice Holmes's opinion, unless Judge Clayton was putting them in prison not for their conduct but for their creed. Yet they were sentenced for their harmless folly to spend the best years of their lives in American jails.[42] The injustice was none the less because our highest court felt powerless to wipe it out. The responsibility was simply shifted to the pardoning authorities[43] and to Congress, which can refuse to revive the Espionage Act of 1918, so that in future wars such a trial and such sentences for the intemperate criticism of questionable official action[44] shall never again occur in these United States.

Notes

The Espionage Act and the Abrams Case

1 Report of the Attorney General, 1917, p. 74; "Civil Liberty in War Time," John Lord O'Brian, 42 Rep. N.Y. Bar Assn. 275, 291 (1919), cited hereafter as O'Brian.

2 Selective Draft Law Cases, 245 U.S. 366 (1918).

3 These statutes are now 18 U.S.C.A. (1926), §§ 4, 6, 88, 550; see *infra* Chapter IV, section 1. World War conspiracy cases thereunder include Emma Goldman *v.* United States, 245 U.S. 474 (1918); Wells *v.* U.S. 257 Fed. 605 (C.C.A. 1919); U.S. *v.* Phillips, Bull. Dept. Just., No. 14 (1917); Bryant *v.* U.S. 257 Fed. 378 (C.C.A., 1919); Orear *v.* U.S., 261 Fed. 267 (C.C.A., 1919); U.S. *v.* Reeder, Bull. Dept. Just., No. 161 (1918).

4 O'Brian, 277. The treason statute is now 18 U.S.C.A. (1926), §§ 1, 2; see Warren. "What Is Giving Aid and Comfort to the Enemy?" 27 *Yale Law Journal* 331 (1918). The legal scope of treason is discussed in Chapter VI, section II. World War treason cases include U.S. *v.* Werner, 247 Fed. 708 (1918); U.S. *v.* Robinson, 259 Fed. 685 (1919); U.S. *v.* Fricke, 259 Fed. 673 (1919).

5 On this Chamberlain bill and similar proposals, see Thomas F. Carroll, "Freedom of Speech and of the Press in War Time: The Espionage Act," 17 *Michigan Law Review* 621, 663 note (1919); cited hereafter as Carroll. The bill seems clearly unconstitutional under *Ex parte* Milligan, 4 Wallace 2 (1866); see note 66 in Chapter I.

6 As to England, see 31 *Harvard Law Review* 296 (by Laski); Laski, *Authority in the Modern State*, p. 101. As to Canada, see Carroll, at 621 note.

7 Act of June 15, 1917, c. 30, Title I, § 3, now 50 U.S.C.A. (1926), § 33. The numerals are inserted by me. As to the provisions of this statute against real spying, see Gorin *v.* United States, 61 Sup. Ct. 429 (1941).

8 See *supra*, Chapter I, at nn. 12, 72; *infra*, Chapter II, at n. 37.

9 4 *American Bar Association Journal*, 306.

[10] The history of the amendment is taken from Report of the Attorney General of the United States (1918), 18; O'Brian, 302. See Montana Laws, 1918, sp., c. II, now Mont. Rev. Stat. (1935); § 10737.

[11] 40 Stat. 553 (1918). As to the repeal in 1921, see 41 Stat. 1359–1360; 60 *Congressional Record*, 293–4, 4207–8.

The Abrams Case

[1] From a letter of 1929, quoted in R. S. Baker, *Woodrow Wilson*, VIII (1939) 284, n. i. See also Secretary Baker's Foreword to Graves, cited in the next footnote.

[2] Graves, *America's Siberian Adventure* (1931), p. 354.

[3] Abrams *v.* United States, 250 U.S. 616 (1919). The sources of the trial are given in my article in 33 *Harvard Law Review* 747 (1920), which contains a fuller statement of the facts; see corrections and additions in 35 *id.* 9 (1921). For the repercussions of this chapter (as first published) upon free speech at Harvard, see S. E. Morison, *Three Centuries of Harvard* (1936), pp. 464 ff.; Henry Copley Green, "A Fight for Freedom, 1921," 8 *History Reference Bulletin*, No. 23, sec. 2 (November, 1934); 35 *Harvard Law Review* 9 (1921).

A valuable analysis of the Supreme Court decision is made by T. R. Powell, "Constitutional Law in 1919–1920," 19 *Michigan Law Review* 283, 288 ff. (1921).

Able comments in support of the majority opinion will be found in Day Kimball, "The Espionage Act and the Limits of Legal Toleration," 33 *Harvard Law Review* 442 (1920); J. P. Hall, "Free Speech in War Time," 21 *Columbia Law Review* 526 (1921); E. S. Corwin, "Freedom of Speech and Press under the First Amendment," 30 *Yale Law Journal* 48 (1920); same, "Constitutional Law in 1919–1920," 14 *American Political Science Review* 635, 655 ff. (1920); H. F. Goodrich, "Does the Constitution Protect Free Speech?" 19 *Michigan Law Review* 487 (1921). A vigorous attack on Justice Holmes's dissenting opinion, which is significant to show how war can upset a first-class thinker, is J. H. Wigmore's "Freedom of Speech and Freedom of Thuggery, in Wartime and Peace-Time," 14 *Illinois Law Review* 539 (1920), which was written after a distinguished military career in Washington as colonel on the staff of the Judge Advocate General. Justice Holmes, who was wounded at Ball's Bluff, Antietam, and Fredericksburg, is said to have remarked after reading this article: "Colonel Wigmore may be a better lawyer than I am, but I think I know a little more about war than he does."

The minority opinion is supported in a note by Sir Frederick Pollock, 36 *Law Quarterly Review* 334 (1920). See *Holmes-Pollock Letters*, II, 29, 31, 32, 42, 44, 45, 48, 65 (1941). American views to the same effect are by K. N. Llewellyn, 29 *Yale Law Journal* 337 (1920); C. E. Clark (now U.S. Circuit Judge), 30 *id.* 68; L. G. Caldwell, 14 *Illinois Law Review* 601 (1920); Gerard C. Henderson, *New Republic,* XXI, 50 (Dec. 10, 1919).

[4] Errors of punctuation, etc., are preserved. Both leaflets measure 12 x 4½ inches, one page, printed on one side.

[5] The conspiracy section of the Espionage Act is Act of June 15, 1917, c. 30, Title I, § 4 [50 U.S.C.A. (1926), § 34]. The 1918 amendment to § 3 is summarized *supra,* Chapter II, section I.

[6] See *supra,* pp. 25 n., 49n.; 42–49; 78–79.

[7] The corresponding clause of the statute resembles the Sedition Act of 1798, but is far more severe in its penalty and its elimination of such defenses as truth and good motives.

[8] 250 U.S. at 619. Compare Stromberg *v.* California, 283 U.S. at 367 (1931), discussed in Chapter XI. The multiplication of overlapping counts in a sedition indictment creates serious risks of unfairness. In tangible crimes like assault with a dangerous weapon, recklessly negligent injury, etc., the jury is familiar with the fences between the different counts and can be trusted to find its way around with discrimination. But a series of charges against a single speech or statute amounts to piling up as many bad names as possible to fling at the accused. The jurymen are only too likely to roll the counts together, and then decide whether the prisoner is an undesirable citizen (or worse yet, an undesirable alien). If so, they may bring in a verdict of guilty all down the line for good measure. So if a fair-minded prosecutor wants to promote freedom of speech but believes that the utterance creates a real danger of disastrous acts, *e.g.,* munition strikes, he should base the indictment on the statutory clause which best describes that danger, and be reluctant to throw in a string of trivial offenses in addition. The first two counts in the Abrams indictment should have been dropped before the trial, not in the Supreme Court.

[9] Mr. Wigmore is a possible exception and may regard all Bolshevism as within the Espionage Act.—14 *Illinois Law Review* 439 ff.

[10] The documents are in R. S. Baker, *Woodrow Wilson,* vol. VIII, chapter iii (1939); Graves, *America's Siberian Adventure* (1931); *Russian-American Relations,* ed. Cumming and Pettit (New York, 1920). See Charles Cheney Hyde, "The Recognition of the Czechoslovaks as Belligerents," 13 *American Journal of International Law* 93 (1919).

[11] *War Information Series, No. 20* (October, 1918); the documents, without the historical report, are in *Bolshevik Propaganda,* etc., p. 1125. The documents appeared in the public press by installments, beginning September 15, 1918. See the *New York Times* of that date. But see R. S. Baker, *Woodrow Wilson,* VIII, 402, n. 2: "The original documents later disappeared. Early in October Balfour sent the President a confidential message

that English experts and authorities had gone over the Sisson papers carefully and had come to the conclusion that they were forgeries."

[12] Page 95, *supra.*

[13] Bolshevik Propaganda, Hearings before a sub-committee of the Judiciary Committee of the U.S. Senate, 65th Cong. 3rd sess. and thereafter, pursuant to Sen. Res. 439 and 469 (1919). This is cited in this book as Bolshevik Propaganda. It contains the testimony of Raymond Robins and others on Russian internal affairs.

[14] Robert Ferrari, "The Trial of Political Prisoners Here and Abroad," 66 *Dial* 647 (June 28, 1919). The same method is pursued in French murder cases where "the honor of the family" is a defense, and perhaps instances like the Thaw trial show it is not wholly unknown in this country. See Walker F. Angell, "A Providence Lawyer at the Caillaux Trial," *Providence Daily Journal,* Aug. 21, 1914.

[15] In 35 *Harvard Law Review* at 13–15 I have set out in full passages in the stenographic minutes of the trial which may have had a slight effect on the jury with respect to the issue of specific intent.

[16] On questioning of witnesses by the trial judge, see 30 *Yale Law Journal* 196 (1920); 4 Reports National Commission on Law Observance and Enforcement (Wickersham Commission) 320 ff. (1931).

[17] 250 U.S. at 622. Bagehot points out the danger of such a test: "The effect of all legislative interference in controversies has ever been to make an approximation to candor compulsory on one side but to encourage on the other side violence, calumny, and bigotry."—*Works,* Longman's ed., X, 127.

[18] The significant passages from both manuscripts are in 250 U.S. at 622.

[19] Judge Clayton's words are taken *verbatim* from the *New York Times,* which on October 18 said editorially, "Judge Henry D. Clayton deserves the thanks of the city and of the country for the way in which he conducted the trial," and praised his "half-humorous" methods.

[20] See the quotation at the head of this section, page 112. On Braxfield's trials of Muir and others for sedition, see Henry Cockburn, *Memorials of His Time;* Brown, *French Revolution in English History;* Robert Louis Stevenson, *Some Portraits by Raeburn* and *Weir of Hermiston; supra* Chapter I, at n. 56.

[21] Abrams and Lachowsky bound books, Lipman produced furs, Rosansky produced hats, Molly Steimer produced shirtwaists.

[22] It would not be treason, for lack of overt acts. (See Chapter VI, section 11.) An actual conspiracy could be punished under the Espionage Act only by the twenty-year sentence here imposed on three of the male defendants. The general statute on conspiracy to destroy by force the government of the United States imposes only six years.—18 U.S.C.A. § 6. Conspiracies to limit the production of necessaries were punished under the Lever Act by two years.—40 Stat. 279.

[23] I have here modified somewhat the views formerly expressed as to the technical legal problems, and am indebted to my colleague Livingston Hall for several very helpful suggestions.

[24] As to the third count Justice Clarke said that "the language of these circulars was obviously intended to provoke and encourage resistance to the United States in the war."—250 U.S. at 624. As proof of this intent, he relied chiefly on the manuscripts which I have already considered to be insignificant. I have not troubled to deal further with this count because my whole chapter indicates that the leaflets did not intend to provoke any resistance to the United States as the third count required. Whatever action was really urged in the leaflets boiled down to munitions strikes to help Russia, and they are covered by the fourth count discussed in the text. Justice Holmes said: "Resistance to the United States means some forcible act of opposition to some proceeding of the United States in pursuance of the war. . . . There is no hint at resistance to the United States as I construe the phrase."—250 U.S. at 629 (1919).

[25] 250 U.S. at 621. Italics mine.

[26] Rex v. Harvey, 2 B. & C. 257 at 264 (1823). *Cf.* Regina *v.* Martin, 14 Cox C. C. 633 (1881). See Jeremiah Smith, "Surviving Fictions," 27 *Yale Law Journal* 147, 156 (1917); H. F. Goodrich, "Does the Constitution Protect Free Speech?" 19 *Michigan Law Review*, 487, 497 (1921).

[27] In People *v.* Landman, 103 Cal. 577, 580 (1894), Garoutte, J., said: "When a specific intent is an element of the offense, no presumption of law can ever arise that will decide this question of intent."

[28] Hibbard v. United States, 172 Fed. 66 (C. C. A. 7th, 1909), noted in 18 Ann. Cas. 1044. To the same effect are Dobbs's Case, 2 East P. C. 513 (1770); Rex *v.* Knight, 2 East P. C. 510 (1782); Baender *v.* Barnett, 255 U. S. 224 (1921); United States *v.* Moore, 2 Lowell (U. S.) 232 (Mass. 1873); Hairston *v.* State, 54 Miss. 689 (1877); and many other decisions.

[29] Cf., Rex *v.* Pembliton, 12 Cox C. C. 607 (1874). A shooting analogy is given in 33 *Harvard Law Review* 444 n.

[30] State v. Clark, 69 Iowa 196 (1886).

[31] Justice Brandeis considered that Wilson's public statement about intervention in Siberia was "unnatural" to him and that it "marked the beginning of his mistakes, all of which came in the latter part of his administration, and were due to physical and mental overstrain."—R. S. Baker, *Woodrow Wilson*, VIII, 316 n.

[32] It is significant that Justice Clarke omits this clause in quoting the indictment and possibly he overlooked it altogether and assumed that intent to advocate curtailment of war essentials was the only intent specified in the Act.

[33] Holmes, J., 250 U.S. at 627; "When words are used exactly, a deed

is not done with intent to produce a consequence unless that consequence is the aim of the deed—unless the aim to produce it is the proximate motive of the specific act. . ." The Sabotage Act of 1918 punishes defective manufacture of war essentials only if there is intent to interfere with the war or reason to believe that the act will interfere with it.—40 Stat. 534; 50 U.S.C. A § 102. The Amendment of Nov. 30, 1940, which includes peacetime sabotage, requires intent to interfere etc., with national defense. See S. B. Warner. "The Model Sabotage Prevention Act," 54 *Harvard Law Review* 602, 624 ff. (1941).

[34] "Justice Holmes' Dissent," 1 *Review* 636 (Dec. 6, 1919). The interrelation between intent and motive is discussed and illustrated by W. Cook. "Act, Intention and Motive," 26 *Yale Law Journal* 645 at 654 ff. (1917).

[35] See these two cases in Report of the Activities of the War Department in the Field of Industrial Relations During the War (Washington, 1919), 32–35.

[36] 40 Stat. 279.

[37] 250 U.S. at 619.

[38] 244 Fed. 535, 538 (1917). See pp. 43–44, *supra.*

[39] Secretary of War Newton D. Baker wrote in 1929: "The expedition [to North Russia] was nonsense from the beginning and always seemed to me to be one of those side shows born of desperation and organized for the purpose of keeping up home morale rather than because of any clear view of the military situation. . . ."—R. S. Baker, *Woodrow Wilson,* VIII, 284 n.

[40] "The Espionage Act and the Limits of Legal Toleration," 33 *Harvard Law Review* 442 (January, 1920), by Day Kimball.

[41] Mill, *Liberty,* chap. 2.

[42] See Morley's indignation at the "thundering sentences" for sedition in India. *Recollections,* II, 269.

[43] In November, 1921, the prisoners were released on the condition of their return to Russia at their own expense.—Report of the Attorney General, 1922, p. 398. See *id.* 1921, p. 717.

[44] On armed intervention without Congressional authority, see the state papers of Seward and Fish in J. B. Moore, *Digest of International Law,* VI, 23 ff., and Moorfield Storey, "A Plea for Honesty," 7 *Yale Review* 260 (1918): "If any nation were to do any of these things to the United States, we should not doubt that it was making war on us."

Selective Bibliography

Censorship and Social Structure

Boorstin, D. *The Image Or, What Happened to the American Dream*. New York: Atheneum, 1962.

Cassirer, E. *The Myth of the State*. New Haven, Conn.: Yale University Press, 1946.

Deutsch, K. W. *The Nerves of Government: Models of Political Communication and Control*. New York: Free Press, 1963.

Hymes, D., ed. *Language and Culture in Society*. New York: Harper, 1965.

Shibutani, T. *Improvised News: A Sociological Study of Rumor*. New York: Bobbs-Merrill, 1966.

Censorship and Aesthetics

Barfield, Owen. *Speaker's Meaning*. Middletown, Conn.: Wesleyan University Press, 1967.

Lowenthal, L. *Literature, Popular Culture, and Society*. New York: Prentice-Hall Spectrum Books, 1961.

Widmer, D. and Widmer, E., eds. *Literary Censorship: Principles, Cases, Problems*. Belmont, Calif.: Wadsworth Publishing Co., 1961.

Censorship and Conflict

Allport, G. W. *Personality and Social Encounter*. Boston: Beacon Press, 1960.

Marcel, G. *Man Against Mass Society*. Chicago: Gateway Edition, 1962.

Shils, E. *The Torment of Secrecy*. New York: Free Press, 1956.

Van den Haag, E. *Passion and Social Constraint*. New York: Stein & Day, 1963.